ADOBE® PHOTOSHOP®
LIGHTROOM®
EDIT LIKE A PRO

2ND EDITION

OCTOBER 2020 RELEASE
COVERING VERSIONS:

Windows / Mac: 4.0

iOS / Android: 6.0

VICTORIA BAMPTON

Adobe Photoshop Lightroom—Edit Like a Pro (2nd Edition)

Publication Date 20 October 2020

ISBN 978-1-910381-10-6 (eBook Formats)
ISBN 978-1-910381-11-3 (Color Paperback)

TABLE OF CONTENTS

ACKNOWLEDGMENTS

A lot of people have contributed to this project, and although I'd love to thank everyone personally, the acknowledgments would fill up the entire book. There are some people who deserve a special mention though.

First and foremost, my heartfelt thanks go to Paul McFarlane, who has worked closely with me on this book yet again.

I also have to thank the entire Lightroom team at Adobe, especially Tom Hogarty, Sharad Mangalick, Josh Haftel, Ben Warde, Jeff Tranberry, Thomas Knoll, Eric Chan, Max Wendt, Josh Bury, Simon Chen, Matt Johnson, Ben Zibble, Jeffrey Andrew, Julie Kmoch, Becky Sowada, Kelly Castro, Rikk Flohr and Rick Spaulding. Their vision for the future of Lightroom is exciting!

I'd like to thank David duChemin for challenging the way I think about photography, and sparking many of the ideas in this book. There's always more to learn!

Thanks are also due to the team of Lightroom Gurus, who are always happy to discuss, debate and share their experience, especially Jim Wilde, Laura Shoe, Jeff Schewe, Martin Evening, Andrew Rodney, Peter Krogh, Ian Lyons, John Beardsworth, George Jardine, Rob Sylvan, Jeffrey Friedl, Linwood Ferguson, Johan Elzenga, Kitty van Gemert, Linda Alschuler, Sam Cox, and the rest of the crew!

I'm also grateful to the members of the various Lightroom forums and my social media followers, who constantly challenge me with questions, problems to solve, and give me ideas for this book.

Special thanks have to go to my Dad. He's been a professional photographer for more than 40 years, and if it wasn't for him, I would never have become involved with photography.

And finally I have to thank you, the Reader. Over the years, you've honed my writing and teaching skills, and you continue to do so. The lovely emails you send me, and the reviews you post online, make all the late nights and early mornings worthwhile—so thank you.

Victoria Bampton—Isle of Wight, England, October 2020

IMPROVE THE BOOK!

This book is constantly being updated. We'd love to hear about what you like and what you think could be improved.

You can send us your feedback using the Contact form on the website at https://www.lightroomqueen.com/contact. We promise to read every email, even if we can't reply to them all personally.

CONNECT ON SOCIAL MEDIA

We'd love to connect with you on:

The Forum: https://www.lightroomqueen.com/community/

Facebook: https://www.facebook.com/lightroomqueen

Twitter: https://twitter.com/LightroomQueen

The Newsletter: https://www.lightroomqueen.com/newsletter/

INTRODUCTION

1

For many years, Lightroom has been the industry standard for photo editing. When Lightroom was first introduced to the world in 2006, editing your photos meant sitting down at a desk at a "proper" computer. Mobile phones were used for phoning people and sending text messages, and iPads didn't even exist. How times have changed!

Lightroom Beta (2006)

In 2017, Adobe announced that the Lightroom family was growing and being reorganized. Like a human family, the Lightroom family of apps all share the same foundation, called the Camera Raw engine. But like the members of a human family, the individual apps have different strengths and weaknesses.

THE LIGHTROOM CLOUD ECOSYSTEM

The Lightroom cloud ecosystem, with its desktop, mobile and web interfaces, has been redesigned and rewritten from the ground up to meet the needs of today's photographers.

Lightroom

These cloud-based apps retain the best of Lightroom's heritage, including the world-class non-destructive editing tools, but also add cutting-edge image-analysis artificial intelligence, allowing you to find your photos by subject, even if you haven't manually added that information.

They're cloud-native, which means that the

Lightroom Classic

photos are stored safely on Adobe servers in the cloud. The photos are available on all of your devices, so you can work on them wherever you are, without having to worry about file management.

LIGHTROOM CLASSIC

The traditional folder-based version of Lightroom, now known as Lightroom Classic, has been refocused on its greatest strength—being a really advanced desktop app. It's had many years of development, so it has a lot of advanced features, and a steep learning curve to match.

Lightroom Classic is a distant cousin of the Lightroom cloud ecosystem. Its communication with the cloud is limited as it's focused on single-desktop editing, so we won't demonstrate Lightroom Classic in this book, other than how to migrate to and from Lightroom Classic.

Lightroom Classic is covered in detail in another of our books, *Adobe Lightroom Classic - The Missing FAQ*.

THE BOOK FORMAT & BONUS DOWNLOADS

This book is broken up into topic-based sections, each containing bite-sized lessons. It's written in a logical workflow order, with each lesson building on the previous lesson. You can skip around, but you'll get more out of the book if you read it in order.

DIAGRAMS & CROSS REFERENCES

Wherever possible, I've used annotated illustrations and graphics rather than thousands of words, so you can grasp the information quickly.

Likewise, instead of constantly repeating the same information, page references link to related topics, and these are clickable links in the eBook formats.

At the end of the book, you'll find a glossary of unfamiliar terms (page 375) and a full index (page 379), so you can easily look up information again later.

MULTIPLE OPERATING SYSTEMS

Lightroom runs on multiple operating systems and devices. The same principles of use apply, but the user interface varies due to screen size, and some behavior varies depending on the operating system.

To keep things simple, if there are only minor differences, they'll be listed inline, for example, *action (Windows) / action (Mac) / action (mobile)*. If there are more significant differences, we'll discuss the desktop behavior first, and then the mobile apps. We'll come back to the web interface on page 23 and Apple TV app on page 352.

FOCUS ON EDITING

A large portion of the book is focused on editing photos, because that's why most of us are using the software. Unlike most books, we won't just discuss what the individual sliders do, but also how the sliders work together, and the way professional photographers *think* as they're editing their own photos.

NEW LESSONS & UPDATES

As Lightroom is subscription software, Adobe adds new features every couple of months. This means all printed books will be out of date within a few months of release—but don't worry, I've got you covered. I'm constantly updating the eBook formats for changes and new features, and these are available to download from the Lightroom Cloud Premium Members Area.

A year's access to the Lightroom Cloud Premium Members Area is included in your book purchase, and you can extend your access at a low cost, so you always have the most up to date information.

ACCESS TO THE PREMIUM MEMBERS AREA

If you purchased this book direct from my Lightroom Queen website, your Members Area access will have been set up automatically at the time of purchase, and login details sent to you by email.

If you purchased your book from Amazon, Barnes & Noble or another retailer, you'll need to register your copy of this book to gain access to the Members Area. For instructions, turn to page 378.

WORKFLOW

2

Before we start using the software itself, let's talk briefly about workflow. It's one of the most popular topics among photographers, but why? What does it actually mean?

WHAT IS WORKFLOW?

The term workflow simply describes a series of steps undertaken in the same order each time. For photographers, this workflow runs from the time of shooting (or even before), through adding your photos to Lightroom, sorting and selecting your favorites, editing and retouching them, and then outputting to various formats, whether on screen or in print.

WHY HAVE A CONSISTENT WORKFLOW?

If you do the same thing in the same order every time, you reduce the risk of mistakes. Photos won't get lost or accidentally deleted, metadata won't get missed, and you won't end up redoing work that you've already completed.

There's no perfect workflow for everyone, as everyone's needs and priorities are different. The following pages (starting on page 6) guide you through the workflow we'll follow through the pages of this book, and we'll come back to more detailed diagrams of specific stages, such as rating your photos (page 92) and editing your photos (page 138). As you gain experience, you can start to build your own ideal workflow.

Once you've settled on a good workflow, that isn't the end of the story. You'll likely find that you continue to tweak it, as you discover slightly more efficient ways of doing things. It'll continue to build with time and experience, as well as with the introduction of new Lightroom tools. The principles, however, remain the same.

IN THIS SECTION, WE'LL CONSIDER:

- The basic steps of a Lightroom workflow.

THE LIGHTROOM FAMILY WORKFLOW

Find your existing photos and video clips, wherever they're currently stored (page 26), and capture new photos using your mobile device (page 38) or camera (page 42).

Add them all to Lightroom on your desktop (page 28) or mobile device (page 31).

Sync with the cloud so you can access all of your photos from any device, whether you're at your desktop or laptop (page 56) or traveling with a mobile device (page 59), and store a copy locally so they're available even when you're offline.

View the photos on a desktop as a grid of thumbnails (page 62) or full size photos (page 65) or on a mobile device (page 67).

Now take that untidy bunch of photos, delete the bad ones (page 84) and organize the rest by date (page 74), and group them into albums (page 76) and stacks (page 82).

Add metadata to help you find photos
again later, such as:
stars and flags (page 89),
descriptive text (page 94),
keywords (page 99),
people's names (page 102),
a map location (page 98),
and dates (page 97).

Display only your best photos by filtering using stars,
flags, keywords and other metadata (page 110), or
send Adobe's AI robot to search for you (page 108).

Then it's time to start editing, but you don't want to waste time going in circles, so first analyze the photo (page 119) and make a plan, just like the pros.

There's a whole array of editing tools (page 137), so in the Editing sections, we'll learn how to pick the right tool for the job.

the right tool
FOR THE JOB

Once we have all the pieces of the puzzle, practice makes perfect, so we'll try a series of start-to-finish edits (page 293) to improve your editing skills.

Looking great? Now you'll want to share your photos with the world!

Save the edited photos to your hard drive (page 324) to email them to friends, or upload the photos to be printed at an online lab.

From your mobile device, email your editing photos or share them on social media (page 324) and other photo sharing websites.

Log into the Apple TV app (page 352) to display a slideshow.

Or share entire albums as web galleries (page 339), so your friends, family and clients can view your photos, wherever they are in the world.

And don't worry, there's no need to get frustrated when your computer misbehaves, as we'll discuss standard troubleshooting steps too (page 355).

Ready to learn? Let's get started...

GETTING STARTED

3

I'm sure you're excited to get started, but you may also be a little apprehensive if you're not completely comfortable with computers. Even if you consider yourself computer literate, every program is different, and you won't want to risk losing any of your photos or create additional work for yourself.

APPS RUN LOCALLY

Although Lightroom stores the photos in the cloud, the application itself installs and runs on your computer or mobile device. This means that you can still use Lightroom even if your internet connection goes down.

The apps automatically sync with the cloud, uploading new photos to your Lightroom library, so you have access to all of your photos everywhere.

In this section, we'll briefly run through the basics of installing Lightroom and finding your way around, before we move on to adding photos in the next section.

LIGHTROOM ON THE WEB

If you're using someone else's computer or device, there's no need to install the Lightroom app. You can access your photos using Lightroom Web, by navigating to https://lightroom.adobe.com in any modern web browser and logging in with your Adobe ID (page 23). You can also share web gallery links with family, friends and clients, to allow them to view your photos and add their own (page 339).

IN THIS SECTION, WE'LL CONSIDER:

• The computer/device specification you'll need.

• How to install Lightroom on all of your devices.

• How to find your way around the interface.

WHAT DO YOU NEED TO USE LIGHTROOM?

Ready to get started? You'll need...

• A trial or active subscription that includes Lightroom and cloud storage space.

• A computer or mobile device that meets (or preferably exceeds) the minimum specification.

• A reliable internet connection.

SUBSCRIPTION

There are multiple Adobe Creative Cloud subscriptions, each including different apps and amounts of cloud storage space.

The Lightroom subscription, which includes Lightroom (for Windows, macOS, iOS, iPadOS, tvOS, Android, ChromeOS and Web) and 1TB cloud storage space, is ideal for many photographers. If you later run out of space, you can pay for additional cloud storage. As your skills progress, you can add Photoshop too.

If you don't already have a subscription, here's the link to sign up: https://www.Lrq.me/LRCC.

Whichever subscription you choose, you're not locked in. If you choose to cancel your subscription in the future, you'll have a year to download all of your photos to your desktop computer before they're deleted from Adobe's servers.

DESKTOP SYSTEM REQUIREMENTS

Adobe publishes minimum system requirements (shown as bullets below, correct at the time of publication), but these are a bare minimum to make Lightroom

run. Higher specification hardware significantly improves performance. These minimum specifications are occasionally updated as new operating systems and features are released, so to check the latest system requirements, visit https://www.Lrq.me/cc-sysreq

If you've purchased your computer in the last 2-3 years, it's likely to be able to run Lightroom. However, if you're considering buying a new computer, it helps to have a basic understanding of what these specifications actually mean, so let's take a closer look...

Operating System

• *Required: Windows 10 (64-bit) Version 1903 or later, or macOS 10.14 (Mojave) or later.*

If you're running an older operating system, you'll need to upgrade to run Lightroom. Support for new operating systems is added when they're released to the public.

CPU / Processor

• *Required on Windows: Intel® or AMD processor with 64-bit support. 2 GHz or faster processor.*

• *Required on Mac: Multi-core Intel processor with 64-bit support.*

The CPU is the "brains" of the computer. It tells the other computer components what to do, depending on the instructions given by the software and the user.

CPU's come in different clock speeds (measured in GHz), which determine how quickly computations are made, so higher numbers are generally better.

CPU's are also available with different numbers of cores, which allow them to do lots of different things at once. Lightroom makes good use of multiple cores for image processing tasks such as editing and exporting photos, so a quad-core processor is a great choice if you're buying a new computer.

RAM / Memory

• *Required: At least 8GB of RAM, but ideally 16GB or more.*

RAM, or Random Access Memory, is short-term storage for the data the CPU's working on, allowing it to be quickly stored and retrieved as it's needed.

When your computer runs out of space in RAM, it has to write the data out to the hard disk, which is much slower.

I'd recommend 16GB if you're buying a new computer and your budget will stretch.

GPU / Graphics Card

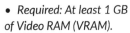

• *Required: At least 1 GB of Video RAM (VRAM).*

• *Minimum required to take advantage of GPU acceleration on Windows: DirectX 12 support,* at least 2GB VRAM, and a driver released in the last few months.

• *Minimum required to take advantage of GPU acceleration on Mac: At least 2GB VRAM and Metal support.*

The GPU, or graphics card, does more than just display the image on screen. It's designed to do thousands of calculations at once, but just for graphics-related tasks.

The GPU needs somewhere to temporarily store all of this information, and this is where the VRAM (or video memory) comes into play. The bigger the screen, the more information it needs to store in VRAM, so the more VRAM you need.

Lightroom can use the GPU to speed up certain tasks, such as how quickly the image preview updates on the screen when you switch photos or move an Edit slider. This is called GPU acceleration. We'll discuss this on page 364.

Hard Drive Space

• *Required: At least 2GB of available hard drive space.*

• *Note, the Mac version can't install on a volume that uses a case-sensitive file system or on removable flash storage devices (such as USB sticks).*

The hard disk drive is long-term storage. This is where you store all of your files, including the computer's operating system, the program files and your photos.

Hard drives can be stored inside your computer (internal drives) or connected using a cable (external drives). SSD's are faster than traditional spinning disks, so they're a better choice for your computer's boot drive.

Lightroom requires a relatively small amount of disk space, as most of the photos are stored in the cloud and they're just downloaded as you need them. However, although the minimum specifications state only 2GB is required, more space may be needed on the boot drive if you have tens of thousands of photos.

It's worth keeping at least one local copy of all of your photos as a backup. To do so, you can simply buy and plug in an external drive, and tell Lightroom to store the original files there, and the rest happens automatically. We'll learn about this on page 57.

MOBILE SYSTEM REQUIREMENTS

The mobile apps also have minimum system requirements, and again, higher specification hardware significantly improves performance.

On iOS, you need to be running *iOS 12.3 or later* on a recent iPhone, iPad or iPod. These include iPhone 5s and later, all iPad Air and iPad Pro models, iPad 5th generation and later, iPad mini 2 and later and iPod touch 6th generation.

Android devices need to be running *Android OS 5.0.x or later* with this minimum specification:

• *Processor: Quad Core CPU with 1.5 GHz frequency and ARMv7 architecture (2.2 GHz or higher recommended).*

• *RAM: 1 GB (2 GB recommended).*

• *Internal storage: 8 GB.*

Some features are only available on high specification devices, for example, on iOS, only devices with a 12MP+ camera can capture in DNG format, and on Android,

only a few phones can capture HDR (high dynamic range) images.

For Adobe's latest system requirements for mobile devices, check https://www.Lrq.me/ccmob-sysreq

INTERNET CONNECTION

• *Adobe says: Internet connection and registration are necessary for required software activation, validation of subscriptions, and access to online services.*

As Lightroom uploads all of your photos to the cloud, you do need a reasonably fast unmetered internet connection (or a lot of patience).

Lightroom continues to work when you go offline, whether your connection drops or you go on vacation. It asks you to connect briefly every so often (about every 30 days) to confirm your subscription status, but it will usually allow you to postpone this check for up to 99 days.

Some features don't work without an internet connection, including:

• Photos/videos can't download from the cloud for viewing/editing if they're not already stored locally.

• New photos/videos and edits can't sync up to the cloud.

• New photos/videos added on other devices and edits made on other devices can't sync down from the cloud.

• Searching for photos/videos using the text search field won't work.

• The map in the Info panel and reverse geocoding (address lookup) won't work.

If you know you're going to be offline, you can store smart previews or originals locally while you still have an internet connection, so the photos are available for viewing and editing offline. (See page 57 and page 60.)

PRIVACY CONCERNS

No one has access to your photos unless:

• They have access to your Adobe account.

• They have access to your computer/ mobile device.

• You choose to share them.

By default, Adobe does automatically collect some usage information to help the engineers improve the software. This includes your computer specifications and which tools you use in Lightroom, but not your photos or other personal information.

Adobe also utilizes machine learning, which means you can search the content of your photos in Lightroom without having to manually tag them.

If you want to learn more about how this information is used, or adjust your preferences, log into your account on Adobe's website, and go to *Manage Account > Security & Privacy > Privacy*.

INSTALLING & OPENING LIGHTROOM ON THE DESKTOP

You can activate Lightroom on two desktop computers at any one time if you have a *Photography Plan 20GB/1TB* or *All Apps* subscription, or five desktop computers if you have the *Lightroom 1TB* plan, in addition to your mobile devices.

INSTALLING USING THE CC APP

The desktop app installation and updates are managed using the Creative Cloud app (often shortened to CC app), which is a small app that runs constantly in the system tray (Windows) or menu bar (Mac).

To install the CC app, follow Adobe's instructions at https://www.Lrq.me/ccinstall When the installation completes, sign in with your Adobe ID and password.

To install Lightroom, select the *Apps* tab in the CC app, find Lightroom (not Lightroom Classic) and click the *Install* button to start the installation.

After installation, Lightroom opens automatically. To open Lightroom again in future, click the *Open* button in the CC app, or go to *Start menu > Adobe Lightroom* (Windows) / *Applications folder > Adobe Lightroom > Adobe Lightroom.app* (Mac).

While Lightroom's open, let's set up a shortcut for easier access. On Windows, right-click on the icon in the Taskbar and select *Pin to Taskbar*. On macOS, right-click on the icon in the Dock and select *Options > Keep in Dock*.

THE CREATIVE CLOUD APP (WINDOWS/MAC)

WELCOME SCREEN & TIPS

When Lightroom opens for the first time, it displays some welcome screens, followed by a series of tips to introduce you to the main features.

If you've already synced photos to the cloud, previews immediately start downloading.

If Lightroom Classic or an earlier version of Lightroom is installed on the computer, Lightroom may ask whether you wish to migrate your catalog. If so, say no for now, as we'll cover this process in detail on page 44, avoiding some potential problems.

DESKTOP WORKSPACE BASICS

Once the welcome screens are out of the way, you're looking at the Lightroom workspace. You might also hear it called the UI, or user interface.

In the center is the preview area, where your photos are displayed.

Down the left and right sides are panels, which are opened and closed using the buttons along the outside edges. The panels on the left are used for organizing photos, and the panels on the right contain the metadata and editing tools.

On the following two page spread, there's

a quick reference guide to the workspace, so you can learn the names of the main elements. There's nothing more frustrating than looking for something in a book's index when you don't know its name! The page references link to pages where the different elements are discussed in more detail.

CHECKING FOR UPDATES

Lightroom is updated regularly, adding new camera support, new features and bug fixes. To check for updates within Lightroom, go to *Help menu > Updates*. This automatically opens the CC app, where you can click the *Update* button to start the update installation.

WINDOWS VS. MAC

The screenshots in this book were captured using a Mac, but Lightroom works the same way on Windows. Any exceptions, for example, file paths or keyboard shortcuts, are noted.

KEYBOARD SHORTCUTS

Throughout the book, we'll focus primarily on which buttons to click to accomplish a task, but many tools are also available as menu commands or keyboard shortcuts. As you become more familiar with Lightroom, the shortcuts will help to increase your efficiency. For your easy reference, I've added a Keyboard Shortcut list to your Members Area downloads.

THE LIGHTROOM WORKSPACE (WINDOWS/MAC)

Show/Hide
Left panels

menu bar

Progress bar

Search
(page 108)

Window buttons (on
the right on Windows,
left on mac)

Add Photos (page 25)

Tutorials (page 320)

All Photos navigate
by date (page 61), by
people (page 102) or by
connection (page 349)

Albums (page 76) &
Sharing (page 339)

Filmstrip (page 62)

Panel Tracks
When you open the panels
on one side, the other
side closes. To change
this behavior, go to
Preferences > General >
Panel Tracks > manual

Left panels
for organizing photos

Toolbar
(page 61)

Refine View (page 110)

Share/Save a Copy (page 323)

Sync Status (page 56)

Recent Activity (page 344)

Help

Sliders

Crop (page 153)

Healing Brush (page 279)

Adjustment Brush (page 242)

Linear Gradient (page 249)

Radial Gradient (page 249)

... menu (page 137)

To show/hide panels on the right of the screen, click the buttons down the edge.

Activity panel (page 344)

Keywords panel (page 99)

Info/metadata panel (page 87)

Preview Area (page 65)

Right panels for editing photos and adding metadata

INSTALLING THE MOBILE APPS

The Lightroom mobile apps can be downloaded onto all of your mobile devices, to provide easy access to your photos wherever you are.

INSTALLING THE APPS

To install Lightroom on your phone or tablet, visit the Apple App Store (iOS) or Google Play Store (Android), as you would for any other app. Here are the direct links:

iOS: https://www.Lrq.me/ios

Android: https://www.Lrq.me/android

Once the installation completes, return to your Home screen and tap on the app icon to open Lightroom. You need to be connected to the internet while setting it up.

The first time you open Lightroom on mobile, it displays a series of welcome screens, highlighting the main features.

To sync your photos with the cloud, you'll need to sign in using your Adobe ID and password or a social login. If you've already synced photos to the cloud, previews immediately start downloading.

The first time Lightroom uses a device feature, such as the camera or notifications, it asks for permission. These permissions can be granted or revoked again later in *Settings app > Lightroom* (iOS) / *Settings app > Apps > Lightroom* (Android).

The future of photography

Make the most of your photography with the power of Adobe Photoshop.

● ○ ○ ○   Skip

"Lightroom" Would Like to Access Your Photos

Lightroom needs access to the photos on your device so you can browse and edit them.

Select Photos...

Allow Access to All Photos

Don't Allow

Allow **Lightroom** to take pictures and record video?

1 of 2   DENY   ALLOW

MOBILE WORKSPACE BASICS

The iOS and Android apps use a series of screens, due to their smaller screen size. There's a brief overview on page 22, and we'll explore the individual screens in more detail a little later in the book. The Library view (page 80) is used for organizing photos into Albums. The Grid (page 70) and Detail (page 72) views allow you to browse and edit photos.

few keyboard shortcuts you can use, for example, to assign a star rating to your photo. For your easy reference, I've added a Keyboard Shortcut list to your Members Area downloads.

IOS VS. ANDROID

There are slight differences between the iOS and Android apps, due to operating-system-specific features, and also between phones and tablets due to their screen sizes. Different teams work on developing the apps in parallel, so some features are available on one operating system before the other. Where there are significant differences, these are noted.

One of the most notable differences is the Settings (Preferences). We'll come back to the individual settings on page 359 (iOS) / page 361 (Android). To find them on iOS, tap the cog icon if you're in Library view, or ... *icon* > *Settings* in Grid or Detail view. On Android, tap the hamburger icon in the top left corner of the Library view.

View Settings (Preferences)

KEYBOARD SHORTCUTS

If you're using an external keyboard with your phone or tablet, there are a

THE LIGHTROOM WORKSPACE (IOS/ANDROID)

1. Select Library view

2. Tap All Photos or an album to open it into Grid view

3. Tap a photo to open it in Detail view

5. Tap arrow to go back

4. To switch between Detail views, tap the menu at the top on small devices, or the buttons down the side on tablet apps

ACCESSING LIGHTROOM ON THE WEB

You can also access your photos using Lightroom Web, by navigating to https://lightroom.adobe.com in any modern web browser and logging in with your Adobe ID. If you click on the Cloud Sync icon on the desktop, there's a link to take you straight there.

The web interface will be familiar by now, because it's designed to look like the desktop apps.

Using the web interface, you can do many of the same tasks as the desktop and mobile apps, including organizing the photos into albums and folders, adding metadata, sharing galleries with friends, family or clients, and even do some editing.

There are a few tools available in the web interface that aren't found in the desktop or mobile apps. Advanced customization for shared web galleries is explored on page 347, and if you're having problems syncing, a *Sync Errors* album appears below *All Photos*, offering additional clues about which photos are stuck and why.

THE LIGHTROOM WORKSPACE (WEB)

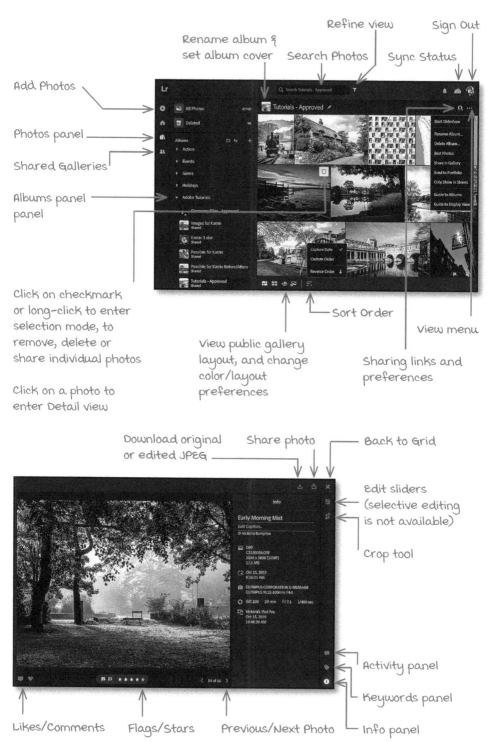

Refine view

Sign Out

Rename album &
set album cover   Search Photos   Sync Status

Add Photos

Photos panel

Shared Galleries

Albums panel
panel

Click on checkmark
or long-click to enter
selection mode, to
remove, delete or
share individual photos

Click on a photo to
enter Detail view

View public gallery
layout, and change
color/layout
preferences

Sort Order

View menu

Sharing links and
preferences

Download original
or edited JPEG

Share photo

Back to Grid

Edit sliders
(selective editing
is not available)

Crop tool

Activity panel

Keywords panel

Likes/Comments   Flags/Stars   Previous/Next Photo   Info panel

ADDING PHOTOS & VIDEOS

4

Before you can start organizing and editing your photos, you need to get them into Lightroom.

ALL OR NOTHING

It's worth adding all of your photos to Lightroom, wherever they're coming from, because:

• You'll be safe in the knowledge that you won't lose any photos, even if your computer crashes or your phone is lost or stolen.

• You'll have all of your photos in one place, so they'll be easy to browse.

• You'll be able to access them on any device, so you can share them with others.

• You can improve your photos using industry standard editing tools.

• You can become a better photographer by studying your previous photos.

• You can see how your photography skills are improving over time.

FILE FORMATS

Lightroom can manage a wide range of file formats. There's a full list at https://www.Lrq.me/file-formats

In addition to photos, many photographers also shoot short video clips on their mobile devices. Lightroom allows you to view and organize some video formats, but you can't edit them using Lightroom. For simplicity, we'll refer to adding photos, but the same principles apply to adding videos.

IN THIS SECTION, WE'LL CONSIDER:

• Where you might find your existing photos.

• How to add photos to Lightroom.

• How to capture photos on mobile devices.

• Camera settings that affect editing flexibility.

• How to migrate photos and edits from other programs.

FINDING YOUR EXISTING PHOTOS

You likely already have a large number of photos stored on your computer's hard drive or in another company's cloud. Before you can add them to Lightroom, you need to find them.

WHERE ARE YOUR PHOTOS?

I can't tell you where you've stored your photos, but these are the most frequent places to check:

• Your phone or tablet.

• Your camera's memory card.

• The Pictures or Photos folder on your computer.

• Other internal or external hard drives.

• DVD's/CD's.

• Cloud services, such as Google Photos, Dropbox or iCloud.

• Organized using other software that stores the files in its own library, such as iPhoto, Aperture or Photos.app.

• In boxes, albums or slide trays of photos shot on film. (You might consider photographing or scanning them to create digital files.)

Importing from your phone/tablet, camera, memory card reader or hard drive is very straightforward using the instructions on page 28, but there are a few things to look out for when importing from other photo editing software...

IMPORTING FROM LIGHTROOM CLASSIC/1-6

If you're migrating from Lightroom Classic or earlier, turn to page 44 to use the migration tool. This retains most of the organization and edits done in Lightroom.

A word of warning before you start: the migration is a one-way process. Continuing to use and sync Lightroom Classic after migration is a recipe for disaster.

If you're unsure whether Lightroom offers all of the functionality you require, don't migrate until you're certain. Instead, use Lightroom Classic to sync smart previews to the cloud so you can view/edit them in Lightroom. This will allow you to fully test Lightroom before committing to switching over completely. See the Cloud

Sync chapter of my book, *Adobe Photoshop Lightroom Classic - The Missing FAQ* to avoid potential problems. I've also published a feature comparison at https://www.Lrq.me/lightroom-cc-vs-classic-features/

IMPORTING FROM PHOTOSHOP ELEMENTS

Lightroom can automatically migrate your Photoshop Elements 2019 or 2020 catalog. Turn to page 48 to use the migration tool.

IMPORTING FROM CLOUD SERVICES

If your photos are on a cloud service, you'll need to download them to your computer to add them to Lightroom, as there are no direct transfer tools. These are a few frequent services:

Google Photos—Use Google Takeout to download the photos to your computer.

Dropbox—Use the Dropbox desktop app to download the photos to your computer.

iCloud Photos—Use iCloud for Windows app or Photos app for macOS to download the photos to your computer.

IMPORTING FROM APPLE PHOTO APPS

Lightroom can import your photos directly from Apple Photos, as long as the photos are already downloaded to your Mac desktop or laptop.

If you have an older iPhoto or Aperture library, you'll need to first open it into Photos. To do so, hold down the Opt key while starting Photos and select the iPhoto or Aperture library. Once the Photos conversion is complete, you can then use

Lightroom's migration tool discussed on page 51.

IMPORTING FROM OTHER SOFTWARE

If you've previously used other software to organize and edit your photos, you may want to preserve these edits, where possible.

Some editing software can write the metadata (that's things like titles, captions, keyword tags and star ratings) back to the files using a standardized format called XMP, which Lightroom can understand.

To check whether your software can write some or all of the metadata to the files, search the web for the name of your software and XMP, for example, *Picasa XMP*.

Some photo editing software stores the edits non-destructively, so these image adjustments are not applied to the originals. To retain these edits, save a copy of the photos as JPEG format and add these to Lightroom along with the unedited original.

ADDING PHOTOS ON THE DESKTOP

Once you've found your photos, you're ready to start adding them to Lightroom. You're in control of which photos (or videos) you import, and the same principles apply whether you're adding existing photos from your hard drive or new photos from your camera.

STEP-BY-STEP

1. If your photos are not currently stored on the computer, plug in the mobile phone, tablet, camera or memory card reader. (Card readers are generally more reliable than camera cables.)

2. Click the **Add Photos** button at the top of the left panel.

3. To add photos from a memory card or mobile device, select the device from the pop-up.

4. To add photos from your computer's hard drive, select **Browse...** from the pop-up to show the standard file browser for your operating system. (If no memory cards or mobile devices are connected, Lightroom skips the pop-up and immediately opens the file browser for you.)

Select a folder (such as the Pictures folder) or individual photos then click **Choose Folder** (Windows) / **Review for Import** (Mac) to move to the next window.

If your photos are currently organized into folders by topic, you may want to add one folder at a time (rather than selecting the parent folder) so you can create an album per folder, retaining your topic-based organization.

Alternatively, you can select the files in Explorer (Windows) / Finder (Mac) and then drag and drop them onto Lightroom's Grid view. The Import dialog opens with only these photos selected for import. This is particularly useful if you want to filter the photos before importing, for example, only the raw files from raw+JPEG pairs.

5. The thumbnails start to appear in a Grid view. There's a larger labeled diagram on page 30.

6. Select the photos you want to import by clicking the **checkmark** in the top left corner of each thumbnail. To select or deselect all of the photos at once, toggle the **Select All** checkbox.

To check a series of consecutive photos, click on the first of the photos so it shows a white border. Hold down the Shift key and click the last photo in the series, so they're all surrounded by a white border, then click the checkbox on one of the selected photos to check them all.

7. If the selected photos are all from the same shoot or topic-based folder, you may want to group them into an album (page 76) to make them easy to find later.

In the **Add to Album** pop-up, select *New* to create a new album, or select an existing album from the list. (A quick tip: if you select the album in the Albums panel *before* opening the Add Photos dialog, the album is automatically selected in the *Add to Album* pop-up.)

8. Click **Add X Photos** to start importing the photos into Lightroom.

9. The dialog closes and a progress bar

appears in the top left corner of Lightroom, showing the current status. Float over it to see the image count. If more than one task is in progress, click on it to see the individual tasks.

10. The photos appear in the preview area, and you can start looking through them immediately (page 61). If you run into any problems adding photos or videos, turn to page 366.

CLEANING UP AFTER ADDING PHOTOS

Adding photos to Lightroom doesn't remove them from their previous location, so you may want to clean up after adding them to Lightroom.

If your photos were on a camera memory card, keep the photos on the memory card as a backup until they're safely uploaded to the cloud. Once they've finished uploading, reformat the memory card in the camera, rather than simply deleting the photos. This helps to avoid card corruption.

If the photos were stored on the hard drive, you may choose to delete the original folders once the photos/videos are safely in Lightroom, to free up space on your computer. Before you delete these folders, double-check all of the photos imported into Lightroom and the folders don't contain any non-photo/video files, for example, Word documents or other file formats that aren't supported by Lightroom.

THE ADD PHOTOS DIALOG (WINDOWS/MAC)

Select Add Photos in the left panel →

Browse computer hard drives

memory cards, cameras, phones, tablets

Return to dialog to change source

Thumbnails of photos in selected source

File type badge

Add to Album

Select all thumbnails

Close dialog without adding photos

Add the selected photos to Lightroom

Photos without previews may still import ok (page 366)

Photo selected to be added to Lightroom

Hover cursor to show tooltip containing photo info

Faded thumbnails are duplicates of photos already in Lightroom (page 366)

ADDING PHOTOS ON IOS/ANDROID

Rather than having to plug your mobile device into your desktop computer, you can add photos directly into the Lightroom mobile apps. The photos can be added to your library automatically or you can add photos manually.

ADDING PHOTOS AUTOMATICALLY

To automatically add new photos captured using other camera apps, go to Lightroom's *Settings*.

On iOS, select *Import* and toggle the *Photos*, *Screenshots* and *Videos* switches to the right.

On Android, select *Preferences > Enable Auto Add* and toggle the *Auto add from device* switch, along with the *JPGs/PNGs*, *Videos* and *Raws* switches. You can also choose whether to automatically *Import from all locations*, or select specific device folders for Auto Add.

Adding photos automatically saves you having to remember to upload your photos. On iOS, you must open the Lightroom app occasionally to allow the photos to import, whereas on Android, the import happens in the background.

ADDING PHOTOS MANUALLY

Auto Add only adds new photos automatically, but you can add older photos using the *Import/Add Photos* button. The process varies slightly by operating system:

iOS

1. Tap the *Import* button at the bottom of the Library or Grid view.

2. Lightroom asks whether to add photos from the *Camera Roll*, *Files* or *All Photos* (if you're viewing an album), so select *Camera Roll*. (Alternatively, selecting *Files* allows you to import photos from cloud storage such as iCloud or Dropbox or external storage units like Gnarbox or WD My Passport Wireless.)

3. Lightroom displays the photos stored on your mobile device. At the top of the grid, select the album of your choice, for example, *Camera Roll*. Photos already imported into Lightroom have a LR icon in the corner. Tapping the ... icon allows you to filter the photos by file type and change the thumbnail size.

4. Drag your finger across the photos to select them (shown by a blue border), or tap the ... button to select all. (If you just tap on a photo, it opens into the Edit view, and doesn't import the photo until you tap the checkmark.)

5. When you've finished selecting the photos to import, tap the *Add* button at the bottom of the screen to confirm your selection.

Android

1. Tap the blue *Add Photos* button at the bottom of the Library or Grid view.

2. If you were viewing an album, Lightroom asks whether to add photos from the *Device*, *All Photos* or *Files*, so select *Device*. (Alternatively, selecting *Files* allows you to import photos from cloud storage such as GoogleDrive or Dropbox, or external storage units like Gnarbox or WD My Passport Wireless.)

3. At the top of the grid, select the grouping of your choice, for example, *Time* or *Device Folders*. Tapping the ... icon allows you to filter the photos by file type.

4. Tap the photos individually, a segment at a time, or tap the ... button to select all. Selected photos have a blue border.

5. When you've finished selecting the photos to import, tap the *Add* button to confirm your selection.

IOS SHORTCUTS

The iOS Shortcuts app, which is available from the App Store, is designed to automate a series of steps. Lightroom's integration is currently limited to adding photos, but there are a few potential advantages, compared to the standard *Auto Add* switches:

• Apply a preset to the new photos as they're added to Lightroom. (Only the default presets at this time.)

• Filter the photos to only add specific file formats (by extension), those marked as favorites in Photos app, or those in a specific album. There's a scrollable list of criteria.

• Send multiple photos from another app (e.g. Google Photos, or some tethering apps) directly to Lightroom.

• Automatically delete photos from the Camera Roll once they're added to Lightroom.

Let's try **building a simple workflow**:

1. Download the Shortcuts app from the App Store.

2. Open the Shortcuts app and click + to create a shortcut. Here's one I made earlier...

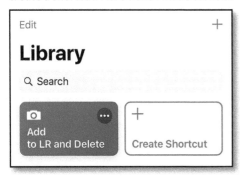

3. Scroll down the list to the Photos & Videos section, or type *Photos* into the Search field.

4. Select the source of the photos, for example, **Get Latest Photos** (*selects a specific number*), *Get Last Import* (if you've just imported from an SD card), *Find Photos* (to filter for specific photos) or another option. You may need to give permission to access these photos.

5. Scroll through the list again, or search for **Import to Lightroom**.

6. (Optional) Toggle the *Apply Preset* switch and select a preset to apply to the photos during import. You may prefer to select *Ask When Run* to choose the preset each time the workflow runs.

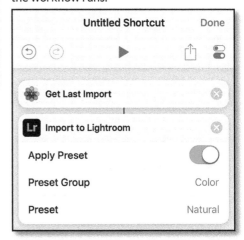

7. Scroll through the list again, or search for **Delete Photos**. Adding this step moves them to the *Recently Deleted* album, which works like a Recycle Bin / Trash. It asks for permission each time the workflow runs, so you can change your mind later.

8. Tap the toggle switch icon (top right) to access the workflow settings, and give the shortcut a name. You can also change the icon and add a shortcut to the home screen for easy access.

To **run the workflow**, tap on it in the Shortcuts app, or on the home screen shortcut, if you created one.

ADDING DSLR/MIRRORLESS PHOTOS ON IOS/ANDROID

If you're shooting with a separate camera, for example, your DSLR or mirrorless camera, you can add the photos to Lightroom on your mobile device instead of the desktop. This is particularly useful when traveling without a laptop, allowing you to start viewing, editing and sharing them.

STEP-BY-STEP

Due to differences in the operating systems, the steps are slightly different:

iOS 13.2 or later

iOS/iPadOS 13.2 and later allow you to browse files stored on a memory card and import them directly into Lightroom, without needing to go through the Photos app. You'll need a Lightning to USB adapter

and a cable to connect your camera, or you'll need a Lightning to SD card reader.

1. Insert the memory card into the SD card reader, or connect the camera and turn it on. The first time, Lightroom asks permission to access the connected device.

2. On the Device Connected screen, tap *Continue*.

3. Lightroom reads the card and presents an import dialog, where you can select

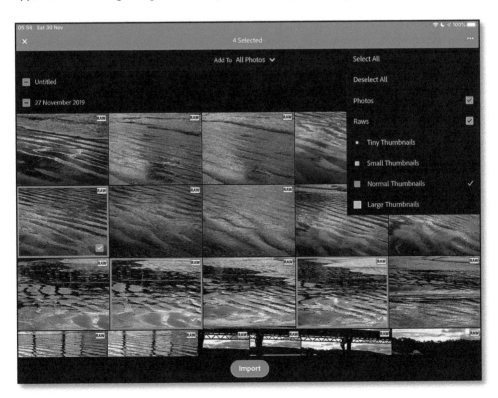

specific photos. Tap the checkmarks on individual photos, date segments, or tap the ... menu to *Select All*. The ... menu also allows you to filter specific types.

4. At the top of the dialog, choose whether to add the photos to *All Photos* or a new album.

5. Tap *Import* to begin the import process. Don't remove the card/camera or switch to another app until the import completes.

6. Tap the *X* to close the Direct Import dialog and return to Lightroom.

One word of warning: At the time of writing, direct import on iOS does not copy videos. Check that you have all of the photos and videos before you format the card.

iOS 13.1 or earlier

If you're using an older version of iOS, or you need to import videos, you'll need to import via the Photos app, due to operating system limitations. You'll need a Lightning to USB adapter and a cable to connect your camera, or you'll need a Lightning to SD card reader.

1. Insert the memory card into the SD card reader, or connect the camera and turn it on.

2. Open Photos app, if it doesn't open automatically, and select *Import* at the bottom.

3. In the top right corner, tap *Import All*, or tap specific photos then tap *Import*.)

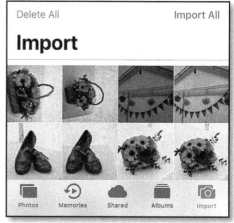

4. When Photos app finishes importing the photos, you can choose to *Keep* the photos on the memory card or *Delete* them. I'd recommend keeping them on the card, at least until they're safely uploaded to the cloud, so that you have a backup. Also note that Photos app might not import photos or videos from all cameras, so it's worth double checking everything has copied before clearing the memory card.

5. Once the photos have safely imported into Photos app, you can add them to Lightroom automatically (using Auto Add) or manually. Once they're safely in Lightroom, you can delete them from Photos app to free up space on your iPhone/iPad (but I'd still suggest keeping a copy on the memory cards as a backup).

Note that Lightroom only adds the raw file from raw+JPEG pairs. This is an iOS limitation.

Android

You'll need a supported OTG cable or adapter, and you may need a cable to connect to your camera.

1. Connect the camera to the mobile device using a supported OTG cable/adapter. Ensure the camera is turned on and is in PTP or MTP mode.

2. In the app picker, select Lightroom. If your device automatically opens another app, you'll need to check your device manufacturer's documentation to clear the default setting.

3. Tap specific photos to select them (shown by a blue border), or tap the ... icon to *Select All, Select None* or filter by file type. Once you've selected the photos, tap *Add.*

4. Lightroom asks whether to add the photos to *All Photos,* to a specific album or to create a new album. By default, *All Photos* is selected. Once you've made your choice, tap *Add* again.

5. Lightroom displays a progress dialog while it copies the photos to your Android device. When it's finished importing the photos, you can disconnect the camera. I'd recommend keeping the photos on the card, at least until they're safely uploaded to the cloud, so that you have a backup.

CAPTURING PHOTOS USING THE LIGHTROOM CAMERA

The iOS app and Android phone app include a built-in camera which has some specific advantages over other camera apps. (The camera isn't currently available on Android tablets.)

BENEFITS OF LIGHTROOM'S CAMERA

Manual camera controls—In addition to the standard Auto mode, there's a Pro mode offering manual controls such as shutter speed, ISO, white balance, and manual focus point.

Shoot-through presets—Unlike the default camera apps, the shoot-through presets are non-destructive. For example, if you want to preview the photo in B&W when shooting, and then later decide you'd prefer the photo in color, you can simply reset the edit settings.

Non-destructive crop for zoom—If you zoom in while composing the photo, it's stored as a non-destructive crop that can be changed later, when you realize you've cropped out something important.

Raw capture—On iOS devices with a 12MP camera, and also on some Android phones, the raw data can be saved as DNG format for greater editing flexibility.

HDR capture—Small mobile device camera sensors have a much more limited dynamic range than many traditional cameras, so highlight or shadow detail can be clipped. On some devices, Lightroom can capture multiple exposures and automatically merge them to create an image with much greater dynamic range, while retaining the editing flexibility of raw data.

Long Exposure—Introduced as a technology preview on iPhones, and hopefully coming to Android in a future release, Lightroom can capture multiple sequential images and merge them into something that looks like a long exposure image, blurring any motion. Unlike a traditional long exposure image, it's smart enough to figure out which areas of the photo are really moving and which bits are blurred due to camera shake, so you can even capture 5 second exposures hand-held.

Depth   Capture—Introduced   as   a technology preview on iPhones with dual cameras, the Depth capture mode creates a depth map that can be used to darken or blur backgrounds using the selective editing tools, like Apple's Portrait mode.

(To enable technology previews, go to *Settings > Technology Previews* and enable the features you want to try.)

Auto Import—The photos are automatically added to Lightroom, and synced to the cloud, so you never need to worry about losing your photos.

On the following pages, there are diagrams demonstrating the location of each of these settings. Some of the settings are only available on more powerful devices due to the complexity of the image processing involved, or the limitations of the operating system.

EASY ACCESS

To open Lightroom's camera, tap the camera icon in Library/Grid view.

 ← Camera

On iOS, you can use the Lightroom camera widget for quicker access. To view the widgets, swipe right over the Home screen, Lock screen, or while you're looking at your notifications. To add the Lightroom widget, scroll down to the end of the widgets and tap *Edit*, then tap the + next to Lightroom and drag it into the order you prefer.

On Android, the Lightroom Camera is available as a separate widget which can be added to the Home Screen for fast access. To do so, touch and hold an empty space on a Home Screen. Tap *Widgets*, then swipe to find the Lightroom Camera widget. Hold your finger on the widget and drag to the location of your choice.

LIGHTROOM'S CAMERA (IOS)

Available options vary depending on the device used

Back to Lightroom

Flash On/Off/Auto

File Format (JPEG/ DNG/HEIC, if available)

Front/Rear Camera

... button to Show/ Hide menu. menu options from left to right are:

Pro Capture Settings... from left to right:

Exposure Compensation (also swipe left <> right)

Shutter Speed

ISO

White Balance

Auto / Manual Focus (tap on photo to auto focus, hold finger to lock focus). Manual Focus shows green focus peaking mask.

Reset (or double-tap individual settings)

Recent Captures

Shooting mode Auto/Pro/HDR/Long Exposure/ Depth (if available)

Crop to Aspect Ratio (non-destructive)

Self-Timer

Grid Overlay and Level

Highlight Clipping Warning (zebra lines)

Camera Settings dialog (below)

Apply Preset (non-destructive)

Exposure Lock

Lens (Ultrawide/ Wide/Telephoto, if available)

Shutter (also use volume keys)

Pinch/Spread to zoom in/out (non-destructive crop)

Increase screen brightness while using camera

Add GPS location data

When shooting HDR/ long exposure, save unedited photo too

LIGHTROOM'S CAMERA (ANDROID)

Available options vary depending on the device used

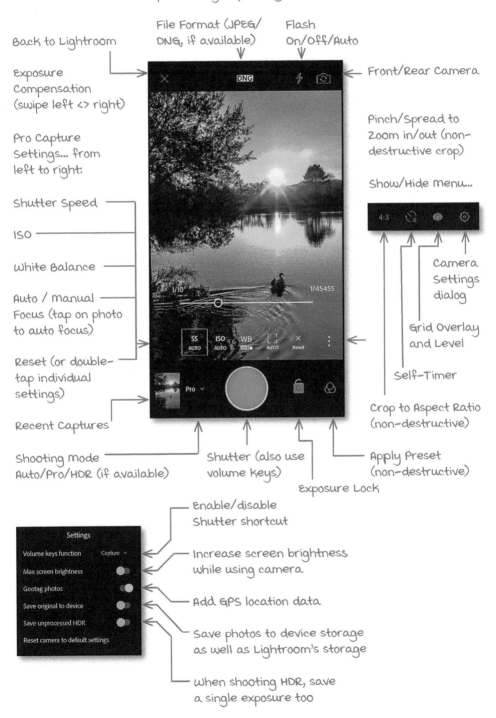

File Format (JPEG/
DNG, if available)

Flash
On/Off/Auto

Back to Lightroom

Exposure
Compensation
(swipe left <> right)

Front/Rear Camera

Pinch/Spread to
zoom in/out (non-
destructive crop)

Pro Capture
Settings... from
left to right:

Show/Hide menu...

Shutter Speed

ISO

White Balance

Camera
Settings
dialog

Auto / Manual
Focus (tap on photo
to auto focus)

Grid Overlay
and Level

Reset (or double-
tap individual
settings)

Self-Timer

Recent Captures

Crop to Aspect Ratio
(non-destructive)

Shooting Mode
Auto/Pro/HDR (if available)

Shutter (also use
volume keys)

Apply Preset
(non-destructive)

Exposure Lock

Enable/disable
Shutter shortcut

Increase screen brightness
while using camera

Add GPS location data

Save photos to device storage
as well as Lightroom's storage

When shooting HDR, save
a single exposure too

SET A GOOD FOUNDATION WITH YOUR CAMERA SETTINGS

Whether you're shooting with a mobile device or a separate camera, your settings will affect the ease of editing your photos as well as the quality of the end result. This isn't a camera manual, so we won't go into detail, but there are a few main settings to look out for...

RAW VS. JPEG—WHAT'S THE DIFFERENCE?

Arguably, the most important decision is your file format.

JPEGs are already processed by the camera in the way the camera manufacturer thought the photo should look. (The same applies to Apple's newer HEIF format.)

Raw files are the unprocessed sensor data, ready for you to process the way you prefer.

Raw vs. JPEG creates a bit of a religious war on the internet, and the decision is yours, but consider a few pros and cons...

WHY SHOOT JPEG/HEIF

Most photographers start out with JPEGs, and many phones and compact cameras only offer JPEG format. Newer Apple devices default to HEIF format. There are some advantages:

Space—JPEGs are much smaller than raw files, and HEIF files are smaller still. That means you can fit a lot more photos on your memory card or phone.

Speed—JPEGs and HEIF files come out of the camera ready to go, whereas raw files require editing. Speed shooters, such as sports photographers, often prefer JPEG for this reason.

Camera Settings Applied—The photos look exactly the same as they did on the back of the camera.

Compatibility—All image editing software understands JPEG format, whereas raw files must first be converted to standard image formats using software like Lightroom. HEIF files are not widely supported yet.

WHY SHOOT RAW

Raw files are bigger, and you do have to edit them, but there are some huge advantages:

Image captured with incorrect white balance and overexposed

Edited JPEG. The clipped highlights couldn't be recovered and the color is unnatural

Edited raw file. Notice the detail recovered on the nose and head, and natural colors

Dynamic Range—Raw files have a much wider dynamic range than JPEGs. This means that clipped highlight or shadow detail can often still be recovered from a raw file, whereas in the JPEGs, that detail's gone forever. You can see the difference in the dog's face.

Mistake Recovery—We all make mistakes, and if you have to make significant exposure changes, there's far more data to work with in a raw file, resulting in a higher quality image.

White Balance—Raw files can have their white balance adjusted while editing (page 204), whereas it's already applied to the pixels of JPEGs. This gives much more flexibility when editing, as you can see in the photo of the dog.

IF YOU'RE SHOOTING RAW

If you're shooting raw, there are a few things to bear in mind:

Unprocessed Raw Data—When you shoot in your camera's raw file format, the data isn't fully processed by the camera. Each raw processing software (like Lightroom) interprets the raw data in a slightly different way. As a result, the photos won't look exactly the same in Lightroom as they did on the back of the camera. There isn't a right or wrong rendering—they're just different.

Camera Picture Styles—While many cameras offer picture styles such as Portrait, Landscape and Monochrome, these editing presets only apply to the JPEGs (and the preview you see on the back of the camera), not the raw data. When you add the raw photos to Lightroom, these effects disappear, ready for you to edit the photos in whatever style you like.

ETTR—Short for "expose to the right," consider setting the exposure to be as bright as possible without clipping the highlights to pure white in order to retain the largest amount of data. Search the web for ETTR for more information on this concept.

Low ISO—To minimize noise, use the lowest ISO possible, balanced against the shutter speed and aperture, and avoid underexposing the photos.

Turn Off Smart Camera Settings—Some camera settings apply shadow brightening to the JPEG preview and histogram on the back of the camera, but not to the raw data. This may fool you into accidentally underexposing the photo, so these settings are best left disabled when shooting raw. Every manufacturer uses a different name, such as Auto Lighting Optimizer (Canon), Active D-Lighting (Nikon), Dynamic Range Optimization (Sony), Shadow Adjustment Technology (Olympus) and Intelligent Exposure (Panasonic).

IF YOU'RE SHOOTING JPEG/HEIF

If you're shooting JPEG/HEIF, there's less flexibility when editing, so you need to get your photo as perfect in-camera as possible.

Set White Balance—Make sure the white balance is about right when capturing the photo, using a WB preset (sunny, cloudy, etc.) or custom white balance. If the white balance is completely wrong, it won't be possible to fix it.

Expose Accurately—Overexposure results in clipped highlights (white areas with no detail) and this can't be recovered later. Underexposure results in lots of noise and blocked shadows (black areas with no detail) that can't be recovered.

MIGRATING FROM LIGHTROOM CLASSIC

If you're migrating from Lightroom Classic or an earlier Lightroom version, the migration tool makes it easy to move your photos to the cloud without losing the organization and edits done in Lightroom.

ONE-TIME MIGRATION

A word of warning—the migration is a one-way process. Continuing to use and sync Lightroom Classic after migration is not recommended because it won't let you migrate the same catalog again, and not all data syncs, so you'll end up with new metadata or photos orphaned in the Lightroom Classic catalog. Be sure of your decision before migrating.

NOT EVERYTHING MIGRATES

Many Lightroom Classic features don't exist in Lightroom. Some of the data gets transferred but remains hidden, and some information simply doesn't transfer.

Data that doesn't transfer to the Lightroom database includes:

• Folders and folder hierarchy (but you can convert to collections before migrating, which become albums in Lightroom).

• Develop History States (but the current Develop settings do transfer).

• Snapshots (but you could manually convert to virtual copies before migrating).

• Custom metadata from plug-ins.

• Creations (books, slideshows, prints and web galleries).

• Map module saved locations (but the GPS data itself does transfer).

• Smart collections.

• Shared web galleries will need to be shared again after migration, so the URL's may change.

Some data gets converted to Lightroom's format.

• Color labels become keywords.

• Virtual copies become real copies.

• Collection sets become album folders.

• Collections become albums.

WHAT YOU'LL NEED

To run the migration, you'll need:

• Lightroom Classic, Lightroom CC 2015 or Lightroom 6. If you're migrating from an earlier Lightroom version (1.0-5.7.1), you must first install a trial of Lightroom Classic and allow it to upgrade a copy of your catalog to Lightroom Classic format before running migration.

• On your boot drive (e.g., C:\ or Macintosh HD), you need space for the catalog and smart previews, which can be as much as 20% of the size of your Lightroom Classic catalog and original files.

• The migration process creates a copy of your images, so you'll need free space for all of the originals, either on the boot drive or on another internal/external hard drive or NAS (network accessible storage). You can set the location of the originals in

Preferences > Local Storage before opening the migration tool (page 58). This extra space is only needed temporarily, as the local cache can be cleared once the files have safely uploaded.

• Enough cloud storage space to hold all of your photos, otherwise Lightroom won't be able to upload your photos. The Photography Plan includes 20GB or the Lightroom plan includes 1TB. If you have a larger library, you can add extra storage space on your account page on Adobe's website.

• You can only migrate each catalog once, so make sure everything's set up before moving forward.

PREPARING YOUR CATALOG IN LIGHTROOM CLASSIC

Before you start the migration, there's some prep work to do in Lightroom Classic.

1. Go to *File menu > Optimize Catalog*.

2. Go to *Library menu > Find Missing Photos* to check that all of the originals are available. If some photos are marked as missing, follow the instructions at https://www.Lrq.me/lightroom-photos-missing-fix/ to locate the missing originals.

3. Create a smart collection to search for metadata conflicts. (Criteria is *Other Metadata > Metadata Status > is > Conflict Detected*.)

In the smart collection, click on the metadata icon in the corner of each thumbnail to fix the conflict. If you're happy that the catalog's metadata is correct (which is usually the case), click *Overwrite Settings*.

4. If you organize your photos into named folders in Lightroom Classic and wish to retain that organization, create collections/collection sets to replicate your folder structure (up to 4 deep). The quickest way to do this is to right-click on the parent folder and select *Create Collection Set "xxx"*. and repeat until all of your chosen folders have been replicated in the Collections panel.

TRANSFERRING PRESETS

Develop presets designed for Lightroom 4 or later will also work in Lightroom, so you may want to import your profiles and presets.

1. Create a folder, perhaps on the desktop, to temporarily store the presets and profiles.

2. Copy any DCP format profiles, XMP format profiles and XMP format presets by:

On Windows, open the Start menu search box and type *%appdata%\Adobe\CameraRaw*.

On macOS, go to *Finder > Go menu > Go to Finder* and paste *~/Library/Application*

Support/Adobe/CameraRaw.

Copy the contents of the *CameraProfiles* and *Settings* folders to the folder you just created on the desktop.

3. If you're using Lightroom 6, Lightroom CC 2015, or Lightroom Classic 7.2 or earlier, also...

On Windows, open the Start menu search box and type *%appdata%\Adobe\Lightroom*.

On macOS, go to *Finder > Go menu > Go to Finder* and paste *~/Library/Application Support/Adobe/Lightroom*.

Copy the contents of the *Develop Presets* folder to the folder on the desktop.

4. Check if there's a *Lightroom Settings* folder next to your catalog, and if so, copy the contents of the *Develop Presets* and *Settings* folders to the temporary folder.

5. In Lightroom, go to *File menu > Import Profiles & Presets* and navigate to the folder on the desktop, then press *Import*. A progress bar displays at the top of the Preset and Profile Browser panels while they're importing.

MIGRATING A CATALOG

Now it's time to start the migration itself...

1. Quit Lightroom Classic / Lightroom CC 2015 / Lightroom 6 and open Lightroom.

2. In Lightroom, select *File menu > Migrate*

From > Lightroom Classic Catalog.

3. In the information dialog that appears, click *Continue*.

4. Review the information in the Before You Begin dialog and click *Continue*.

5. Select the catalog that you want to migrate, then click *Start Scan*.

6. Lightroom scans the catalog and launches the migration tool, displaying a progress bar for you to monitor. This step may take some time to complete, depending on the size of your catalog.

7. Review any exceptions that the migration tool reports, for example, if you don't have enough cloud or local storage space available. If you've prepared your library in advance, there may not be any exceptions. Stop and fix the problems, then click *Check Again*, or ignore the exceptions by clicking *Continue Anyway*.

8. Review the information in the Catalog Ready for Migration dialog. If necessary, click *Open Log File* to check the details of any errors. Then click *Start Migration* to begin the migration process.

A progress bar is displayed during the migration process. Depending on the catalog size and your computer specifications, this step may take some time to complete (e.g., many hours, or even a few days if you have tens of thousands of photos), as it copies all of the photos into Lightroom's own storage space, ready for upload to the cloud.

9. When migration is complete, Lightroom displays a confirmation dialog. If there are exceptions, click *Open Log File* to review what went wrong. Otherwise, you're all done, and ready to start using Lightroom. Photos may take hours, days or weeks to sync to the cloud, depending on the speed of your internet connection and the number and size of the photos.

10. If you have more than one Lightroom Classic catalog, you can repeat the process. An album folder is created for each catalog, so you can identify the source of the photos.

11. Once you're happy that everything's safely in Lightroom's storage space and you have a local backup of the originals (page 57), you may choose to delete the Lightroom Classic catalog and photos to free up hard drive space, or move them to a disconnected hard drive as an extra backup.

MIGRATION ERRORS

You may run into errors with the migration, since it's a relatively complex process. The most frequent issues and their solutions are listed at https://www.Lrq.me/migration-errors

MIGRATING FROM PHOTOSHOP ELEMENTS

If you're migrating from Photoshop Elements Organizer 2019 or 2020, the migration tool makes it easy to move your photos to the cloud without losing the organization and edits.

NOT EVERYTHING MIGRATES

Some Photoshop Elements features don't exist in Lightroom. Data that doesn't transfer to the Lightroom database includes:

- Events.

- Mobile albums.

- Hidden images.

- Audio-only files.

- Creations (books, calendars, etc.).

WHAT YOU'LL NEED

To run the migration, you'll need:

- Photoshop Elements 2019 or 2020. If you're migrating from an earlier version, you must first install a trial of Photoshop Elements 2020 and allow it to upgrade a copy of your catalog to the current format before running migration.

- On your boot drive (e.g., C:\ or Macintosh HD), you need space for the catalog and smart previews, which can be as much as 20% of the size of your original files.

- The migration process creates a copy of your images, so you'll need free space for all of the originals, either on the boot drive or on another internal/external hard drive or NAS (network accessible storage).

You can set the location of the originals in *Preferences > Local Storage* before opening the migration tool (page 58). This extra space is only needed temporarily, as the local cache can be cleared once the files have safely uploaded.

- Enough cloud storage space to hold all of your photos, otherwise Lightroom won't be able to upload your photos. The Photography Plan includes 20GB or the Lightroom plan includes 1TB. If you have a larger library, you can add extra storage space on your account page on Adobe's website.

- You should only migrate each catalog once, as repeating the process can create duplicates, so make sure everything's set up before moving forward.

PREPARING YOUR CATALOG IN PHOTOSHOP ELEMENTS

Before you start the migration, there's some prep work to do in Elements Organizer.

1. Go to *File menu > Manage Catalogs*. Select your catalog and then click *Optimize*.

2. Go to *File menu > Reconnect All Missing Files* to check that all of the originals are available. If Elements can't find them all automatically, you may need to give it a helping hand.

3. Go to All Media view then go to *View menu > Hidden Files > Show Only Hidden Files*. Select all of the files, and go to *Edit menu > Visibility > Mark As Visible*, otherwise they'll be missed by the migration process. You may want to add a keyword or add them to an album to remind you which files were previously hidden.

4. If you organize your photos into named folders in Elements Organizer and wish to retain that organization, create albums/album folders to replicate your folder structure (up to 4 deep) before starting the migration.

MIGRATING A CATALOG

Now it's time to start the migration itself...

1. Quit Photoshop Elements and open Lightroom.

2. In Lightroom, select *File menu > Migrate From > Photoshop Elements Catalog.*

3. In the information dialog that appears, click *Continue.*

4. Review the information in the Before You Begin dialog and click *Continue.*

5. Select the catalog that you want to migrate, then click *Start Scan.* (If you can't find your catalog, briefly open Photoshop Elements Organizer and go to *Help menu > System Info.* Don't forget to quit Elements Organizer again before continuing.)

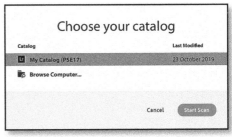

6. Lightroom scans the catalog and launches the migration tool, displaying a progress bar for you to monitor. This step may take some time to complete, depending on the size of your catalog.

7. Review any exceptions that the migration tool reports, for example, if you don't have enough cloud or local storage space available. Stop and fix the problems, then click *Check Again*, or ignore the exceptions by clicking *Continue Anyway.* If you've prepared your library in advance, there may not be any exceptions.

8. Review the information in the Catalog Ready for Migration dialog. If necessary, click *Open Log File* to check the details of any errors. Then click *Start Migration* to begin the migration process.

A progress bar is displayed during the migration process. Depending on the catalog size and your computer specifications, this step may take some time to complete (e.g., many hours, or even a few days if you have tens of thousands of photos), as it copies all of the photos into Lightroom's own storage space, ready for upload to the cloud.

9. When migration is complete, Lightroom displays a confirmation dialog. If there are exceptions, click *Open Log File* to review what went wrong. Otherwise, you're all done, and ready to start using Lightroom. Photos may take hours, days or weeks to sync to the cloud, depending on the speed of your internet connection and the number and size of the photos.

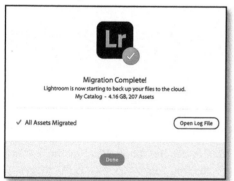

10. If you have more than one Photoshop Elements catalog, you can repeat the process. An album folder is created for each catalog, so you can identify the source of the photos.

11. Once you're happy that everything's safely in Lightroom's storage space and

you have a local backup of the originals (page 57), you may choose to delete the Photoshop Elements catalog and photos to free up hard drive space, or move them to a disconnected hard drive as an extra backup.

MIGRATION ERRORS

You may run into errors with the migration, since it's a relatively complex process. The most frequent issues and their solutions are listed at https://www.Lrq.me/migration-errors-pse

MIGRATING FROM APPLE PHOTOS

If you're using Apple Photos on a Mac desktop/laptop computer, the migration tool makes it easy to move your photos to Lightroom without losing the organization and metadata edits done using Photos.

However, they're tools from two different companies, so it's worth being aware of what doesn't transfer before you start. Continuing to use Photos after migration is not recommended.

WHAT DOES MIGRATE

Standard metadata migrates from Photos to Lightroom.

• Photos Folders and Albums become Lightroom Folders and Albums.

• Photos marked as Favorites are grouped into a Favorites album, so you can choose to flag or star them after migration.

• EXIF metadata such as the Capture Date/Time, GPS location and Camera model, shutter speed, ISO etc. are found in the Info panel.

• Titles and Captions are found in the Info panel.

• Keywords are found in the Keywords panel.

• Named people are found in the People view and Keywords panel.

Duplicate checks are not done during migration, so photos that are already in Lightroom as well as Photos may end up in Lightroom twice.

WHAT DOESN'T MIGRATE

Some Apple Photos features are not currently supported in Lightroom, so they don't get migrated:

• **Hidden** photos/videos are not migrated.

• **Recently Deleted** photos/videos are not migrated.

• **iCloud Storage**—Photos/videos stored in iCloud but not stored locally are not migrated. (We'll download these while preparing the Photos Library.)

Some data is partially migrated:

• **Edits**—Only the untouched originals are migrated. The edits are not migrated.

• **Bursts**—Only the key frame is transferred. If you want to keep all of the individual frames, unstack them using Photos before migration.

• **Live Photos**—The still key frame and video are migrated, but they're no longer combined as a live photo.

• **Portrait Mode**—The unedited original is migrated, without the depth effect.

PREPARING APPLE PHOTOS

OS Updates—Ensure your operating system has the latest updates installed.

System Library—Most people only have one Apple Photos Library, but if you have more than one, open the one you want to migrate in Apple Photos and go to *Preferences > General tab > Library Location > Use as System Photo Library* before proceeding with the migration. Then repeat this process for each of the other libraries.

Download originals from iCloud—Photos need to be stored locally before they can be migrated to Lightroom. To ensure you have a local copy, go to *Photos Preferences > iCloud* tab. If *iCloud Photo Library* is checked, select *Download Originals to this Mac*.

Select the Photos view and scroll to the end, where it shows upload/download status, and wait for the download to complete before starting migration.

HEIF Processing—If your library has HEIF images, Photos runs a background task to process these photos. The migration tool can't import these photos until this processing is complete.

STEP-BY-STEP

Now it's time to start the migration itself...

1. Quit Photos and open Lightroom.

2. In Lightroom, select *File menu > Migrate From > Apple Photos Library*.

3. In the information dialog that appears, click *Continue*.

4. Review the information in the Before You Begin dialog and click *Continue*.

5. Lightroom scans the Photos library and launches the migration tool, displaying a progress bar for you to monitor. This step may take some time to complete, depending on the size of your library.

6. Review any exceptions that the migration tool reports, for example, if you don't have enough cloud or local storage space available. If you've prepared your catalog in advance, there may not be any exceptions. Stop and fix the problems, then click *Check Again*, or ignore the exceptions by clicking *Continue Anyway*.

7. Review the information in the Photos

Library Ready for Migration dialog. If necessary, click *Open Log File* to check the details of any errors. Then click *Start Migration* to begin the migration process.

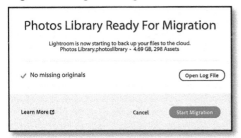

A progress bar is displayed during the migration process. Depending on the catalog size and your computer specifications, this step may take some time to complete (e.g., many hours, or even a few days if you have tens of thousands of photos), as it copies all of the photos into Lightroom's own storage space, ready for upload to the cloud.

8. When migration is complete, Lightroom displays a confirmation dialog. If there are exceptions, click *Open Log File* to review what went wrong. Otherwise, you're all done, and ready to start using Lightroom. Photos may take hours, days or weeks to sync to the cloud, depending on the speed of your internet connection and the number and size of the photos.

9. Once you're happy that everything's safely in Lightroom's storage space and you have a local backup of the originals (page 57), you may choose to delete the

Photos library to free up hard drive space, or move it to a disconnected hard drive as an extra backup.

MIGRATION ERRORS

You may run into errors with the migration, since it's a relatively complex process. The most frequent issues and their solutions are listed at https://www.Lrq.me/migration-errors-apple

SYNCING WITH THE CLOUD

5

Once you've added photos, Lightroom automatically uploads them to the cloud whenever you have an internet connection, and downloads changes made on other devices. The upload prioritizes photos that are flagged or starred, so your most important photos are backed up to the cloud as quickly as possible, and available on your other devices.

Lightroom's smart about minimizing the amount of space it uses on your computer's hard drive, so you don't need to worry too much about file management, but there are a few preferences that you may want to adjust, depending on your usage.

The sync and caching behavior is slightly different, depending on whether you're using a desktop (Windows/Mac) or mobile device (iOS/Android) so we'll look at each in turn.

IN THIS SECTION, WE'LL CONSIDER:

• How to control syncing on the desktop.

• How to control syncing on mobile.

• How to store photos locally for offline use.

SYNCING ON THE DESKTOP & WORKING OFFLINE

Lightroom handles the syncing and file management, but the desktop apps give you a few options to tailor the sync and local cache to your own needs, depending on your internet connection, available hard drive space, performance priorities, etc.

CHECKING SYNC STATUS

You can check the **overall sync status** by clicking the cloud icon in the top right corner. **Synced and Backed Up** means the local database cache is in sync with the cloud. **Syncing X Photos** means originals and/ or edits are currently being synced to/from the cloud.

The **sync status of individual photos** displays in the lower right corner of their thumbnail in Square Grid view (page 62).

The badge style varies depending on the sync status:

- Synced and Backed Up (managed by Lightroom)
- Synced and Backed Up (Original Stored Locally)
- Syncing
- Smart Preview Only

The Sync Status section of the Info panel (page 95) gives further information about the type of file that's stored in the cloud and currently downloaded to your computer.

Original refers to the original file format. Lightroom uploads all originals to the cloud and downloads them when they're needed, for example, when zooming into 1:1 view or exporting full size files. The originals may also be cached locally, depending on your preference settings and range of behind-the-scenes criteria, such as how recently you've viewed the photo.

A **Smart Preview** is a smaller (2560px) proxy file that can be used in place of the original file for editing when the original isn't available.

If Lightroom says there's only a smart preview in the cloud, it's because you synced the photo using Lightroom Classic. In this case, you won't be able to access the full-size original until you add it to Lightroom (page 28).

PAUSING/RESUMING SYNC

If you're on a limited bandwidth connection, for example, on vacation or tethering a mobile phone, or you have a more urgent upload underway, you may want to temporarily pause sync.

To do so, click the cloud icon and float over the sync status line to display the **Pause Syncing** button. Later, return to the same location to resume syncing.

MANAGING THE LOCAL CACHE

Lightroom stores a local copy of the cloud database, along with small previews (and by default, some originals) at:

Windows—C:\Users\[your username]\AppData\Local\Adobe\Lightroom CC\Data

Mac—Macintosh HD / Users / [username] / Pictures / Lightroom Library.lrlibrary

Lightroom automatically manages the amount of space it uses for its local cache, but it's a balancing act. Lightroom can use a larger amount of hard drive space to keep lots of previews and originals locally, or it can save local space by downloading files from the cloud as they're needed.

You can control the balance using the *Use photo cache size equal to X% of your remaining disk space* value in *Preferences > Local Storage*. This determines how much of the available disk space Lightroom can use on your main hard drive to store smart previews and/or originals.

It's a target rather than a hard limit. For example, if you've added new photos that haven't uploaded to the cloud yet, Lightroom may need to use more space than you've specified, at least until it's finished uploading them.

STORING PHOTOS LOCALLY

Although   Lightroom   is   smart   about

managing its local cache, it gives you some control over which originals are cached locally. There are a few reasons you may want to determine which files are stored locally, including:

Performance—It's usually faster to load a photo or video from a local hard drive than download it from the cloud.

Bandwidth—Working from a local cache means Lightroom doesn't need to download the files from the cloud, reducing your internet usage.

Work Offline—A local cache means you can continue working on your photos without an internet connection.

Backup—While extremely unlikely, something could go wrong with Adobe's servers, so it's worth having a local copy.

You may decide to only store specific albums locally, for example, the albums you're currently working on, or the albums containing your best photos. To mark an album for local storage, right-click on the album and select **Store Album Locally**. Unchecking it reverts to automatic management.

To keep a copy of all originals locally, check the **Store a copy of all originals at the specified location** checkbox in *Preferences > Local Storage*.

The **Store a copy of all smart previews locally on C:/ or Macintosh HD** checkbox retains a local copy of the smaller smart previews. This can be valuable for performance and offline work, especially if you don't have a local cache of all originals.

STORING ORIGINALS ON ANOTHER HARD DRIVE

By default, Lightroom stores any downloaded originals along with its database and preview files in its local cache.

Original photos can take a significant amount of disk space, but you can select another hard drive (e.g., an internal/external hard drive, or a network drive) to avoid filling up your main boot drive. The local database cache and previews still remain on the main hard drive. Only the originals move to your selected location.

To change the location of the original photos, click **Browse** in *Preferences > Local Storage* and navigate to another drive. Lightroom automatically moves any downloaded originals to the new location, so you don't have to do anything else. If you change your mind, the **Reset** button moves the photos back to the main hard drive.

When that location is unavailable (e.g., the external drive is disconnected), Lightroom obviously can't access the originals stored there, so it downloads them from the cloud as needed and stores them in the default location, along with any new photos you add to Lightroom. When you next restart Lightroom with the drive attached, Lightroom automatically moves any originals to your custom location.

SYNCING ON MOBILE & WORKING OFFLINE

Like the desktop apps, Lightroom handles syncing and file management on iOS and Android devices, but there are a couple of preference settings to adapt Lightroom to your own workflow.

CHECKING SYNC STATUS

You can check the **overall sync status** by tapping the sync icon in the top right corner. Initially it tells you how many photos are still syncing, and when it's done, it changes to *Synced and Backed Up*.

PAUSING/RESUMING SYNC

If you're on a limited bandwidth connection, you can temporarily **pause sync**, tap the sync icon in the top right corner and then tap *Pause Syncing* button. Later, return to

the same location to resume syncing.

Syncing photos, especially full size originals, can quickly use up your cellular data allowance, so you may want to limit Lightroom to **WiFi only**. To do so, go to *Settings > Cloud Storage & Sync* (iOS) / *Settings > Preferences* (Android) and toggle *Use Cellular Data* to the left to disable it. It doesn't completely stop cellular data usage, but it's minimized.

DOWNLOADING PREVIEWS

To minimize the amount of space needed on your mobile device, Lightroom is very selective about what it downloads.

Initially, Lightroom just downloads a local cache of its database, containing a list of your albums and photos.

SYNC STATUS (IOS/ANDROID)

When you start to view the photos in Grid view, Lightroom downloads the thumbnails, and as you flip through the photos in Detail view, it then downloads the smart preview for those photos too.

Lightroom doesn't download the full size original from the cloud unless you do one of two things:

• In Detail view, tap on the sync icon and tap *Get This Original* (iOS) / *Download Original* (Android).

• You've disabled *Only Download Smart Previews* in *Settings > Cloud Storage & Sync* (iOS) / *Preferences > Settings* (Android) and you then view the photos in Detail view or store the album locally. (For screenshots of the various Settings screens, see page 359 for iOS or page 361 for Android.)

CACHING FILES TO WORK OFFLINE

If you're going to be offline, you can store albums locally, so you can still view and edit the photos without an internet connection by downloading them in advance.

Go to Library view and tap the ... icon next to the album you wish to store locally, then select *Store Locally*. The photos download while you still have an internet connection, and the album cover photo is marked with a small blue arrow when the download is complete.

RECLAIMING SPACE

You can check how much space Lightroom's using on your device by going to *Settings > Local Storage* (iOS) / *Settings > Device Info & Storage* (Android).

On your Android device, you can make more space by moving the Lightroom data to your **expansion storage** (SD card). To do so, go to *Settings > Device Info & Storage > Use SD Card*. (Unfortunately there isn't a similar option for iOS, due to operating system limitations.)

If you need to **clear some space** on your device, you can clear Lightroom's cache using the *Clear Cache* buttons. This only clears cached files that are already safely in the cloud, so you don't need to worry about originals that haven't uploaded yet.

It also retains any albums marked to store locally. To **clear the locally stored albums** on iOS, select the album's ... icon again and select *Disable Store Locally* and then *Clear Cache* from the same menu. On Android, select the album's ... icon and toggle *Store Locally* off. Then go to *Settings > Device Info & Storage > Manage Storage*, check the albums you want to clear and tap *Clear*.

VIEWING & ORGANIZING

6

Having added your photos to Lightroom, you naturally want to view them, and you probably want to start organizing them too.

On the desktop, click the *Photos* button above the left panel or press the P key to show the Photos panel. On mobile, select the Library view, which is the first view you see when you open Lightroom.

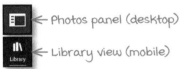

← Photos panel (desktop)

← Library view (mobile)

Select **All Photos** to display all of your photos in the central preview area (desktop) / Grid view (mobile). *All Photos* is useful for scrolling through your photos or searching.

All Photos   48,190 ⌄

Your photos are automatically organized by the date they were captured. You can also choose to group specific photos into albums, album folders and stacks, so you can easily find them again later.

The Grid views allow you to view thumbnails of multiple photos, whereas the Detail view displays a much larger view of a photo, so you can take a closer look and zoom in to check it's perfectly in focus.

IN THIS SECTION, WE'LL CONSIDER:

• How to view your photos and videos in Grid and Detail views.

• How to change the sort order.

• How to select multiple photos.

• How to view photos grouped by date.

• How to group photos into albums.

• How to group similar photos into stacks.

• How to delete photos (carefully!)

GRID VIEWS & SELECTIONS ON THE DESKTOP

The Grid views allow you to view and select multiple photos at once, so you can see them in context and quickly scroll through them, looking for specific photos.

GRID VIEW OPTIONS

There are two kinds of grid view—the Photo Grid and the Square Grid. To **switch between the Grid views**, use the buttons in the toolbar below the grid or press the G key.

Photo Grid   Square Grid

The **Photo Grid** displays the photos in a mosaic pattern. It's a distraction-free view that doesn't waste any space, but vertical photos are smaller than horizontal photos, and panoramic photos can appear stretched.

The **Square Grid** view displays the photos in a grid of square cells with extra icons showing useful information, such as flags, stars, file type and sync status.

The **size of the thumbnails** can be changed

using the slider at the bottom of the grid.

Video length
Stack
Thumbnail
White border = selected
Star Rating
Flag Status
File Type
Sync Status
Has Edits

CHANGING THE SORT ORDER

You can change the order of the photos, for example, to see your vacation photos in the order that they were captured.

To **change the sort order**, click the sort order button in the toolbar below the grid. Your chosen sort order is saved with the selected album, so different albums can have different default sort orders. The options are:

Capture Date sorts the photos by capture date/time. If multiple photos were captured

Photo Grid
Square Grid

GRID VIEW TOOLBAR (WINDOWS/MAC)

↑ Sort Order ↑ Flags ↑ Star Ratings ↑ Thumbnail Size
↑ Detail view
↑ Square Grid view
↑ Photo Grid view

Capture Date	✓
Import Date	
Modified Date	
File Name	
Star Rating	
Custom Order	
Reverse Order	↑ᴬᴢ

select one or more photos in Grid view and drag to a new location. As you drag, a blue line appears between the photos, showing where the photo will drop.

in the same second, the file name is used as a secondary sort to ensure they're in the right order.

Import Date sorts the photos based on when you added them to Lightroom.

Modified Date sorts the photos based on whether you've changed their metadata or edited them.

File Name sorts the photos based on their file name.

Star Rating sorts the photos based on their star rating, from 0-5.

To **reverse the sort order**, for example, from oldest to newest photos first, select **Reverse Order**.

Finally, **Custom Order** displays the photos in a manual sort order for the album. Simply

SELECTING PHOTOS

In the Grid views, you can select the photos you want to view, edit and share. Selected photos have a white border.

Selected   Not Selected

If you select multiple photos in Grid view, your actions apply to all of the selected photos. For example, you can select 10 photos and add your copyright or star rating to them all in one go.

When you switch to the Detail view

(page 65), most actions only affect the single photo you're viewing. (A few functions, such as saving edited photos to your hard drive, apply to all photos regardless of view mode.)

To **select one photo**, simply click on it, and the border becomes highlighted in white.

To **select a consecutive series of photos**, click on the first thumbnail, hold down the Shift key and click on last thumbnail in the series.

To **select multiple scattered photos**, click on the first thumbnail, hold down the Ctrl key (Windows) / Cmd key (Mac) and click on each of the other thumbnails, so they all have white borders.

To **select all** of the photos in the current view, go to *Edit menu > Select All* or use the keyboard shortcut Ctrl-A (Windows) / Cmd-A (Mac).

If the photos are already selected, you can deselect them, removing the white border.

To **deselect one or more photos**, hold down the Ctrl key (Windows) / Cmd key (Mac) and click on the thumbnails.

To **deselect all photos**, go to *Edit menu > Select None* or use the keyboard shortcut Ctrl-D (Windows) / Cmd-D (Mac).

DETAIL VIEW & ZOOMING ON THE DESKTOP

The Detail view displays a much larger view of the photo, so you can see every detail.

To **switch to Detail view**, click the button on the toolbar or press the D key. You can move between photos using the left/right arrow keys on your keyboard.

Detail view

FILMSTRIP

Below the main Detail preview is the Filmstrip, which displays thumbnails of your photos. This allows you to select a different photo without returning to the Grid view or using the keyboard.

To **show or hide the Filmstrip**, click the button in the toolbar or use the / shortcut.

Right-click on the Filmstrip to select *Filmstrip Style > Photo* or *Filmstrip Style >*

The Filmstrip has two styles:

The Detail view toolbar is the same as Grid view, except the Thumbnail Size slider is replaced with these buttons:

Zoom Ratios

Show/Hide Filmstrip

Before/After Edits

Square from the context-sensitive menu to **change the Filmstrip style**.

ZOOMING IN

To **zoom in** to see more detail, click on the photo or click the **100%** button in the toolbar. *100%* was called *1:1* in earlier Lightroom versions, and it displays the individual pixels.

If you click the arrow next to the zoom percentage, you can **select from a variety of different zoom ratios**, from 6% to 1600%.

When you're zoomed in, click and drag the photo to move it around to see hidden sections of the photo. If you're using an editing tool, such as the brush (page 242), hold down the Spacebar key while clicking and dragging.

To **zoom out**, click on the photo again or click *Fit* to zoom out. *Fit* view fits the whole photo in the preview area.

There are a few more options for easy zooming:

The Spacebar key toggles between the last

two zoom ratios you clicked on, so by default, it toggles between *Fit* and *100%* view. The Ctrl = (Windows) / Cmd = (Mac) and Ctrl - (Windows) / Cmd - (Mac) shortcuts zoom in and out through all of the zoom ratios.

Scrubby Zoom and *Box Zoom* are both useful when you want to zoom in on a specific area of the photo.

To use **Scrubby Zoom**, click and hold the mouse to show the Scrubby Zoom cursor, then drag right/left to zoom-in/out continuously.

To use **Box Zoom**, hold down Ctrl (Windows) / Cmd (Mac) and click and drag on the image to draw a rectangular marquee.

Lightroom zooms in to fill the preview area with the selected area of the photo.

PLAYING VIDEOS

Most photographers shoot short video clips on their mobile phones, even if they're not "into video."

While Lightroom is primarily designed for photographs, it is able to store and play many popular video formats.

The videos are identified using a small icon and timestamp at the top of the thumbnails.

When you open a video into Detail view, a play button appears in the center of the preview.

To **play the video**, click the triangular play button. Additional video controls appear below, allowing you to pause and scrub through the video timeline.

VIDEO PLAYBACK (WINDOWS/MAC)

Play/Pause

Timestamp on thumbnail

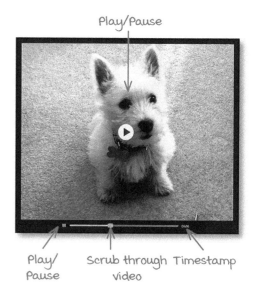

Play/Pause   Scrub through video   Timestamp

VIEWING PHOTOS ON A MOBILE DEVICE

Viewing photos in the iOS/Android apps follows the same principles, but because the interface is small, the panels are replaced with a series of screens, as demonstrated on page 22.

As you'll know the basics of your own phone/tablet operating system, we'll just cover a few less obvious features...

LIBRARY VIEW

Like the Photos panel on the left of the Windows/Mac apps, the Library view (illustrated on page 80 and page 81) allows you to organize your photos into albums and album folders. We'll come back to managing albums on page 76, but for now, tap on *All Photos* and we'll start viewing some of your photos.

The Library view is split into the standard Photos view and the Sharing view (page 345). On an iPad, you can **show/hide the Library panel** by tapping the buttons at the top.

GRID VIEW OPTIONS

Using the Grid view (illustrated on page 70 and page 71), you can view multiple photos, filter them and change the sort order.

On iOS, you can change the **thumbnail size** by going to ... *menu > View Options > Small/Normal/Large Thumbnails* or by using a pinch/spread gesture. If you two-finger tap on the thumbnails, you can cycle through a series of **metadata overlays**. (These features aren't currently available on Android.)

CHANGING THE SORT ORDER

To **change the sort order**, click the ... icon in Grid view to show the menu, then select *Sort by ...*. In the following menu, you can select the sort order of your choice. To **reverse the sort order**, for example, from oldest to newest photos first, select *Reverse Order*.

You can manually rearrange the photos into a **custom sort order**. Select *Custom* from the Sort menu, then tap *Edit* (iOS) / pencil icon (Android).

On iOS, tap photos to select them, then hold your finger on one of the selected photos and drag them to a new location between two photos. Tap *Done* when you're finished.

On Android, hold your finger on a photo and drag it to a new location between two photos, then release your finger. (You can only move one photo at a time on Android.) Press the X to return to Grid view.

DETAIL VIEW

The Detail views (illustrated on page 72 and page 73) are used for viewing and editing photos. It's split into 5 (iOS) / 4 (Android) view modes, each designed for different tasks.

Rate & Review mode is used for viewing photos and adding flags and star ratings (page 72).

Info view displays photo metadata and allows you to add a Title and Caption (page 96).

Keywords view on iOS allows you to view, add and delete keywords. On Android, keywords are found at the bottom of the

Info view (page 96).

Edit view gives you access to all of the profiles, presets and sliders, as well as the crop and selective editing tools (page 144).

Activity view shows likes and comments from shared web galleries (page 344).

To **view a photo in Detail view**, tap on it in the grid. To **zoom in or out**, double-tap on the photo, or use a spread/pinch gesture.

To **switch between these Detail views** on a phone, tap the pop-up at the top of the screen. On a tablet, tap the buttons on the right to show/hide the panels, as you would on a desktop.

There's a filmstrip at the bottom of the Detail views on tablets, to allow you to view and select nearby photos without returning to the Grid view. You can **show/hide the filmstrip** using the Filmstrip button.

The Filmstrip is also available in Rate & Review mode on iPhones, and you can show/hide it by going to *... menu > View Options > Filmstrip*.

The mobile apps can **play videos** imported from the device or downloaded from the cloud. Tap the play button in the center of the screen, or scrub along the timeline at the bottom of the screen.

SELECTING PHOTOS

On mobile, you can't select multiple photos to apply the same action to all of them at once, for example, to add the same keyword to multiple photos. However, there are a few things you can do to multiple photos, including:

- copy or move photos between albums

- remove photos from albums

- delete photos from the cloud

- share or save photos

- apply some metadata such as Copyright

On phones, show/hide Detail view modes using the pop-up at the top

On tablets, show/hide Detail view panels and Edit tools using the buttons on the right

Show/Hide Filmstrip

(currently Android only)

• copy/paste edit settings

Hold your finger on a photo in Grid view to **activate selection mode** (or go to ... *menu > Select*). Tap the photos to select them, or hold a finger down on a photo and then swipe across other photos to select multiple, and then tap an icon at the bottom (iOS) / top (Android) of the screen to share, remove, delete, or add/copy them to other albums.

GRID VIEW (IOS)

On an iPad, the Library panel (page 80) and Grid view can be active at the same time. Tap the Photos button to show/hide the Library panel.

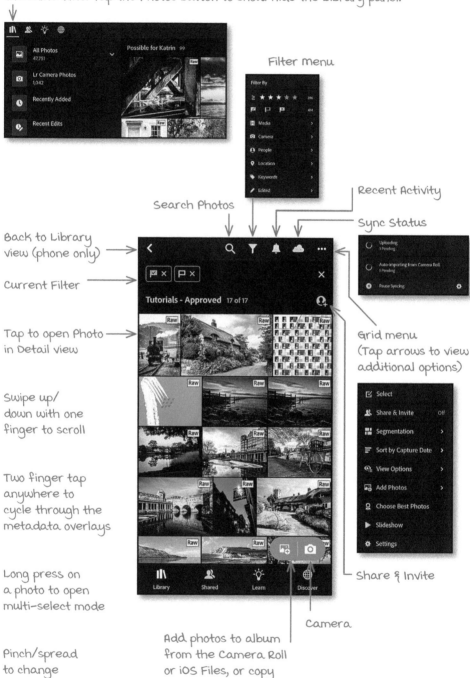

Filter menu

Search Photos

Recent Activity

Sync Status

Back to Library view (phone only)

Current Filter

Tap to open Photo in Detail view

Grid menu
(Tap arrows to view additional options)

Swipe up/ down with one finger to scroll

Two finger tap anywhere to cycle through the metadata overlays

Long press on a photo to open multi-select mode

Share & Invite

Camera

Pinch/spread to change thumbnail size

Add photos to album from the Camera Roll or iOS Files, or copy from All Photos

GRID VIEW (ANDROID)

Filter menu

Recent Activity

Search Photos

Back to
Library view

Current Filter

Tap to open Photo
in Detail view

Swipe up/
down with one
finger to scroll

Long press on
a photo to open
multi-select mode

Grid menu
(Tap arrows to view
additional options)

Camera

Add photos to album
from the Device or
copy from All Photos

DETAIL VIEW (IOS)

Share menu

Sync Status

Tap to switch between
Edit, Info, Keywords, Rate &
Review and Activity views

Help

Back to Grid view →

Two finger tap
anywhere to cycle
through metadata
overlay & histogram,
metadata only,
histogram only
or neither

← menu

Sub menus:

One finger tap on
metadata cycles
metadata views

Swipe left <>
right on the photo
with one finger
to view the next/
previous photo

Double-tap
anywhere or
pinch/spread to
zoom in and out

Tap on the photo
to hide controls

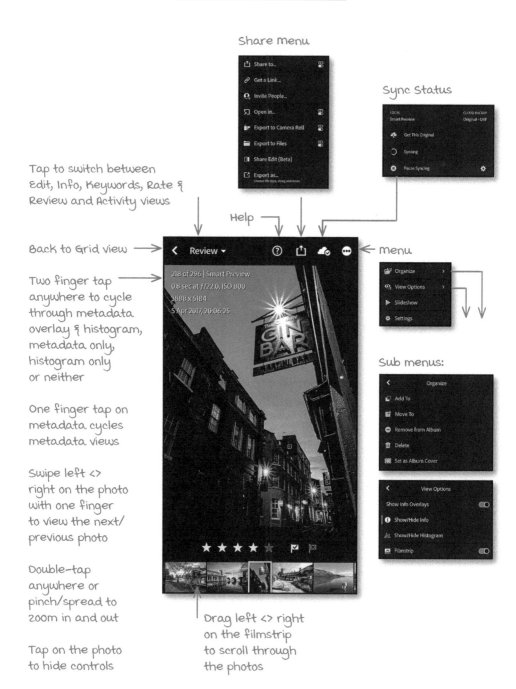

Drag left <> right
on the filmstrip
to scroll through
the photos

DETAIL VIEW (ANDROID)

Sync Status

Share menu

Tap to switch between
Edit, Info and Rate &
Review and Activity views

Back to Grid view ⟶

Enable metadata ⟶
or histogram
in the menu

One finger tap on
metadata cycles
metadata views

Swipe left <>
right on the photo
with one finger
to view the next/
previous photo

Double-tap
anywhere or
pinch/spread to
zoom in and out

Tap on the photo
to hide controls

menu

← Drag left <> right
on the filmstrip
to scroll through
the photos

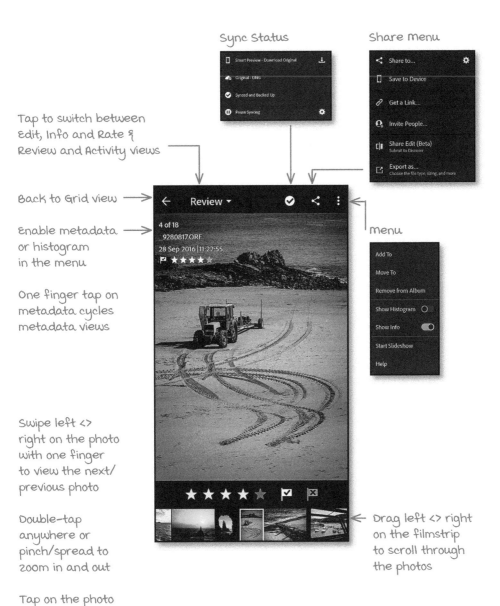

VIEWING PHOTOS GROUPED BY DATE

If you remember the date, month or even just the year that a photo was taken, you can use that information to narrow down the photos in the current view, rather than having to scroll through everything.

DATE VIEWS ON THE DESKTOP

Lightroom automatically groups the photos by date. Click on *All Photos* to show:

Recently Added displays the photos added during your five most recent imports. This is useful when you've just added photos shot on multiple dates.

By Date groups your photos by the date they were captured. You can display the entire year, month, or narrow it down to a

specific day. This is particularly useful when you remember when you shot a photo, for example, the date of your wedding or vacation.

Click on the text or number to **display the photos captured in that year** or month, or click on the arrow to collapse/expand sub-dates.

To **display photos from multiple dates** at once, for example, multiple vacation days, click on one date and then either hold down Ctrl (Windows) / Cmd (Mac) and click on each of the other dates, or hold down the Shift key and click on the first and last dates in the series.

If you're already viewing a photo, and want to see other photos captured on the same date, right-click on the photo and select **Show Photos from Same Date**.

SEGMENTED VIEW ON MOBILE

On mobile, if you go to the *All Photos* collection, you can **segment the grid by date** (or other metadata).

On iOS, tap the ... menu icon, select *Segmentation* and then select *Auto, Years,* *Months, Days, Hours, Flags, Star Ratings or File Types*.

On Android, tap the ... menu and toggle *Grid Segmentation*, then go to *Segment by...* to select the time period.

Tap the arrow on the right to collapse or expand individual segments.

VIEW BY DATE (iOS/ANDROID)

← In Library view, tap All Photos.

← Tap ... menu and select Segmentation (iOS) / Grid Segmentation (Android).

← Tap arrow to show or hide additional photos.

GROUPING PHOTOS IN ALBUMS

In the left panel on the desktop, or in Library view on mobile, are your albums. Albums allow you to group photos for a specific purpose, for example:

- Your best photos as a portfolio.

- Photos to share with someone, perhaps as an online gallery.

- Photos of an event, such as a vacation.

- Photos of specific genre.

- Photos you've published on social media.

- Photos for output as a slideshow, prints, or a photobook.

The same photo can appear in lots of different albums. Even if a photo is not in an album, it's still available in the *All Photos* and *By Date* views.

CREATING ALBUMS

To **create an album**, click/tap the **+** button at the top of the panel, select *Create Album*, then give the album a name.

If you have a folder selected, you can place the album inside that folder by checking the *Inside folder* checkbox (desktop only). On mobile, the new album is automatically added to the selected folder. Folders are a way of grouping related albums, for example, family vacations. We'll come back to folders later in the lesson.

While creating an album on the desktop, you can also choose to include any photos that are currently selected.

Create Album

> Album Name

☑ Include the selected photo
☑ Inside folder "Holidays"

Cancel   Create

To **add photos to an existing album** on the desktop, select the photos in Grid view (or in the Filmstrip) and drag them to the album in the Albums panel.

On mobile, hold your finger on a photo in Grid view to activate selection mode (or go to ... *menu > Select*). Tap the photos to select them, or hold a finger on a photo and then swipe across other photos to select multiple photos. On iOS, tap the *Add To* button, or on Android, tap the ... menu and select *Add To*. Finally, select the target album, and tap *Add*.

If you're viewing an album on iOS/Android, there's an additional *Move To* option that removes the photos from the current album while adding them to a different album, which can be handy if you have an album of photos you need to sort into topic-based albums.

To **find photos that aren't organized into an album** yet, go to the Search field (which we'll discuss on page 108), type *album:* and wait... When the pop-up appears, scroll right to the end and select *Not in any album*. (This currently only works on the desktop apps.)

TARGET ALBUM

If you're scrolling through your photos, looking for ones to add to a specific album, dragging them over to the Albums panel can be slow. On the desktop, there's a customizable shortcut that can help, called the Target Album. To **set an album as the Target Album**, right-click on the album and select *Set [album name] as the Target Album*. To **add the selected photos to the Target Album**, simply press the T key. You can change the target album to a different album by repeating the process.

MANAGING ALBUMS

Your photo groupings are likely to change over time, so you'll need to know how to remove photos and manage the albums.

If you're viewing a photo on the desktop, check the Info panel to see **which albums contain that photo**. Click on an album name to view the rest of the album.

To **remove photos from an album** on the desktop, select the photos in the Grid view, then right-click and choose *Remove Photos* or press the Backspace key (Windows) / Delete key (Mac).

On mobile, hold your finger on a photo in Grid view to activate selection mode, select the photos and then tap the trashcan icon and select *Remove from Album*.

Remove from Album just removes the photos from the selected album, but the photos remain available in the *All Photos* and *Date* views, as well as in any other albums that contained the photo. *Delete*, on the other hand, actually deletes the photos everywhere (page 84), so be careful to select the right option!

All of these *Remove from Album* options are also available in Detail view, but only apply to single photos.

To **delete an album**, right-click on the album (desktop) / tap the album's ... menu (mobile) and select *Delete*. This deletes the album, but not the photos inside the album.

To **rename an album**, right-click on the album (desktop) / tap the album's ... menu (mobile) and select *Rename*, then type the new name.

If the album name is too long to display in the Albums panel (desktop) / Library view (mobile), float the mouse cursor over the album name to show the full name in a tooltip on the desktop, or rotate your mobile device to horizontal view.

To **change the cover photo** on the desktop, click on the album, then right-click on a photo in Grid view and choose *Set as Album Cover*. On iOS, select the photo in a Detail view (e.g., Rate & Review), tap the ... menu and select *Organize menu > Set as Album Cover*. On Android, hold your finger on the photo in Grid view to select it, then tap the

... menu and choose *Set as Cover*.

The cover photos always show on mobile, but to **show/hide the cover photos** on the desktop (in order to minimize the vertical height required), click the view menu button at the top of the Albums panel.

Album Names vs. Names & Cover Photos

While you're in the albums view menu, you can also **change the sort order** of the album list.

GROUPING ALBUMS IN FOLDERS

As your list of albums grows, it can be hard to find specific albums. Like folders on your computer's hard drive, you can group the related albums into folders. For example, you may want to group all of your vacation albums together in a folder, and perhaps create another folder for albums related to your photography projects.

To **create a folder**, click the **+** button, select *Create Folder*, then give the folder a name.

To **move an album into a folder** on the desktop, or to nest folders inside of other folders (up to 5 deep), select it and drag it onto the folder, which turns blue, and release the mouse.

On mobile, tap on the album/folder's ... menu, then select *Move to Folder*. Select the folder to place it inside, then tap *Move*. (You can also create a new folder by clicking the + button, and then select it.)

To **move an album/subfolder out of folders**, and back up to the top of the list, drag the album/subfolder to the left, until a blue bar appears, and then release the mouse.

On mobile, tap on the album/folder's ... menu, then select *Move to Folder*. This time, don't select a folder before tapping *Move*.

To **open/close a folder** to see the albums inside, toggle the arrow to the left of its name (desktop) / tap the folder (mobile).

If you can't remember where you stored an album, rather than opening all of the folders in turn, simply select the *All Photos* view and start to type the album name in the search field (desktop only).

To **view all of the photos** contained in all of the albums inside a folder, click on the folder name (desktop only).

To **delete a folder**, right-click on the folder (desktop) / tap the folder's ... menu (mobile) and select *Delete*. The folder and any albums inside the folder are deleted, but the photos themselves are not.

ALBUMS (WINDOWS/MAC)

Show menu to create
New Album or Folder

Show menu to change sort
order and view options

Album Folder

Toggle arrows
to expand/
collapse folders

Album

Album Cover
Photo

Album photo
count

Right-click on folder or
album to rename/delete

Right-click on Album to share
using Lightroom Web

Drop the album/folder on
a folder to nest them

Drag an album/folder to the left to
show the blue bar to un-nest them

LIBRARY VIEW (IOS)

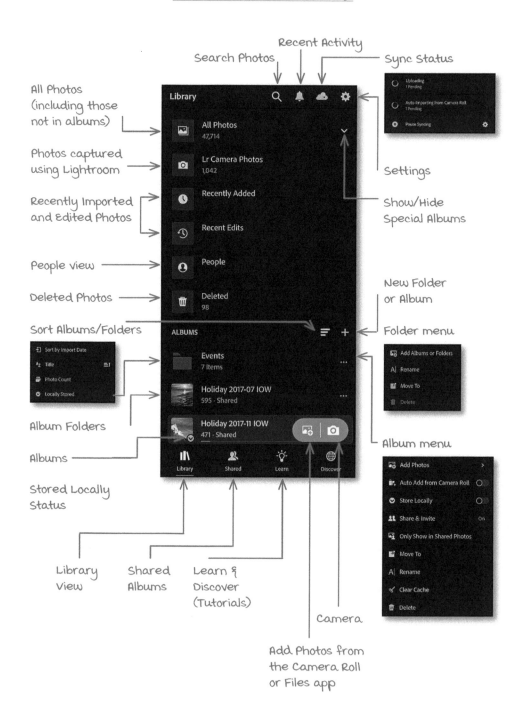

Recent Activity

Search Photos

Sync Status

All Photos
(including those
not in albums)

Library

All Photos
47,714

Uploading
1 Pending

Auto-Importing from Camera Roll
1 Pending

Pause Syncing

Photos captured
using Lightroom

Lr Camera Photos
1,042

Settings

Recently Imported
and Edited Photos

Recently Added

Show/Hide
Special Albums

Recent Edits

People view

People

New Folder
or Album

Deleted Photos

Deleted
98

Sort Albums/Folders

ALBUMS

Folder menu

Sort by Import Date

Title

Photo Count

Locally Stored

Events
7 Items

Add Albums or Folders

Rename

Move To

Delete

Holiday 2017-07 IOW
595 · Shared

Album Folders

Albums

Holiday 2017-11 IOW
471 · Shared

Album menu

Library   Shared   Learn   Discover

Add Photos

Auto Add from Camera Roll

Store Locally

Share & Invite   On

Only Show in Shared Photos

Move To

Rename

Clear Cache

Delete

Stored Locally
Status

Library
View

Shared
Albums

Learn &
Discover
(Tutorials)

Camera

Add Photos from
the Camera Roll
or Files app

LIBRARY VIEW (ANDROID)

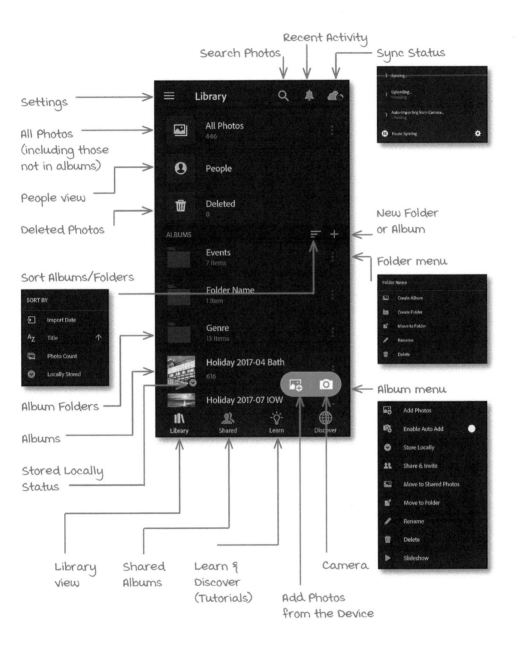

Search Photos

Recent Activity

Sync Status

Settings

All Photos
(including those
not in albums)

People view

Deleted Photos

Sort Albums/Folders

Album Folders

Albums

Stored Locally
Status

New Folder
or Album

Folder menu

Album menu

Library
view

Shared
Albums

Learn &
Discover
(Tutorials)

Add Photos
from the Device

Camera

GROUPING PHOTOS USING STACKS

Sometimes you might shoot a series of similar photos, for example:

• A high speed burst to capture action.

• A series of photos to merge into a panorama.

• Bracketed exposures for HDR.

• Raw+JPEG pairs of photos, because you like the in-camera picture style.

• An original photo plus the TIFF you edited in Photoshop.

You may not want to delete the similar photos, but these groups of photos can clutter the grid view, making it hard to see the wood for the trees.

Stacking allows you to group similar photos and display them as a single photo in the Grid view. It's currently only available on the Windows/Mac apps.

MANAGING STACKS

To **stack photos**, select the photos in the Grid, right-click and select *Group into Stack*.

To **view the photos in a stack**, click on

the stack icon. The thumbnails appear in a special Filmstrip at the bottom of the preview area.

To **view the hidden photos in Detail view**, first open the stack by clicking on the stack icon, then switch to Detail view. The Filmstrip at the bottom of the preview area displays the stacked photos until you collapse the stack.

To **collapse the stack**, click the X button in the Filmstrip, or click the stack icon in the Grid again.

To **ungroup the stack** of photos, changing them back into separate photos, right-click on the collapsed stack and select *Ungroup*.

To **remove one or more photos** from a stack without ungrouping the whole stack, select the photos you want to remove, right-click and select *Remove Photo(s) from Stack* or select the photos and press the Backspace key (Windows) / Delete key (Mac).

To **change the stack cover photo**, which is the one that shows in the main Grid view, right-click on your chosen photo and select *Set as Stack Cover* or drag the thumbnail onto the small square to the left of the stack.

STACKS ARE ALBUM-SPECIFIC

Stacks are album-specific, so stacking photos in one album doesn't stack them in another.

If you create a stack in *All Photos*, and then add the stack to an album, it's stacked in the new album too, however the photos aren't automatically stacked in other existing albums.

If you create a stack in an album, it's displayed as a stack in *All Photos*, but not in other albums.

EDITING STACKS

In some situations, your actions affect all of the photos in a stack, whereas other actions only affect the cover photo.

The principle is that organizing tasks (such as adding or removing a stack from an album) apply to the whole stack, whereas editing tasks (metadata edits or slider adjustments) apply only to the cover photo.

To apply metadata to all of the photos inside a stack, you must expand the stack and select the photos and then apply your keyword or other metadata edits.

STACKS (WINDOWS/MAC)

DELETING & RESTORING PHOTOS

Whether your finger slipped, the camera settings were incorrect, or you just missed the moment, some photos simply aren't worth keeping.

While you could mark bad photos as rejects and hide them, completely deleting the really bad photos frees up space on your hard drive and in the cloud.

REMOVE VS. DELETE

In an earlier lesson, we discussed how to remove photos from an album (page 76), and in the last lesson (page 82), how to remove photos from a stack.

It's worth noting the difference in terminology between removing photos and completely deleting them.

Remove just removes the photos from the selected album or stack, but the photo remains available in the *All Photos* and date views.

Delete deletes the photos from your computers and mobile devices. If they were already synced to the cloud, they're temporarily placed in the cloud trash.

DELETING PHOTOS

On the desktop, to **delete photos from All Photos**, select them, right-click and choose **Delete Photos**, go to *Edit menu > Delete Photos* or use the shortcut Alt-Backspace (Windows) / Opt-Delete (Mac), then confirm your choice.

On mobile, hold your finger on a photo to activate multi-select mode (or go to ... *menu > Select*). Tap the photos to select them, or hold a finger down on a photo and then swipe across other photos to select multiple photos, then tap the trashcan icon and select *Delete*.

If you're viewing a single photo in a Detail view on iOS, tap the ... menu and select *Organize menu > Delete*. On Android, tap the Detail view's ... menu, select *Remove from Album* and then choose *Delete*.

The confirmation dialog on desktop, or the bar at the top of the screen on mobile, confirms the number of photos you're deleting. Always double-check this number!

SAFELY DELETING PHOTOS

When you're sorting through photos, don't try to delete one photo at a time. It's inefficient, because you have to keep confirming your decision, and it's easy to make a mistake. Instead, mark them with a reject flag (instructions coming up on page 89), then use Refine View to show only the rejected photos (instructions to follow on page 108), select them all, double-check you definitely want to delete them, then go ahead and delete.

RESTORING ACCIDENTAL DELETIONS

Deleted photos remain in the cloud trash for 60 days, unless you restore them or empty the trash. They don't count towards your cloud storage quota.

There are currently a couple of limitations to be aware of:

• If the photos were only low resolution smart previews synced from Lightroom Classic, then only smart previews can be restored.

• It may take some time to restore photos down to your desktop or mobile app, if they need to be downloaded from the cloud again. If you're offline, the photos may not be fully restored until you're next online.

• Album membership and almost all metadata and edits are restored with the photo. The exception is stack membership (page 82).

If you accidentally delete some photos, select the **Deleted Photos** view on the desktop, mobile or web app.

DELETED PHOTOS (WINDOWS/MAC)

View Deleted Photos

Time left until permanently deleted automatically

Sync status

Restore photo

Permanently delete photo

View menu to restore all photos or clear the trash

To **restore a single photo** on the desktop/web, click the undo icon below the thumbnail. On mobile, long press on one or more photos to enter selection mode and tap *Restore*.

To **permanently delete a single photo** on the desktop/web, click the trash icon.

To **restore or permanently delete multiple photos** on the desktop/web, click the checkmark to select them, then select the restore or delete icons from the blue bar at the top. Having checked the first photo, you can hold down the Shift key and click on the last photo in a series to select multiple consecutive photos, like selections on the desktop. On mobile, long press on a photo to enter selection mode, tap to select multiple photos, then tap the *Restore* or *Delete* icons.

To **manually empty the trash** or restore all of the deleted photos, click/tap the ... icon and select **Permanently Delete All** or **Restore All** from the menu.

DELETED PHOTOS (IOS/ANDROID)

←View menu to restore all photos or clear the trash

... menu > Select or long press to enter selection mode and select photos

Restore or permanently → delete selected photos

ADDING METADATA & SEARCHING

7

Using the Info and Keyword panels, you can view and add metadata.

To show the Info and Keyword panels on the desktop, click the button in the right panel bar, or press the I key for Info or the K key for Keywords.

Keywords panel

Info panel

On a mobile device, tap on a photo to open into Detail view, then select the Info or Keywords view from the pop-up at the top of the screen on a phone, or the icons down the sidebar on a tablet.

< Info ▾

⚙ Edit

★ Rate & Review

💬 Activity

🏷 Keywords

ℹ Info

WHAT IS METADATA?

Metadata is often defined as 'data describing data.'

As far as photos are concerned, There are two main types of metadata:

EXIF data is technical information added by the camera at the time of capture. It includes camera and lens information such as the make and model, and image information such as the capture date/time, shutter speed, aperture, ISO, and pixel dimensions.

IPTC data is added by the photographer to describe the photo, for example, title, caption, keywords and the photographer's name and copyright.

Lightroom also stores all of your edits as metadata, which means that it records your changes as a set of text instructions (e.g., *Exposure +0.33, Highlights −30, Shadows +25*, etc.) instead of applying them directly to the image data. This means you can edit the photo again later without degrading the image quality.

WHY VIEW & ADD METADATA?

Metadata can help you find photos again later and examining the camera settings can also help you learn to become a better photographer. For example, if you find blur caused by movement in a photo, your shutter speed was too slow, or if the photo is too noisy (grainy), check the ISO value.

IMAGE ANALYSIS

In addition to the metadata you add manually, Adobe's computers scan your images looking for recognizable content. Like any artificial intelligence, it's not perfect, but it allows you to search for photos even if you haven't manually added metadata to describe the content.

IN THIS SECTION, WE'LL CONSIDER:

• How to flag and star rate photos.

• How to view metadata added by the camera.

• How to add titles, captions and copyright.

• How to view and add location metadata.

• How to add keywords.

• How to use Lightroom's image-analysis to search for specific subjects, without having to manually add metadata to the photos.

• How to refine the current view based on your flags or star ratings, keywords, camera models, locations and more.

FLAGGING OR STAR RATING PHOTOS

Marking the best photos with flags or star ratings makes them easy to find again later.

WHICH PHOTOS ARE WORTH KEEPING?

How you decide which photos are deserving of a specific ranking is a personal decision, but there are a few questions that may help:

- Does the photo immediately grab you?

- Does the photo trigger a strong emotion or a memory?

- Does the photo tell a story or capture a special moment?

- Do you have a similar photo that's better?

- Is the subject (person/animal) making eye contact? Does it capture their personality?

- Are there significant technical issues, for example, is it in focus?

Move fast and don't agonize over decisions. Your gut instinct is often right.

FLAGS VS. STARS

Lightroom offers two different ways of ranking your photos:

Flags have three different states—flagged (picked), unflagged and rejected. Most people use flags to mean:

- ○ Flagged—photos worth keeping

- ○ Unflagged—not sorted yet

- ○ Rejected—to be deleted

Star Ratings are used by photographers worldwide. Most use 5 stars for their very best portfolio images and 0 stars for unsorted photos.

APPLYING FLAGS OR STARS ON THE DESKTOP

There are multiple ways of applying a flag or star rating. On the desktop, these include:

- Click the icons in the toolbar beneath the photo in Grid or Detail view.

- Click the icons on the thumbnail border in Square Grid view. The icons appear as you float the mouse cursor over the border.

- Use the keyboard shortcuts: Z to flag, U to unflag, X to reject. 0-5 for 0-5 stars. Add the Shift key to these shortcuts to automatically move to the next photo.

APPLYING FLAGS OR STARS ON MOBILE

On mobile, tap on a photo to open into a Detail view, then select the Rate & Review view from the pop-up at the top of the screen on mobile phones, or the star icon in the sidebar on tablets. You can then:

• Tap the icons in the toolbar beneath the photo in Grid or Detail view.

• Swipe up/down on the left of the screen for stars or on the right for flags.

• If you have an external keyboard connected, you can use the keyboard shortcuts: P to flag, U to unflag, X to reject and 0-5 for 0-5 stars.

BEST PHOTOS

Best Photos is an Adobe Sensei-based artificial intelligence which analyzes your photos and tries to figure out which it thinks are your best photos. At the time of writing, it can be accessed from the iOS, Android and Web apps.

To **see Lightroom's recommendations**, select an album with 10-2000 photos. Go to the Grid view and select ... menu > Choose Best Photos. Lightroom analyzes the photos and then displays a grid of thumbnails. At the bottom is a slider to increase or decrease the quality threshold..

If you **agree with Lightroom's selection** of the best photos, tap the ... menu and select

BEST PHOTOS (IOS/ANDROID)

Back to normal Grid view

... menu

Suggested best photos

Other photos

Threshold of included photos

Create Album to create an album of these best photos, Flag as Picked to flag them, or simply export them. Alternatively, you can remove the other photos, either using Flag as Rejected or Remove from Album.

If you only agree with some of the selections, you can open individual photos into the Detail view to flag/reject them.

RATING WORKFLOW

Everyone has a different system. Some photographers use Grid view and others prefer Detail view. Some like to rate their photos in a single pass, and others like multiple passes. Some like flags and some prefer stars. Whatever you pick, just be consistent.

Flexibility is a wonderful thing, but so much choice can be confusing, so I've included my tried and tested desktop rating workflow on the following pages to help you get started.

MY RATINGS MEAN...

	meaning	What's Next...
⚑✕	Really bad photo worthy of deletion	Nothing (deleted)
★	Should be deleted really, but I'm a packrat	Nothing (ignored)
★★	Triggers a memory, but not great as a photo The hotel room, a meal out with friends, etc.	A fast edit and a few keywords. They might end up in a photo book or slide show, but they'll never be great photos in their own right
★★★	A decent photo I'd be willing to show someone	
★★★★	Good photo, might end up on the wall or social media	A careful edit, possibly some Photoshop work, titles/ captions and more extensive keywords. These are the photos that will end up on the wall or on social media
★★★★★	Best photos I've ever taken. Rare!	

MY DESKTOP RATING WORKFLOW

STEP I—FIND THE BEST AND WORST PHOTOS

Start off in Grid view with large thumbnails.
It's easier to make decisions when you're
not bogged down in the details

Just flag or reject the ones you really like
or don't like. Leave the rest unflagged

"Yeah, keep that!"   "Boring..."   "Ooops!"

STEP 2—DELETE THE REALLY BAD ONES

Click the Refine View button
to show the filters

 ← Refine view

Click the Rejected button

Select all (Ctrl-A / Cmd-A)

Go to Edit menu > Delete Photos to delete them
from your computer and the cloud (page 84)

STEP 3—HIDE THE PHOTOS THAT DON'T EXCITE YOU

Click the X button in the search bar to clear the previous filter

Click the Unflagged button

Select all (Ctrl-A / Cmd-A)

Press the number I key to give them I star,
meaning that you'll keep them for now,
but not waste further time on them

STEP 4—GO BACK THROUGH THE GOOD ONES

Click the X button in the search bar
to clear the previous filter

Click the flagged button to
show only flagged photos

Go back through the Flagged photos
again, occasionally switching to
Detail view to check focus

Press the number 2, 3 or 4 keys to
give them 2, 3 or 4 stars, depending
on how much you love the photo

"It's a bad photo but
it sparks a memory
or tells the story."

"I like that!"

"I LOVE that! I'd hang
that on my wall!"

STEP 5—ALLOW TIME TO PASS

Some months later, go back through
the 3 and 4 star photos and see if any
need to be upgraded or downgraded

It's easier to make an objective
decision when time has passed

ADDING TITLES, CAPTIONS & COPYRIGHT

Some photographers like to add descriptive text to the photos to remind them of the story behind the photo.

The **Title** and **Caption** fields do have official IPTC definitions (http://www.iptc.org/), but many photographers simply use *Title* for a short image title (e.g., "Blue Eyes") and *Caption* for a more descriptive paragraph (e.g., "Kanika, the Amur Leopard cub, has piercing blue eyes").

Title
Three's Company

Caption
Three swans walk out of the water in a row

Copyright
© Victoria Bampton

APPLYING METADATA

To **open the Info panel**, click the i button in the right panel bar (desktop/tablet), press the I key (desktop) or select **Info** from the pop-up at the top of a Detail view (phone).

← Info panel

To **add metadata** to a single photo, simply type in the Info panel.

To **add the same metadata to multiple photos** on the desktop, first select the photos in Grid view, and then type the metadata in the Info panel. From the Android Grid view, hold your finger on a photo to enter selection mode, tap to select the photos you want to edit, and then go to ... *menu > Edit Info*. Enter the metadata and tap the checkmark to confirm. (Not currently available on iOS.)

Some cameras automatically add text into a metadata field, for example, Olympus cameras add *OLYMPUS DIGITAL CAMERA* as the caption. To **delete the metadata from multiple photos** on the desktop, select them in Grid view, click in the *Caption* field and delete the text. On Android, select the photos in the Grid view, go to ... *menu >Edit Info* and tap the X at the end of the field to

clear the existing metadata and then tap the checkmark to confirm.

ADDING COPYRIGHT

It's important to add your copyright to your photos. While it doesn't prevent theft, it does make it easy to identify you as the photographer, especially if you post the photos online.

In many countries, the **Copyright** notice requires the copyright symbol ©, the year of first publication and then the name of the copyright owner, for example, © *2020 Victoria Bampton*. Copyright laws vary by country, so please check your local laws for exact specifications.

You can have your copyright automatically applied to photos as you add them to Lightroom, so you don't forget. On the desktop, check *Preferences > General > **Add copyright to imported images***. It's smart enough to only add copyright to new photos that don't have an existing copyright entry. For the equivalent setting on iOS, go to *Settings > General > Add Copyright*, or on Android, go to *Settings > Preferences > Photo Import Options > Add Copyright*.

But how do you type that © symbol? On the desktop, it's automatically entered for you. If you accidentally delete it, type Ctrl-Alt-C (Windows) / Opt-G (Mac). On iOS,

PHOTO INFO/METADATA (WINDOWS/MAC)

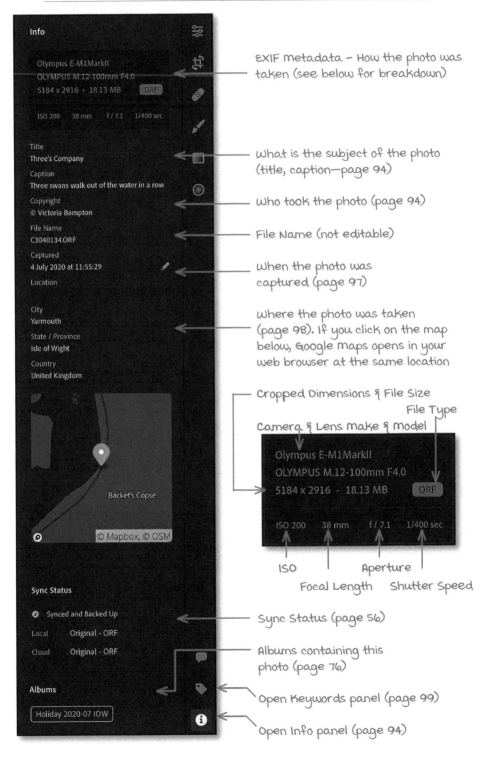

EXIF metadata - How the photo was taken (see below for breakdown)

What is the subject of the photo (title, caption—page 94)

Who took the photo (page 94)

File Name (not editable)

When the photo was captured (page 97)

Where the photo was taken (page 98). If you click on the map below, Google Maps opens in your web browser at the same location

Cropped Dimensions & File Size

File Type

Camera & Lens make & model

ISO   Aperture

Focal Length   Shutter Speed

Sync Status (page 56)

Albums containing this photo (page 76)

Open Keywords panel (page 99)

Open Info panel (page 94)

you can type (c) followed by a space, and it's automatically converted. On Android, the copyright symbol may be found with the emojis or symbols on some third-party keyboards, or you can simply do a web search for *copyright symbol* and copy/paste from a web page.

PHOTO INFO/METADATA (IOS/ANDROID)

iOS

Android

On iOS, keywords are in a separate view mode

On Android, keywords are at the bottom of the Info view

FIXING THE CAPTURE DATE & TIME

We've all done it... you go on vacation abroad, or Daylight Savings Time starts, and you forget to change the time stamp on the camera. It's not a problem though, as Lightroom on the desktop makes it easy to correct the time stamp. (This isn't currently available on mobile.)

STEP-BY-STEP

1. Select the photos in the Photo Grid or Square Grid.

2. Go to *Photo menu > Edit Date & Time* or click the pencil icon next to the date field in the Info panel.

Captured
30 January 2018 at 14:02:06 ✏

3. In the Shift Date Range dialog, enter the correct date and time for the most recent photo in the selection. Other selected photos automatically shift by the same increment, rather than all being set to the same time.

Shift Date Range   22 photos

Current date range
30 January 2018 at 13:56:55 - 30 January 2018 at 14:53:06

Change end of range
31   January ⬍   2018   PM ⬍   02 : 53 : 06

This is the most recent capture date in the group. Other selected photos will automatically shift based on this new date.

Reset   Cancel   Change

VIEWING & EDITING THE PHOTO LOCATION

Location information on a photo can be useful for:

• Searching for photos by location, for example, vacation destinations.

• Knowing exactly where a photo was taken, so you can replicate it, perhaps at a different time of day or a different season.

This is currently only available on the desktop apps, and there isn't a way to copy a location to another photo.

AUTOMATIC GPS DATA

If your phone or camera embeds GPS metadata into the photos, the *City*, *State/Province* and *Country* fields are automatically populated, and the map appears below. This reverse geocoding is done on the server and then synced to your computer, so there may be a delay before the fields are populated.

MANUALLY ADDING A LOCATION

If your camera doesn't record the location, you can enter an approximate location manually. If you type the postal code / zip code into the *Location* field and the country into the *Country* field, Lightroom automatically looks up the rest of the address and displays the map.

MAP STYLES

If you right-click on the map, you can choose between *Road Map*, *Satellite*, *Hybrid* and *Terrain* map views. The *Hybrid* option is shown in this screenshot.

VIEWING IN GOOGLE MAPS

The small map is useful to see the approximate location, but sometimes you need more detail. If you click on the map, Lightroom opens your default web browser to the same location in Google Maps.

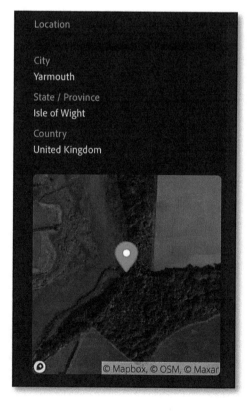

ADDING KEYWORDS

Keyword tags are text metadata used to describe the content of a photo.

Lightroom's image analysis technology is already able to identify many subjects, reducing the need for keywords. However, it's likely to be some time before software can correctly name your friends and family without some input from you, or tell the difference between a lesser spotted and great spotted woodpecker, so some keywords are still important.

Focus your efforts on your best photos, as they're the ones you're likely to want to find again in future.

TYPES OF KEYWORDS

If you've never keyworded photos before, you may be wondering where to start. There are no hard and fast rules for keywording unless you're shooting for Stock Photography.

Assuming you're shooting primarily for yourself, the main rule is simple—use keywords which will help you find the photos again later! For example, they can include:

Who is in the photo (people). (Lightroom can help with this task. We'll come back to identifying people on page 102.)

What is in the photo (other subjects or objects).

Where the photo was taken (names of locations).

Why the photo was taken (what's happening).

When the photo was taken (sunrise/sunset, season, event).

How the photo was taken (HDR, tilt-shift, panoramic).

CONSISTENCY

For keywords to be really helpful, you need to be consistent, for example:

Capitalization—stick to lower case for everything except names of people and places.

Quantity—either use singular or plural, but avoid mixing them. Either have "bird, cat, dog" or "birds, cats, dogs."

Verbs—stick to a single form, for example, "running, playing, jumping" rather than "run, play, jumping."

APPLYING KEYWORDS ON THE DESKTOP

To **open the Keywords panel** and activate the *Add Keyword* field, click the tag icon in the bottom right corner, or press the K key.

 ← Keywords panel

To **add a keyword**, type directly in the *Add Keyword* field, then press Enter. You can add multiple keywords by separating them using commas.

To **delete a keyword** from a photo, hover over it in the tag cloud so it turns red, then click.

To add to, or delete keywords from, **multiple photos** at once, you must be in Grid view with the photos selected. When you're in Detail view, your actions only affect the single visible photo.

APPLYING KEYWORDS ON MOBILE

To **open the Keywords view** on a mobile device, switch to Detail view and select Keywords view (iOS) / Info view (Android) using the pop-up (mobile) / icons in the sidebar (tablet).

To **add a keyword**, type directly in the text field. You can add multiple keywords by separating them using commas.

To **delete a keyword** from a photo on mobile, tap on the keyword tag.

Unlike the desktop, you can't select multiple photos at once, but on iOS, you can copy keywords from one photo to another, which is useful when you're adding a whole series of keywords. To do so, tap the ... menu, then select *Copy Keywords*. Move to the next photo, return to the ... menu and select *Paste Keywords*. (This isn't currently available on Android.)

There is one more advantage of keywording on a mobile device: voice recognition. By selecting the microphone on your device's keyboard, you can dictate your keywords.

KEYWORDS (WINDOWS/MAC)

To add a keyword, type it here ⟶

These keywords are applied to all of the selected photos ⟶

To delete a keyword from all of the selected photos, click on it when it turns red ⟶

These keywords are applied to some of the selected photos ⟶

To apply a keyword to all of the selected photos, click on it when it turns blue ⟶

KEYWORDS (IOS/ANDROID)

Switch to Keywords view (iOS) or Info view (Android) ⟶

⟵ (iOS only) Tap ... and select Copy Keywords or Paste Keywords. First copy the keywords to the clipboard, then switch photos and paste to save typing them all over again

To add keywords, type them here, separated by commas ⟶

To delete a keyword, tap on it ⟶

IDENTIFYING PEOPLE

Lightroom's image analysis technology can identify many subjects automatically, but it needs a helping hand with the names of your friends and family.

Once the photos are uploaded to the cloud, they're automatically searched for faces. The faces are then grouped into clusters of photos that are very likely the same person. It's not perfect, but it does a pretty good job, even recognizing people as they age.

Click on *All Photos* in the left panel on the desktop or in the Library view on mobile and then select *People* view. Here you can add names, merge photos of the same people captured at different angles, and hide people you don't want to see.

ADDING NAMES

To **name a person**, click on their thumbnail (cover photo) to enter the Person view, and click/tap at the top to enter the person's name. Click/tap the back arrow to return to the People view and repeat for the next person.

Before you get started, consider how you'll handle nicknames or last names for married women. Many people use the married name followed by the maiden name, for example, *Mary Married née Maiden*. Some also like

to add the date of birth for children, for example, *Katie Smith 2018-10-15*.

If you have as much trouble remembering names as I do, you might want to name them with clues that might prompt your memory later, such as *Katie ? née Smith, married to Michael Jones* or *Emma Brown's oldest son*. You can then fix their name later when you remember or someone else can tell you the answer!

If you want **change a person's name**, perhaps to fix a spelling mistake or add extra information, click/tap on name in Person view and type the correct name. On the desktop, you can also right-click on the person in People view and select *Rename Photo*, which saves a little time loading all of the photo thumbnails.

MERGING PEOPLE

If Lightroom's not sure that photos are of the same person, perhaps because they're at a different angle, it errs on the side of caution and leaves them as separate clusters.

To **merge duplicate people**, click/tap the ... icon and select *Merge People*. Check the clusters you want to merge into a single person and click *Merge* desktop or tap the checkmark on mobile.

Lightroom asks for confirmation that these

are the same person, and allows you to correct the name.

On the desktop, there are additional shortcuts. In People view, drag one cluster onto another cluster to merge them, or hold down Ctrl (Windows) / Cmd (Mac) to select multiple people and then click Merge at the top of the screen. In Person view, if you start to type the name of an existing person, Lightroom displays a pop-up, giving you the option to select that person and merge in one go.

When you click on a person to enter Person view, Lightroom displays other clusters of photos it suspects may be the same person, and asks Is this also the same person? If you know the answer, click Yes, Merge or No, but if you're not sure, click the X in the corner.

SPLITTING PEOPLE

Occasionally, Lightroom makes a mistake and includes a photo of a different person.

To **tell Lightroom that this is a different person** on the desktop, right-click on the photo and select Remove Photo from Person or tap the Backspace key (Windows) / Delete key (Mac). On mobile, hold your finger on the photo to enter selection mode then tap the Remove icon, followed by Remove from Person. The photos are then reevaluated and Lightroom takes another guess at who they might be.

If the photo belongs with a different named person, you can move them to the correct person. This saves some double-handling. On the desktop, right-click on the photo and select Move to > the correct name. On Android, hold your finger on a photo to enter selection mode, then go to ... menu > Move To > the correct name. Moving to a different person is not currently available on iOS.

SELECTING A COVER PHOTO

Lightroom picks a default thumbnail for a person, but it's rarely the most flattering choice, so you can **select an alternative cover photo**. On the desktop, click on the person to enter Person view, select a better photo, and then right-click on it (or click the ... menu) and choose Set as Cover Photo. On iOS, from Person view, tap the photo to view it in Detail view, then go to ... menu > Organize > Set as Cover Photo. (This is not currently possible on Android.)

SORTING PEOPLE

As the number of named people grows, you may want to **change the sort order**. From the People view, select the ... menu, then select First Name, Last Name or Count.

HIDING PEOPLE

People view will likely include people you don't know, for example, people who were standing in the background at a tourist location. It only shows clusters of more than 5 photos of the same person to minimize this issue. There may also be people who you know but you don't want to search for, such as friends of friends.

To **hide people**, click the ... menu in the corner of the People view and select **Show and Hide People**. Uncheck the people you want to hide and click *Done*. On the desktop, you can also right-click on a thumbnail in People view and select *Hide Person*.

To **show hidden people**, return to the Show and Hide People view and check their thumbnails again.

EXTRA CONTEXT IN DETAIL VIEW

Sometimes a little extra context can help to identify a person. If you switch to Detail view on the desktop and open the Keywords panel, all of the identified people are listed above the keywords.

Click on *Add Name* to type the name of the person, or click on the X to remove the person from the photo. Clicking on the thumbnail cover photo takes you to the Person view for the selected person.

The thumbnails are a bit small, so to **see who's who** in the photo, float the cursor over a name in the Keywords panel. A rectangular overlay appears on the photo, identifying the person.

TAGGING MISSING PEOPLE

When looking in Detail view, you may find that Lightroom has missed a person, perhaps because the person is facing away from the camera, or their face is partially hidden, or they're simply too small in the photo. There isn't currently a way of drawing a face region, but you can add the missing person's name as a normal keyword (page 99).

STEP-BY-STEP

Let's give this a try...

1. In the left panel (desktop) / Library view (mobile), click on *All Photos* and select *People* view.

2. Click/tap on the thumbnail of a person you recognize to open them into Person view.

3. At the top, click/tap on *Add Name* and type the person's name.

4. If Lightroom suspects other clusters of photos may be the same person, it displays a thumbnail and asks *Is this also the same person?* If you know the answer, click/tap *Yes, Merge* or *No*, but if you're not sure, click/tap the X in the corner.

5. Scroll down to find your favorite photo of that person, then right-click and choose *Set as Cover Photo* (desktop).

6. As you're scrolling, if you spot any photos that don't include that person, right-click and select *Remove Photo from Person* (desktop).

7. Click/tap the Back arrow to return to People view and repeat these steps with the next person you recognize.

8. When you've finished naming all of the people you know, click/tap the ... menu in the top right corner of People view and select *Show and Hide People*. Uncheck any people you haven't named, then click *Done*.

DISABLING PEOPLE

If you don't want Adobe to run the face recognition on your photos, perhaps for privacy reasons, you can disable People view. The switch is found in *Preferences > General tab* on the desktop, or under *Settings > People View* on mobile.

Any faces that have already been identified remain accessible in People view, so you don't lose your work. However, Lightroom deletes its recognition data from the server and stops scanning new photos. If you change your mind, you can enable it again later, and scanning will resume after a short delay (around 90 minutes).

PEOPLE VIEW (WINDOWS/MAC)

Click cover photo to open into Person view (below)

Number of photos of this person

Change sort order

Open People view

menu

Select multiple people (to hide/merge) by holding down Ctrl (Windows) / Cmd (Mac)

Hide a person using right-click > Hide Person or enter Show/Hide People view from ... menu

merge people by dragging a person onto another person or enter Merge People view from ... menu

PERSON VIEW (WINDOWS/MAC)

Back to People view

Type person's name

Merge with existing person by selecting from autocomplete pop-up

Selected photos

Number of photos of this person

menu

Switch between Grid and Detail views

Remove selected photo from this person

Set selected photo as thumbnail cover photo

PEOPLE IN KEYWORDS PANEL (WINDOWS/MAC)

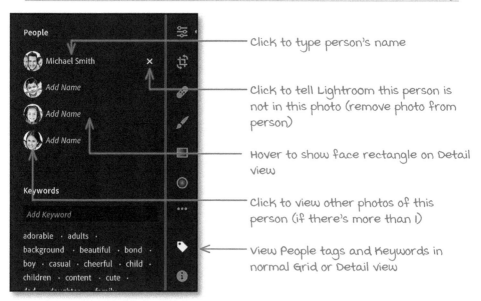

Click to type person's name

Click to tell Lightroom this person is not in this photo (remove photo from person)

Hover to show face rectangle on Detail view

Click to view other photos of this person (if there's more than 1)

View People tags and Keywords in normal Grid or Detail view

PEOPLE VIEW (IOS/ANDROID)

Back to Library view

People menu incl. Show/Hide and merge People

Tap on a person to open into Person view (below)

Benjamin Smith
1 Photos

Isabelle Smith
1 Photos

Michael Smith
6 Photos

Olivia Smith
1 Photos

29 Photos

18 Photos

15 Photos

14 Photos

12 Photos

- 👁 Show & Hide People
- 👤 Merge People
- ☰ Sort by Name >
- ⚙ Settings

PERSON VIEW (IOS/ANDROID)

Back to People view

Person menu

Tap on name to rename person

Tap on photo to open into Detail view

Swipe up/down with one finger to scroll

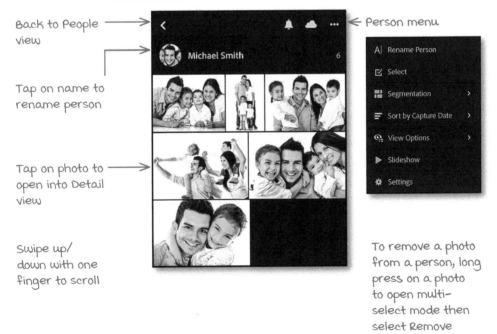

Michael Smith   6

- A| Rename Person
- ☑ Select
- ▦ Segmentation >
- ☰ Sort by Capture Date >
- 🔎 View Options >
- ▶ Slideshow
- ⚙ Settings

To remove a photo from a person, long press on a photo to open multi-select mode then select Remove

SEARCHING FOR PHOTOS

One of the main benefits of having all of your photos in one place is they're easy to search.

ENTERING SEARCH CRITERIA

The text Search field is always found at the top of the Lightroom desktop window, and the shortcut Ctrl-F (Windows) / Cmd-F (Mac) moves the cursor to the Search field. To **access the search field** on mobile, tap the magnifying glass icon at the top of Library/Grid view.

To **search your photos**, simply type the search terms in the search field and press the Enter key.

Lightroom searches the photos in the current view. To **search all of your photos,** select *All Photos* in the left panel (desktop) / Library view (mobile), or select an album to limit the search.

To **delete a search term**, click/tap on its token.

To **cancel the search**, click/tap the X at the end of the search criteria.

SEARCHING CONTENT

If your photos are synced to the cloud, Adobe's artificial intelligence machine learning tool, called Adobe Sensei, can search your photos and take a guess at their content.

This image-analysis allows you to find your photos, even if you never got around to adding keyword tags manually.

This automated tagging is done in Adobe's cloud, so there is a slight delay before they're searchable, and it does rely on you being connected to the internet.

You can search for all sorts of terms, for example:

• **Subjects**, such as *boats, cats, dogs, trees* or *water*, whether they're identified automatically or you've added them as keywords.

• **People** you've named using the People view.

• **Colors**, such as *red* or *blue*.

• **Locations**, such as *London* or *UK*.

• **Cameras**, such as *Canon EOS 6D Mark II, Sony A6500*, or *iPhone X*.

• **Lenses**, such as *75-300mm*.

• **Dates**, such as *October 2017*, or *21 August 2018*.

• **Filenames and extensions**, such as *IMG_2948* or *.jpg*

• **Other words** in the *Title* or *Caption* fields.

As you start typing, Lightroom offers a number of suggestions, just like Google or Amazon.

It's still early days for this type of search, so it will continue to improve over time. In the meantime, some of the suggestions will provide a few laughs. ☺

SEARCHING METADATA

You can also specify which metadata field to search by adding "facets." Type the facet followed by a colon (:) and a list of options pops up.

The available facets in English are:

camera: and *lens:* search the camera and lens models.
f: searches aperture (f-stop).
shutter speed: searches shutter speed.
iso: checks the ISO rating.
focal length: searches the focal length used.
flash: checks whether the flash fired.
depth map: checks whether a depth map was recorded by the camera/phone.
rating: searches the star rating, from 0 to 5.
flag: searches the flagged/unflagged/reject status.
location: searches the GPS fields.
keyword: searches keywords you've manually added to the Keyword panel.
people: searches for people tagged in the People view.
album: limits the search to a specific album. This also allows you to search for photos

that aren't in any album.
type: separates photos, HDR/panos and videos.
extension: searches by file extension, such as jpg or cr2.
orientation: searches for photos that are vertical, horizontal, panoramic or square.
edited: looks for photos that have been edited since importing into Lightroom.

These facets can be combined, for example, you might search for *rating:equal to 5 extension:cr2 camera:Canon EOS 5D Mk III*

It's tricky to remember all of the different facets, so when you click on an empty search field, Lightroom displays a helper screen. Just click on the facet and then select from the options pop-up.

SEARCH LANGUAGE

Lightroom searches based on the language selected in *Preferences > Interface* on the desktop, or based the operating system language on mobile. If you need to search in Spanish, for example, you'll need the Lightroom interface in Spanish too.

REFINING THE CURRENT VIEW

The Refine toolbar filters the current view based on specific criteria, for example, to show all of your photos marked with 4 stars that were shot using your iPhone.

To **show the Refine toolbar** on the desktop, click the Refine button to the right of the Search bar. On mobile, tap the Refine button at the top of the Grid view.

If you're viewing photos from a specific date or album, it only searches those photos. To **search all of your photos**, select *All Photos* in the left panel (desktop) / Library view (mobile).

FILTERING BY STAR RATING

The star filters allow you to show/hide photos and/or videos based on their star rating. For example, to **show only photos with 3 or more stars**, click/tap on the third star.

The **symbol** to the left of the stars allow greater control, so you can filter based on:

≥ rating is greater than or equal to.

≤ rating is less than or equal to.

= rating is equal to.

For example, to display only photos with 0 stars, click/tap on the symbol to the left of the stars, select the = icon, and leave the stars themselves deselected.

FILTERING BY FLAGS

The flag filters allow you to show/hide photos and/or videos based on their flag status.

To **show only flagged photos**, click/tap on the flag so it's highlighted.

To **show both flagged and unflagged photos** (hiding the rejected photos), click/tap on both the flagged and unflagged icons, so they're both highlighted.

To **show only rejected photos**, ready to delete them, click only the rejected flag so it's highlighted.

FILTERING BY METADATA

The *Metadata* filters allow you to refine the view based on additional metadata. This metadata is searchable using the text search field (page 108), however the Refine pop-ups work even if you're offline.

The *Sync Status* criteria on the desktop is particularly useful if you're having sync issues, as it shows which photos are yet to upload. It's also useful if you previously uploaded photos using Lightroom Classic, as it shows which photos only have smart previews available in the cloud.

As they all work the same way, let's use the *Cameras* pop-up to illustrate how they work on the desktop. Click on the pop-up to **show the list** of cameras. They're sorted by frequency, with the most-used camera first.

Click on one of the lines to select it, such as the Olympus E-M1 in the screenshot. Any photos shot with other cameras are hidden from view. You can click to select multiple lines to display photos from more than one camera.

To remove a camera from the selection, click on the line again. To cancel the camera filter and show photos from all cameras, click on the circular number icon on the pop-up.

On mobile, tap the arrow to show the list of cameras (or other metadata) and check the cameras you want to include in your filtered view.

CLEARING FILTERS

To **reset the filters** to show all photos, click the X at the end of the search criteria.

Click/tap the X to reset the filters

Click to show list of keywords, cameras, locations, etc.

Click number to clear all selected cameras

Click one or more white lines to show photos from selected camera

Click blue lines to uncheck cameras

REFINING THE VIEW (WINDOWS/MAC)

Search for photos using text

Cancel search

Show Refine View toolbar

File Type

People

Cameras   Locations

Sync Status

Keywords

Contributed
by Others

Star
Rating

Flag
Status

Photo Counts...

1 of 2,575 photos (2,077 filtered)

Selected — Visible

Hidden by filter

REFINING THE VIEW (IOS/ANDROID)

Clear search criteria

Show Refine View options

Star Rating (swipe left
across stars to set to 0)

Flag Status

Other metadata fields. Tap
arrow to show options:

INTRODUCTION TO EDITING

8

Most photographers want to get on to the fun bit—editing their photos! Editing photos is not about making them look fake or photoshopped, nor is it a new phenomenon. Photographers were editing their photos in the darkroom long before computers existed. Even the Masters, such as Ansel Adams, edited their photos, not to fix mistakes, but because a print can't match the dynamic range of the human eye.

WHY ARE YOU EDITING YOUR PHOTOS?

Before you starting editing, ask yourself why you're editing your photos. Are you editing...

• To fix mistakes? (Yes, even pros make mistakes!)

• To compensate for intentional overexposure (ETTR), done to retain the largest amount of data?

• To adjust the dynamic range of the photo to match the scene you remember?

• To draw the eye to specific areas of the photo?

• To match your artistic vision for the photo?

• For consistency, perhaps across your portfolio or in an album or on the wall?

• To crop in closer, because you didn't have a long enough lens?

The reason you're editing the photos will

affect the editing choices you make, for example:

• If you're figuring out the kind of style you like, you might experiment with lots of different presets.

• If you're aiming for consistency, you'll view the images as a group rather than just individually.

• If you're editing an image to put on the wall, you'll probably spend more time on it than a photo to put on social media.

WHICH PHOTOS SHOULD YOU EDIT?

If you spend hours editing every photo you capture, you'll soon get frustrated. Consider these time-saving tips:

• Don't try to edit everything. Editing won't fix bad photos. They can be improved, but you can't make a silk purse from a sow's ear. Flag/star the photos first, and just edit the best ones.

• Just do a "quick" edit on most of the photos you decide to keep, and focus most of your editing time on the photos you'll be proud to share with the world.

HOW DO YOU USE LIGHTROOM TO EDIT YOUR PHOTOS?

You can get the gist of how Lightroom's sliders work simply through experimentation. It doesn't take a rocket scientist to work out that the *Exposure* slider brightens or darkens the photos.

However, many of Lightroom's sliders do all sorts of clever calculations behind the scenes. Understanding how the sliders work—and how they work together—means you can get the best result.

We're going to focus on analyzing the photos before you start editing, and how to figure out what you need to adjust to fix or enhance them. For example:

• How do you know where to crop a photo?

• How do you know how bright or dark to make the photo?

• How do you decide on the color?

• How much sharpening should you apply?

• How do you know which photos will look better in B&W without testing it on every single one?

In the following sections, we'll answer these questions, and more besides.

IN THIS SECTION, WE'LL CONSIDER:

• Why it's worth learning photo editing skills instead of always relying on presets.

• How to avoid looking like a new photographer.

• The importance of calibrating your monitor.

WHY LEARN TO EDIT PHOTOS USING SLIDERS?

Most new photographers edit photos using profiles, presets and filters. So why bother learning to use the sliders?

PHOTO EDITING IS LIKE A LANGUAGE

Photo editing is a skill, just like any other. If you're trying to learn a language, repeating phrases from a phrase book is only going to get you so far. To become fluent in a language, you have to learn its structure and vocabulary, so you can start to build your own sentences that can apply in any situation.

Editing photos is the same. Profiles and presets are like those pre-built phrases. They'll work okay in some situations, but they'll never be a perfect fit.

Skilled editing can enhance photos in a way that presets simply can't match. Learning which sliders to tweak is also much faster than hunting through hundreds of presets trying to find one that works.

PROFILES & PRESETS HAVE THEIR PLACE

Don't misunderstand me... profiles and presets have their place. Benefits include:

• Selecting a base profile can be a good starting point for your editing.

• Profiles and presets (especially those you've created yourself) can help to ensure consistency over a group of photos, or over your entire portfolio.

• Presets can be really helpful in learning the kind of styles of editing you prefer, and looking at which sliders are adjusted by presets is a great way of learning how to create a specific look.

IT TAKES TIME

Any new skill takes time to develop, and you'll improve with practice. When you first start trying to edit photos with sliders, rather than relying on presets, you won't always be happy with the result initially. But that's ok! That's the benefit of non-destructive editing—you can go back and change them later, as your skills continue to develop. If you've saved a "classic" edit (as opposed to a fashionable look), your future changes will be tweaks, not a complete overhaul.

LEARNING THE LANGUAGE OF EDITING

We'll start by introducing the sliders and tools, like adding new words to your vocabulary.

Then, we'll learn how to combine related sliders to get a specific result, like combining words to make a sentence.

Finally, we'll start combining different sets of sliders into full photo edits, like turning these sentences into whole conversations.

WHAT NOT TO DO WHEN EDITING

There are some weird and wonderful photo effects that are popular with new photographers. Play with them and get them out of your system. But then, if you want to be respected as a photographer, your photos should usually look like photos.

There are a few red flags that make it easy to identify new photographers, and of course, you don't want to look like a newbie, so here are a few things to avoid:

• You don't need to use every single slider on each photo, just as you don't need to use every word in the dictionary in each conversation.

• Less is more. Unless you're intentionally aiming for a surreal look, keep it natural. Sliders rarely need pushing to the ends.

• Be especially careful with photos of people. Glowing eyes, bright white teeth and plastic skin rarely look good.

• Watch your white and black clipping. Most photos benefit from a few pure white and pure black pixels, but you don't usually want large areas of white or black without detail.

• Reduce digital noise, but don't make it so smooth it looks like plastic.

• Avoid using too many different presets, because your photos won't look like "yours".

• Don't crop too far, as you'll cause visible pixelation (obvious square pixels).

• Watch out for halos either side of edges in the photo, whether they're wide halos caused by overzealous use of the *Highlights*, *Shadows* or *Clarity* sliders, or narrow halos caused by too much sharpening or

chromatic aberration (a lens defect).

• Limit your use of the latest fad and fake film presets that go out of fashion again just as quickly as they arrived. Likewise, limit your use of special effects such as selective color (B&W photos with one element in color), as these effects date quickly.

• Don't go out and buy every software program on the market. Master the ones you already have first. "The grass is always greener on the other side of the fence" doesn't always hold true. Often you just need to learn which slider to adjust to make it greener on this side!

• Finally, don't spend hours on every photo. If you get stuck, consider printing it, sticking it on the wall and "living with it" for a while. This makes it easier to see what needs changing.

Don't worry, as you continue through this book, I'll show you how to avoid all of these issues and skillfully edit your photos.

THE IMPORTANCE OF CALIBRATING YOUR MONITOR

When you walk into a TV store and look around, you'll notice that all of the screens are slightly different. Some are a little brighter, some are a little darker, some are more contrasty, others have less contrast, some are more colorful, some are warm, some are cool... the differences go on.

If you display the same image on all of these screens, they'll all look slightly different. The same applies to computer monitors and mobile devices. The same photo will look different, depending on the screen you're using.

THE AIM OF CALIBRATION

The aim of monitor calibration is to adjust all of these different screens to a standard, so the photo looks similar regardless of the screen you're viewing at the time.

When you put your photos out into the world, you can't control exactly how they'll look, because most people don't calibrate their monitors. However, editing your photos on a standardized system gives you the best shot at getting your prints to match the screen, and saves you having to re-edit your photos every time you switch to a different device.

HOW TO CALIBRATE YOUR DESKTOP MONITOR

Monitor calibration on the desktop isn't complicated. You simply need a monitor calibration tool and the software that comes with it. The main players are X-Rite's ColorMunki and i1 Display Pro devices, and Datacolor's range of Spyder devices. The software will differ slightly, but the principles remain the same.

STEP-BY-STEP

Let's use the i1 Display Pro to illustrate:

1. Install the software and drivers that come with the calibration device.

2. Follow the instructions in the software. Most ask you to make a few decisions:

Monitor Technology—Newer monitors are probably *White LED*, while older ones are mainly *CCFL*. The software often selects the right one automatically.

White Point—select *D65* or *6500*.

Luminance—select *120 cd/m2* as a starting point. (You may increase/decrease it later, if your prints are a little darker/lighter than you see on screen.)

Contrast Ratio—select *Native*.

3. Place the calibration device on the screen, ensuring that it's flat against the screen with no ambient light creeping in the sides, and start measuring.

4. The software measures the brightness of the screen, and tells you how bright it is currently. Use the monitor buttons (or *System Preferences > Display* on a Mac with a built-in screen) to increase or decrease the monitor brightness until the line is in the green 'optimum' area. Most monitors are way too bright, so don't be surprised if you have to make a big adjustment.

Adjust the monitor brightness until the line is in the center of the green area

Some high-end monitors make these adjustments automatically. Other monitors may also ask you to adjust contrast or RGB values to match the target values.

5. The calibration software then flashes a series of colors on the screen, measuring each in turn, so it can build a profile.

6. When the calibration finishes, give the profile a sensible name and click the *Save* button, then close the software.

CONTROLLING YOUR SURROUNDINGS

Your surroundings also influence your perception of brightness and color. Ideally, it's best edit your photos in dim light, with the light source no brighter than the screen. This may be as simple as closing the curtains and turning on a small desk lamp holding a daylight bulb.

ADJUSTING MOBILE DEVICES

Mobile devices can't be calibrated at an operating system level using hardware calibration tools. Apple devices display fairly accurate color out-of-the-box, but Android devices can be a bit more variable. In either case, screen brightness is usually too bright and needs reducing to match your calibrated desktop screen. There may also be automatic adjustment settings to consider, such as Auto Brightness or Apple's True Tone color adjustment.

ANALYZING THE IMAGE

9

When you watch a professional photo editor editing a series of photos, it looks like they "just know" what to change. They don't start randomly moving sliders, hoping to hit on the right combination of adjustments. Instead, they first analyze the photo.

Due to years of experience, that analysis may only take a few seconds, and may be a subconscious process, but it happens every time. Without necessarily realizing they're doing so, they're essentially running through a series of questions in their head—and you can ask yourself the same questions. This process of analysis is the focus of this section.

PLAN YOUR JOURNEY

Starting to edit a photo without first taking the time to analyze it is like setting off on a road trip without first looking at a map. You'll end up somewhere, and the trip might still be fun, but you're unlikely to get to the best destination.

You don't have to plan every detail, but having a rough idea of where you want to end up means you can make good decisions along the way, and avoid going in circles.

We're going to break the analysis down into two categories:

- Technical Faults (page 123)

- Artistic Intent (page 131)

ANALYZING YOUR OWN PHOTOS

I've included a checklist and worksheet to help guide you through the process. Printable copies are available for download in the Members Area (page 378), and we'll use these worksheets again later in the book, when we edit some photos from start to finish (page 293).

Analyzing your photos may look like a lot of work, but once you understand what you're looking for, you'll be able to analyze your photo in a matter of seconds, like you do when shooting a photo.

You don't have to complete a written worksheet every time you sit down to edit a photo, but your editing will improve if you run through the process a few times on paper before switching to doing it in your head. As you gain experience, it'll become second nature.

IN THIS SECTION, WE'LL CONSIDER:

• How to analyze the image, looking for technical faults.

• How to analyze the image from artistic point of view.

• How to start to develop your own consistent editing style.

PHOTO ANALYSIS CHECKLIST

Technical

Light & Contrast
- ☐ Is the overall exposure about right?
- ☐ Is there enough detail in the highlights and shadows?
- ☐ Does the photo fill the entire dynamic range?
- ☐ Are the highlights and/ or shadows clipping?

Color
- ☐ Is there a color cast?
- ☐ Do the memory colors look natural?

Detail
- ☐ Is it sharp?
- ☐ Is there noise?
- ☐ Is there moiré patterning?

Optical Distortion
- ☐ Is there vignetting?
- ☐ Is there barrel/pincushion distortion?
- ☐ Is there chromatic aberration or other fringing?

Geometric Distortion
- ☐ Is the horizon straight?
- ☐ Are the vertical lines straight, or do they converge?

Sensor Dust
- ☐ Are there any sensor dust spots?

Output
- ☐ Does the photo need to fit a specific aspect ratio, for example, a frame?
- ☐ Does it need to match the color of another photo?
- ☐ How big is the photo going to be?

Artistic Intent

Purpose
- ☐ Why did I capture the photo?
- ☐ What's important in the photo?
- ☐ What did I want to show the viewer?

Story
- ☐ What's the story I'm trying to tell?
- ☐ How can I use light, contrast, color and saturation to help tell the story?

Mood/Emotion
- ☐ How do I want the viewer to feel?
- ☐ How can I use light, contrast, color and saturation to influence the viewer's response?

Simplify
- ☐ Are there any distractions I can exclude from the scene by cropping, darkening, blurring, etc?

Draw the Eye
- ☐ Can I guide the viewer's eye around the photo by highlighting or diminishing:
  - People
  - Contrasts in Size
  - Contrasts in Brightness
  - Contrasts in Color & Saturation
  - Contrasts in Sharpness
  - Lines
  - Something else?

PHOTO ANALYSIS WORKSHEET EXAMPLE

Good dynamic range, no
notable clipping

TECHNICAL

Exposure
Needs a little more detail
in his clothes. No pure white
expected in the photo.

Color
Color doesn't add to the photo.
The strong lines and stone
texture would work well in B&W.

Detail
Shot at low ISO in good light, so no
notable noise. Texture of stone can
take some crunchy sharpening.

Optical & Geometric Distortion
Horizon needs straightening
(use bricks in background).

Sensor Dust
None found.

Output
Nothing specific planned.

ARTISTIC INTENT

Purpose
The guy looked small and
insignificant against the huge
pillars of the government building.

Story
Is he homeless? Or just waiting for
a friend? He looks cold and lonely.

Mood/Emotion
Very cold day (hat). Feeling lonely?
High contrast B&W with lots of local
contrast for a gritty urban look?

Simplify the Scene & Draw the Eye
Notes scribbled on photo.

Remove the sign from the
door on the left.

Even up lighting on the pillars, front
step and bricks in the background
to reduce background contrast.

Increase contrast on face/
clothing of man to draw the eye
in that direction even more.

ANALYZING THE IMAGE—TECHNICAL FAULTS

One of the aims of the editing process is to get the best possible result from whatever data you captured, so there are some technical issues to look out for. You may not be familiar with all of the terminology, so we'll explain a few new terms as we go along.

Shadows   Highlights

Our eyes are most sensitive in the midtones

Highlights   midtones   Shadows

LIGHT

In the real world, our eyes don't care whether something is light or dark, as they automatically adjust to see detail in both the highlights and shadows, even in high contrast situations such as midday sun.

A photo (and especially a print) is unable to hold that wide a range of tones while still looking natural. Something has to give. Editing photos is a balancing act, determining which range of tones is most important and where you're willing to sacrifice detail.

Is the overall exposure about right? Is there enough detail in the highlights and shadows?

There is no such thing as "correct" exposure, but the human visual system (the combination of our eyes and brain) expects to see an image in a specific way. This means there's room for creative expression, but there's a narrow band of exposure most people prefer.

Our eyes are most comfortable when the main focus of interest is around middle gray (called the midtones). Therefore, the optimum exposure setting may lighten or darken the highlights or shadows to move the most important tones towards the midtones.

What does the histogram tell you?

A Histogram is a bar graph showing the distribution of tonal values. To show the histogram on the desktop, click the ... button in the right panel bar and select **Show Histogram** or use the shortcut Ctrl-0 (Windows) / Cmd-0 (Mac). On mobile, go to Detail view > ... menu > and select *View Options > Show/Hide Histogram* (iOS) / *Show Histogram* (Android).

The brightness of each pixel is measured from 0% (black) to 100% (white), so a histogram runs from the blackest shadow on the left to the brightest highlight on the right. Vertically it shows the number of pixels with that specific tonal value. A color photo is made up of three channels—red, green and blue—so the histogram has a line for each channel.

There's no such thing as a 'correct' histogram. When analyzing your photo, a histogram can provide some really useful information on the exposure values of your photo, but don't get too hung up on it. We're trying to make great photos, not great histograms! However there are a few useful things we can learn from the histogram...

Does the photo fill the entire dynamic range?

The difference between the brightest and darkest tones in the photo is called the dynamic range.

The histogram of a scene that has a much wider dynamic range than the camera could capture shows spikes at both ends. These are pixels that are currently pure white or pure black, but if it's a raw file, there may be detail that can be recovered with careful editing. This is called a **high dynamic range**, and these photos usually have too much contrast.

A histogram stuck in the middle of the range, without reaching the ends is a narrow or **low dynamic range**. In most cases, these photos benefit from stretching to create a real white and black point because they lack contrast. However some photos, such as those shot in thick fog, may not have any true white or black details.

READING THE HISTOGRAM

Number of pixels with that brightness value

0%   25%   50%   75%   100%

Pixel brightness, from pure black (0%) to pure white (100%)

Spikes at the ends = dynamic range too wide, so detail is clipped

Data doesn't reach ends = low dynamic range

missing detail in the highlights and shadows

Low dynamic range   Stretched to full dynamic range

WATCH FOR CLIPPING

Enable/disable
blue Shadows
Clipping warning

Enable/disable
red Highlight
Clipping warning

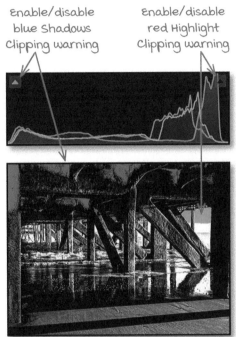

Clipped blacks show as black on a
white background when you hold
down the Alt/Opt key and move
the sliders. Pixels only clipped in
one or two channels show in color

Are the highlights and/or shadows clipping?

If the last pixel on the left or the right of the histogram spikes, it means that a significant number of pixels in your photo are solid white or black without any detail. These are called clipped highlights or shadows, or you may hear them referred to as blown highlights and blocked shadows. Clipping can be a fault or it can be intentional.

To check whether the clipped pixels are in areas of important image detail on the desktop, hold down the Alt key (Windows) / Opt key (Mac) while dragging the *Exposure, Highlights, Shadows, Whites* or *Blacks* sliders to view the clipping warnings. On mobile, drag these sliders using two fingers, or start dragging the slider and then add another finger elsewhere on the image.

In addition to these on-demand clipping warnings, on the desktop you can turn on automatic clipping warnings to show while you work. To do so, click the triangles in

Pure white clipped highlights don't
look out of place on shiny objects

Avoid
clipping
skin tones

the corners of the histogram or press the J key. Clipped highlights turn red and blocked shadows turn blue.

In some areas of the photo, such as bright spots on shiny objects, clipping is expected. Small areas of clipping on a light source, such as a light bulb or the sun, can also look fine, but ideally you don't want large clipped areas, such as a window with no detail. Clipping on skin looks unnatural and is worth avoiding at all costs.

Some studio or product photographers like to clip their backgrounds to pure white or black, and intentionally compressing the shadow detail can be a creative choice. It's not always bad, as long as there's a smooth transition to image detail.

We'll use the tools in the Light and Effects panel to make these adjustments (page 177).

COLOR

Unless you're doing reproduction work, the main aim is visually pleasing color, which may not be the same as perfectly accurate color, due to the way the camera captures the scene. While you can make artistic choices, there are a couple of things to look out for...

Is there a color cast?

A color cast is an unwanted tint in the image, often caused by an incorrect White Balance setting. It makes the photo look muddy and hazy, like you're viewing it through a colored film. We're most sensitive to color casts in lighter tones. If you remove the tint, the other colors usually fall into place.

Do the memory colors look natural?

Some colors are burned forever into our memory. Think about skin tones. We recognize when someone looks jaundiced or ashen, or when they've applied fake tan, because the color of their skin doesn't match the color we expect to see. In the same way, we expect the sky to be blue, grass to be green, and bananas to be yellow.

KEEP COLORS NATURAL

What's wrong with this image? memory colors need to be accurate!

A color cast makes the photo look muddy

CHECK THE DETAIL

This was a grab shot, and the camera focused on the grass instead of his eyes, so it's not perfectly sharp but it sums up Charlie too well to throw away

High noise levels are usually found on high ISO photos

moiré pattern

As long as the memory colors remain natural, you can take liberties with other colors for artistic effect, without the photo looking "wrong".

We'll use the tools in the Color panel to make these adjustments (page 203).

DETAIL

If we have 20/20 vision, everything we look at is perfectly sharp, and our eyes automatically adjust to see detail in the shadows without any noise. Cameras have come on leaps and bounds over the last few years, but they're no match. Whether it's softness caused by imperfect optics or focusing, or noise caused by low light hitting tiny digital sensors, there's room for improvement in the detail of our photos.

Is it sharp?

We all grab photos that aren't perfectly in focus and most will be removed when ranking the photos, but occasionally there's just "something" about them that's worth keeping. You can't fix out of focus photos in Lightroom, but you can certainly improve them.

Is there noise?

If you shot in low light, used a high ISO, your camera has a very small sensor, or you need to significantly brighten the photo, then there's likely to be noise in the photo, making it look very grainy. This can be reduced in Lightroom.

Is there moiré patterning?

Moiré (pronounced mwa-ray) is a rainbow-like pattern which is often seen when photographing fabrics. It's caused by two patterns combining—in this case, the weave in fabric and the grid of the camera sensor—which creates a new pattern.

Sharpening and noise reduction can be optimized using the tools in the Detail panel (page 231) and moiré can be removed using the Brush tool (page 258).

OPTICAL DISTORTIONS

The way the light passes through the camera's lens can result in distortions that can distract from the content of the photo, so it's worth taking a moment to correct them.

Is there vignetting?

Vignetting is a darkening around the edges of the photo, especially in the corners.

Is there barrel/pincushion distortion?

Pincushion distortion causes straight lines to curve inward, while barrel distortion causes straight lines to curve outward. It's particularly noticeable when there are straight lines in the photo.

Is there chromatic aberration or other fringing?

Chromatic aberration (often shortened to CA) is the little fringes of color that can appear along high contrast edges, where the red, green and blue light wavelengths are unable to focus at the same point. It's most noticeable around the corners of photos taken with a lower quality wide angle lens, and doesn't appear in the center of the image.

Compact and mirrorless cameras often fix these issues automatically, but where these distortions are still visible, we'll use the tools in the Optics panel to make these corrections (page 261).

GEOMETRIC DISTORTIONS

When you look around in real life, horizontal lines look horizontal and vertical lines look vertical, and even if you tilt your head, your brain compensates. However, if your camera sensor isn't perfectly aligned with those horizontal and vertical lines, the resulting photo looks wonky.

Is the horizon straight?

Most of us have trouble getting horizons perfectly straight at the time of shooting, and since the edge of the photo acts as a point of comparison, they stand out like a sore thumb.

Are the vertical lines straight, or do they converge?

If you're shooting buildings, have you noticed that they sometimes seem to lean backwards? This is called keystoning and it's caused by tilting the camera to get the whole building into the frame. Some keystoning can look natural, as we're used to looking up at buildings, but you may want to reduce excessive keystoning.

The horizon can be straightened using the Crop tool (page 153), and we'll use the tools in the Geometry panel to make more complex corrections (page 261).

OPTICAL & GEOMETRIC DISTORTIONS

Horizons should be horizontal!

Pincushion distortion curves inward

Barrel distortion curves outward

Due to the camera angle, the building appears to be leaning backwards

Halos of opposing colors (green and magenta here) are caused by chromatic aberration

RETOUCHING

Removing distractions from the photo allows your viewer to focus on the content. Some unnatural distractions, such as sensor dust spots, stand out more than the litter we see around us every day.

Are there any sensor dust spots?

Small spots that are most noticeable in the sky are caused by dust on the sensor. If you have a camera with interchangeable lenses, it's worth keeping your camera's sensor clean. Spots on blank areas on the sky are easy to clean up in Lightroom, but when they fall on more detailed areas, they can be tricky to remove.

We'll use Lightroom's Healing Brush to remove these distractions, or pass the photo to Photoshop for more advanced retouching (page 279).

OUTPUT

Finally, the intended output will affect some of your editing choices, such as...

Does the photo need to fit a specific aspect ratio, for example, a frame?

If a photo will be placed in a specific frame, the aspect ratio used when cropping will be important. You'll need to bear in mind the shape of the frame when cropping the photo (page 153).

Does it need to match the color of another photo?

If the photo is part of a collection that will displayed together on the wall, consistency across the group will be a high priority.

How big is the photo going to be?

If it's a quick snap to email to Granny, you may decide to spend less time editing than you would for a poster-sized print.

LOOK FOR SPOTS

Dust spots on the sensor can be distracting

ANALYZING THE IMAGE—ARTISTIC INTENT

Photography is a form of visual communication. It's not "just a pretty picture." It's up to you to decide what you're trying to communicate through your photo, and ensure that the viewer gets the right message.

The composition, the lighting and the subject of the photo are essential, of course. You can't make a bad photo great through editing, but thoughtful editing can enhance a good photo and turn it into a great photo.

It's easy to look at a photo and say "I like it" but ask yourself WHY you like it. Once you've answered that question, you're well on the way to knowing what needs to be enhanced, to ensure that your viewer sees it the same way. Not sure how to answer? Let's break it down into a series of questions about the purpose of the photo, the story you want to tell, the mood you want to convey, and where you want the viewer's eye to go.

THE PURPOSE

Why did you capture the photo? Or why did you keep the photo? What was it you wanted to show the viewer? For example:

- To capture a specific moment in time.

- To tell a story.

- A specific subject caught your eye.

- The way the light was falling caught your eye.

- Someone commissioned you to shoot it. (What was their purpose?)

- Something else?

What's important in the photo? What's interesting about it? For example, in a photo of a thunderstorm the clouds are most important, or in a portrait, it's the eyes.

THE STORY

They say a picture speaks a thousand words, so what are you trying to communicate through this photo? What kind of story are you trying to tell? What do you want the viewer to think of when they see it? If it's a portrait, does it show the subject's personality?

For example, a portrait of an older man can be edited as a gritty B&W to accentuate the weathered wrinkles on his face, showing that he's worked hard outdoors all his life, or as a soft low contrast color image, showing his softer side.

THE MOOD/EMOTION

How did you feel when shooting the photo, and how do you want the viewer to feel? What emotion are you trying communicate? And then, how can you communicate that mood through your editing?

For example, a high contrast B&W shot of stormy seas may communicate drama, power and a feeling of awe, whereas the colorful blue sky and yellow sand on a paradisaic beach makes us think of relaxation.

Or a country village looks better in peaceful calm tones, whereas edgy architecture looks great with a strong, contrasty look, and a factory can look great with a gritty grainy look.

USING EDITING TO COMMUNICATE MOOD

Was it a bright sunny day at the beach?

Or would you prefer a more moody look?

Or do you want to emphasize the drama of the crashing waves and rocky cliffs?

Words to Describe the Feel of a Photo

Light	airy, bright, clear, dainty, fluffy, glowing, hopeful, radiant, shining, sunny	dark, dull, gloomy, heavy, hopeless, mysterious, sinister, somber
Contrast	dramatic, energetic, gritty, hard, stormy, turbulent, wild	calm, delicate, gentle, mellow, mild, peaceful, smooth, soft
Color	cozy, fresh, happy, summery, rosy, upbeat, warm, yellow	bleak, blue, cold, frosty, icy, miserable, wet, wintry
Saturation	bright, cheerful, colorful, excited, gaudy, lively, loud, rich, vibrant, vivid	calm, dull, delicate, faded, mellow, muted, pale, pastel, sober, subdued

Think of words you'd use to describe the photo, and the brightness, contrast and colors you associate with those words.

SIMPLIFYING THE SCENE

So far we've been talking about the overall feel of the image, but now, let's think about the content.

In a confused scene, your eyes don't know where to look, so it's important to simplify the scene.

What caught your eye, making you take the

photo—and is that the first thing that will catch your viewer's eye? Or will their eye wander off to distractions?

If the eye doesn't go straight there, careful cropping and selective editing can draw the viewer's eye away from the distractions to the right spot.

DRAWING THE EYE USING VISUAL MASS

Once you've removed everything that isn't necessary, think about how your eyes move around the photo. Consider:

• Where does the eye go currently, and in what order?

• Where do you want the viewer's eye to go?

• How can you use editing to draw your viewer's eye along that same path?

In the world of photography and art, there's a concept called Visual Mass. It simply means that some elements attract the eye more than others, and you can use that to draw your viewer's eye around the photo. For example, we're drawn to:

• **People** (especially faces, particularly eyes). Even in landscapes, having a person in the scene creates a sense of scale or draws your eye to a specific spot. This also applies to animals, to a lesser extent.

• **Size**—We look at large objects before small.

• **Contrasts of Brightness**—We're drawn to light things in a mainly dark image, or dark things in a main light image.

• **Color**—We drift towards warm colors before cool colors (unless the scene is primarily warm, then we're drawn to the contrasting cool color), and saturated colors before dull colors.

• **Recognizable Objects**—We look at recognizable objects before those that are less recognizable.

• **Sharpness**—We see sharp objects before soft ones (which is why out of focus backgrounds work so well).

• **Lines**—We follow diagonal or curved lines before straight lines. Diagonal lines are more dynamic, whereas our eyes meander along curved lines.

• **Text**—We always try to read it!

This is massively over-simplified, and these elements are often combined, but you can use this concept to your advantage when editing, as well as when shooting.

Starting on page 241, we'll learn to use the selective adjustment tools to enhance these contrasts, but for now, just start noticing where your eye goes in photos, and where you want the viewer's eye to go to tell your story.

VISUAL MASS TO DRAW THE EYE

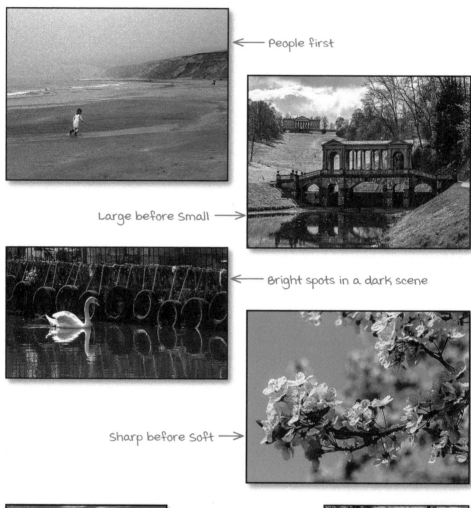

People first

Large before Small

Bright spots in a dark scene

Sharp before Soft

Warm before cold

Diagonal or curved lines before horizontal/ vertical ones

DEVELOPING YOUR OWN STYLE

One of the biggest differences between seasoned photographers and newer photographers is consistency in editing. Would all of your pictures look good hung on the wall together, or are they "all over the place"? Could someone identify a photo as yours, just by looking at it?

THE IMPORTANCE OF EDITING STYLES

If you look at the work of any famous photographer, you may know who the photographer is, long before you see their name. As you scroll through their website or Instagram feed, all of their photos work together as a consistent set.

This is partly due to their choice of subject, lighting, posing, lens, composition and so forth, but their editing style can make or break the consistency. If they applied a different preset to every photo, the photos would no longer be identifiable as theirs.

Professional photographers gradually develop a style and they stick to it. It may change over time, but it's a gradual shift.

If you're an amateur photographer, you don't have to go that far, but any improvement in consistency will make your photos look better together.

HOW DO YOU START TO DEVELOP YOUR STYLE?

To start to define your own preferences, look at lots of people's photos. Notice what you consistently like, and what you consistently don't like, but don't just copy them, because you're unique.

Experiment with different presets to help you learn too, but remember that they're someone else's style.

Start to analyze *what* it is you like or don't like about a photo. Look out for things like:

• Do you love high contrast, or do you prefer photos that look soft and dreamy?

• Do you like highly saturated colors, or softer muted shades?

• How important are creamy skin tones?

• Do you prefer specific color palettes, such as muted greens and blues?

• Do you prefer the darkest tones blocked to pure black, or do you prefer more shadow detail?

When you edit a photo and love the result, add it to a "my style" album. Over time, a theme will start to become apparent. The style you prefer for landscapes may not be identical to the style you prefer for portraits, but there will be similarities.

It won't happen overnight, and as you start to improve your editing, you might find your photos even become a little inconsistent for a while, as you're experimenting. That's part of the learning process. I've edited more than a million photos for professional photographers in their own styles, but I'm still figuring out my own preferences too. That's part of the fun of editing!

EDITING TOOLS   10

In the previous sections, we've discussed the theory of photo editing. Now let's get down to the practicalities of editing in Lightroom.

NON-DESTRUCTIVE EDITING

Lightroom's editing tools are non-destructive. This simply means that the edits are saved as a series of text instructions. If you make an edit one day in Lightroom, and change your mind the next day, you can simply move the slider back, without degrading the image quality.

Non-destructive editing also means that you can make adjustments in whatever order you like, skipping from one tool to the next. However, there are more efficient ways of working, so we'll discuss the editing tools in a logical workflow order. Remember, you don't have to use every tool and slider!

To **show the main Edit sliders** on the desktop, click the Edit button in the right panel bar, or press the E key.

 ← Edit sliders

On a mobile device, tap on a photo to open into a Detail view, then select the Edit view from the pop-up at the top of the screen on a phone, or the icons down the sidebar on a tablet.

WORKFLOW TOOLS

As you start to get better at editing, Lightroom offers tools that can help improve efficiency and consistency over groups of photos, and allow you to experiment with more freedom. They're handy to know about before you get started, so we'll discuss these tools next.

IN THIS SECTION, WE'LL CONSIDER:

• Where to find the global and local editing tools.

• How to undo and reset edits.

• How to compare the photo with the unedited original.

• How to create multiple versions of the same photo.

• How to copy edits to other photos.

EDITING WORKFLOW

It's time to start editing, but we don't want to waste time going in circles, so we've analyzed the photo (page 119) and made a plan, just like the pros.

There's a whole array of editing tools which can look overwhelming (page 137), but we'll work through them in a logical order.

Don't worry about making mistakes, as Lightroom's a non-destructive editor, so you can always undo or start over (page 146).

Ctrl+C   Ctrl+V

And if you do something you love, you can copy the same edits to other photos (page 151) or save them as a preset (page 170).

Start by cropping and straightening the photo (page 153) to remove distractions and improve composition.

Then decide on your "look" (page 161). Do you prefer bright punchy photos? Or soft and subdued? Perhaps you miss the "good old" film days.

Then it's time to balance the light and contrast (page 177).

And perfect the color (page 203).

Or perhaps you'd prefer a B&W or tinted monochrome image (page 219).

How about adding some special effects (page 227), like a vignette to draw the eye, film-like grain, or split toning effects.

Then we need to optimize the detail (page 231) in the photo by sharpening and reducing digital noise.

Most photos benefit from selective adjustments (page 241), like dodging and burning, to minimize distractions and draw the eye around the photo.

There might also be some distortion (page 261) that needs correcting, and of course you'll probably need to tweak the crop again after fixing it.

There's sure to be some distractions that need cleaning up, whether using Lightroom's Healing tools (page 280) or jumping to Photoshop for more advanced editing (page 288).

Done? Give yourself a pat on the back, and keep practicing!

THE EDITING TOOLS (WINDOWS/MAC)

Auto (page 177)

B&W (page 219)

Profile (page 163)

Exposure (page 180)

Contrast (page 182)

Highlights & Shadows (page 185)

Whites & Blacks (page 187)

Tone Curve (page 191)

White Balance, Temp & Tint (page 204)

Vibrance & Saturation (page 208)

Color Mixer (page 209)

Color Grading (page 213)

Texture (page 232)

Clarity (page 189)

Sliders

Crop Tool (page 153)

Healing Brush (page 279)

Brush (page 242)

Linear Gradient (page 249)

Radial Gradient (page 249)

... menu

A dot to the right of the icon shows which tools you've used on the selected photo

Toggle the arrows to open/close panels

Dehaze (page 190)

Vignette (page 228)

Grain (page 230)

Sharpening (page 234)

Noise Reduction & Color Noise Reduction (page 239)

Remove Chromatic Aberration (page 262)

Enable Lens Corrections (page 266)

Defringe (page 262)

Upright (page 268)

Manual Transforms (page 271)

Some sliders break down into further advanced sliders by toggling these arrows (called Disclosure Triangles)

Constrain Crop
(page 270)

Presets (page 170)   Versions (page 148)

← ... menu

← Copy/Paste Edit Settings
   (page 151)

← Before/After Preview (page 148)

← Reset (page 146)

| Histogram (page 123)

← On a small screen, select Single-
   Panel mode to automatically close
   panels as you open another

← Edit in Photoshop (page 288)

EDIT VIEW (IOS)

Tap to switch between Edit, Info, Keywords, Rate & Review and Activity views

Share menu incl. Edit in other apps

Sync Status incl. download full size original (if available)

Back to Grid view

Tap to undo, hold to redo

Two finger tap anywhere to switch between metadata overlay, histogram or neither. One finger tap on metadata cycles metadata views

... menu

Swipe left <> right on the photo with one finger to view the next/previous photo

Sub menus:

Drag left <> right on slider to adjust value

Scroll up/ down to show additional sliders

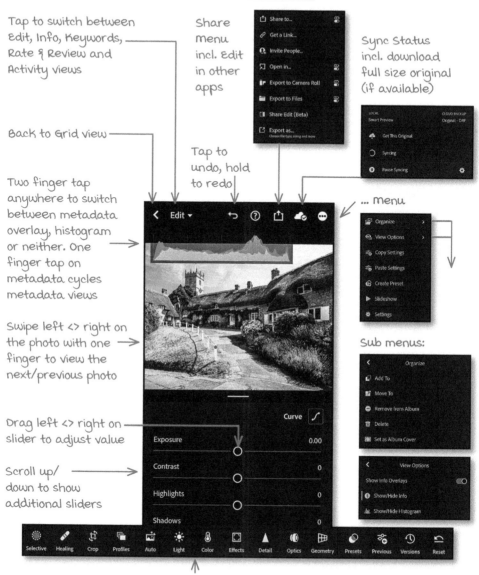

To view clipping warnings, hold two fingers while dragging slider handle

Swipe row left <> right to show all sets of sliders

Hold finger on photo to preview without recent edits

Double-tap slider handle to reset slider

Double-tap anywhere or pinch/spread to zoom in and out

Tap on photo to hide controls

EDIT VIEW (ANDROID)

Tap to switch
between Edit, Info
and Rate & Review
and Activity views

Sync Status
incl. download
full size original
(if available)

Share menu
incl. Edit in
other apps

Back to Grid view

Tap to
undo, hold
to redo

Enable metadata
or histogram
in the menu

One finger tap on
metadata cycles
metadata views

Swipe left <> right on
the photo with one
finger to view the
next/previous photo

Drag left <> right on
slider to adjust value

Scroll up/down to
show additional
sliders

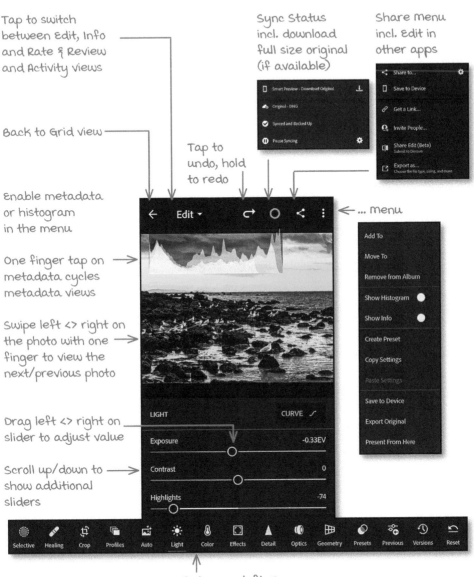

←... menu

To view clipping
warnings, hold two
fingers while dragging
slider handle

Swipe row left <>
right to show all
sets of sliders

Hold finger on photo
to preview without
recent edits

Double-tap
slider handle to
reset slider

Double-tap anywhere
or pinch/spread to
zoom in and out

Tap on photo to
hide controls

UNDOING MISTAKES & RESETTING EDITS

Lightroom is a non-destructive editor. It doesn't apply the settings to the original image data, but just stores your edits as a list of text instructions (*Exposure* +1.2, *Highlights* -40, *Shadows* +40, etc.). This means you can easily undo any edits you've made to your photo in Lightroom, even if it was edited months ago, so you can experiment without fear and try new things. It's a great way of learning.

← Undo Tap to undo, hold to show undo/

← Redo redo pop-up (left)

If you don't like a slider setting, the most obvious solution is to simply move the slider to a new value, but there's also a variety of undo and reset options.

UNDOING / REDOING ACTIONS

To **undo your last action** on the desktop (or the one before that, or the one before that), just keep hitting Ctrl-Z (Windows) / Cmd-Z (Mac) to step back in time.

This doesn't just apply to edits on the selected photo. It remembers most things you've done in chronological order—including adding star ratings, flags, metadata and even switching photos—for as long as Lightroom's open. When you quit Lightroom, the undo history is cleared.

If you go too far, use Ctrl-Y (Windows) / Cmd-Shift-Z (Mac) to redo the last undone action.

On mobile, undo/redo only applies to the edits you've applied since you last switched photos. To undo, tap the undo button at the top of the screen, and just keep tapping to undo previous actions. To redo an action, hold your finger on the undo button to show the redo button.

RESETTING THE EDITS

If you made the change you want to undo some time ago, then the reset options are a better choice. These reset a single slider, a whole section of sliders, a selective adjustment or all of the edits applied to a photo back to their default settings (page 175).

To **reset a single slider**, float over the slider label, which changes to a *Reset* button, then click on it. On mobile, double-tap on the slider handle.

To **reset a whole panel of sliders**, hold down the Alt key (Windows) / Opt key (Mac) and click on the section label (desktop only).

To **reset the entire photo** back to default settings on the desktop, click the ... menu in the right panel bar to show the fly-out menu, then select *Reset Edits*, or use the keyboard shortcut Shift-R.

If you only want to reset the edits from the current editing session (since you switched to the selected photo), select *Reset to Open* from the same menu, or use the keyboard shortcut Ctrl-Shift-R (Windows) / Cmd-Shift-R (Mac).

On mobile, tapping the **Reset** button at the right-hand end of the edit toolbar offers a series of options:

Adjustments resets everything except the Crop.

All resets all settings to the default settings.

To Import resets all of the settings to the settings selected when the photo was first imported to the mobile device or synced to the cloud.

To Open resets the photo to the settings used when you switched to the photo.

COMPARING VERSIONS & CREATING COPIES

While you're learning how to edit your photos, you'll want to compare your edits against earlier versions and experiment without losing the edits you're happy with. Lightroom provides the tools you need.

On mobile, hold your finger on the photo in Edit view to display the Before view. On Android, instead of the original, it shows the photo before you starting editing on the current device.

VIEWING A BEFORE/AFTER PREVIEW

While you're working on editing your photos, you can **compare your edited version with the original**. It retains your current crop and geometry settings to make it easy to compare your other edits.

To view the original on the desktop, click the *Show Original* icon in the toolbar beneath the photo, press the \ key on your keyboard, or use the **Show Original** command in the ... menu in the right panel bar. Repeat to show the edited version again.

 ← Show Original

COMPARING EDITS

Sometimes you'll want to create different versions of the same photo. Perhaps you want to try it in color and in B&W, or you can't decide between a few different presets. Lightroom offers two different options... versions or duplicates.

Remember, you don't need to create a copy before editing, because you can just reset the photo to get back to the unedited version.

SAVING VERSIONS

Versions are like snapshots. They capture the slider settings at the moment of their creation. They're automatically synced to the cloud, so they're available on all of your devices. As they're purely an additional set of edit instructions, they don't take up extra space in your cloud storage. They only appear in the Versions panel.

To **show the Versions panel** on the desktop, select the Edit view then click the **Versions** button in the bottom right corner or use the shortcut Shift-V. On mobile, tap the Versions button in the toolbar.

Versions panel ──↑

VERSIONS (WINDOWS/MAC)

Show menu to clear all versions

Close Versions panel

Switch between Named and Auto versions

Create new version

Show version menu

Float over version to preview settings

Click on version to apply settings

VERSIONS (IOS/ANDROID)

Back to Edit

Version name and date created

Switch between Named and Auto versions

Show menu (to rename/delete selected version)

Apply selected version and return to Edit view

Create Version button is here when Current thumbnail is selected

Tap to preview different versions or go back to the current edits

To **create a version**, click/tap the ***Create Version*** button, then give the version a name to help you remember why you saved it. These show in the ***Named*** tab of the Versions panel.

Lightroom also **creates versions automatically** when you switch to a different photo or switch back to Grid view. These show in the ***Auto*** tab of the Versions panel.

You can **convert an *Auto* version to a *Named* version** by clicking/tapping on the ... menu to the right (desktop) / at the top (mobile) and selecting ***Save as Named Version***.

To **preview a version** on the desktop, float the cursor over the version name. The effect is previewed on the photo in the main preview area, and the sliders move temporarily to their saved positions. On mobile, tap on the version thumbnail.

To **apply the saved settings** on the desktop, click on the version name. On mobile, tap on the version thumbnail and then tap the *Apply* button.

To **rename a version**, click/tap on the ... menu to the right (desktop) / at the top (mobile) and select *Rename*.

To **delete a single version**, click/tap on the ... menu to the right (desktop) / at the top (mobile) and select *Delete* (but take care as it will be deleted from all of your devices). You can't delete the *Original* version.

To **clear all of the versions** (desktop only), click on the ... menu at the top of the panel and select *Delete > All Named Versions* or *Delete > All Autosaves.*.

To **close the Versions panel** on the desktop, click the X in the corner or the *Versions*

button again. On mobile, tap the back button.

CREATING DUPLICATES

Duplicates are real copies of the photos. They take up additional cloud storage space, and appear in the Grid view as separate photos

To **create a copy of a photo** on the desktop, right-click and select ***Duplicate 1 Photo***. You'll also find it in the *Edit* menu. At the time of writing, you can't create a duplicate using the mobile apps.

The duplicate is entirely independent of its original, so you can add different metadata or delete it, just as any other photo.

COPYING & PASTING EDITS

If you're shooting a series of photos in similar light, they're likely to need similar edits. To save time and improve consistency, you can copy and paste the settings.

COPY/PASTE ON THE DESKTOP

To copy and paste settings to one or more photos on the desktop:

1. In Edit view, go to the ... menu in the right panel bar and select **Choose Edit Settings to Copy...** or use the keyboard shortcut Ctrl-Shift-C (Windows) / Cmd-Shift-C (Mac).

2. In the Copy Settings dialog, check the specific panels, sliders or tools you want to copy to the clipboard. In the pop-up above the checkboxes:

All checks all of the sliders, and **None** unchecks the sliders, so you can pick specific sliders yourself.

Default checks the sliders Adobe thinks you'll want to include, or the sliders you've set as defaults. (We'll come back to setting custom defaults shortly.)

Modified checks only the sliders you've edited.

3. Click *Copy* to place the checked settings on the clipboard.

4. If you only want to paste to a single photo, you can stay in Detail view and go to the ... menu > **Paste Edit Settings** or use the shortcut Ctrl-V (Windows) / Cmd-V (Mac).

If you want to apply the settings to multiple photos, switch back to the Grid view, select the photos, and then use the same shortcut.

There's a secret shortcut that allows you to paste the settings to multiple selected photos in Detail view, but be careful if your Filmstrip is hidden, as you might not realize that multiple photos are selected. The secret shortcut is Ctrl-Shift-V (Windows) / Cmd-Shift-V (Mac).

DEFAULT COPY SETTINGS ON THE DESKTOP

You can **skip the Copy Settings dialog** by going to ... menu > **Copy Edit Settings** or using the shortcut Ctrl-C (Windows) / Cmd-C (Mac). This copies the default copy settings.

Adobe's own defaults copy the Profile, Light panel, Color panel, Effects panel, Detail panel and Chromatic Aberration checkbox. It skips the Crop, Healing, Brush and Gradient tools, as well as the Lens Profile and Geometry adjustments, as these are more likely to be in different positions on different photos.

You can **change the copy defaults** by checking your chosen checkboxes in the Copy Settings dialog, clicking the ... icon on the right and then selecting **Set as Default**.

COPY/PASTE ON MOBILE

To copy and paste settings to one or more photos using a mobile device:

1. In Edit view, tap the ... menu and select **Copy Settings**. (On iOS, you can also copy the default settings to the clipboard from the Grid selection view.)

2. In the Copy Settings menu, check the groups of settings you want to copy, or tap the arrow to check/uncheck individual sliders. Tap *OK* to place the settings on the clipboard.

3. If you only want to paste to a single photo, stay in Edit view. Switch to the next photo, tap the ... menu and select **Paste Settings**.

If you want to apply the settings to multiple

photos, switch back to the Grid view, select the photos, and select **Paste Settings** from the toolbar (iOS) / ... menu (Android). Turn back to page 68 for a reminder of how to quickly select multiple photos.

COPY FROM PREVIOUS ON MOBILE

There's an additional **Previous** button at the right hand end of the Edit view toolbar, which copies some or all edits from the previously selected photo onto the current photo, without having to go through the Copy Settings dialog.

Copy from Previous

Adjustments copies everything except for the crop, whereas **All** includes the crop.

CROPPING &
STRAIGHTENING

11

In an ideal world, you'd have the time to make sure a photo was perfectly composed in the camera at the time of shooting. Unfortunately, few of us live in an ideal world, and by the time you've perfected the shot, you've missed the moment.

Cropping is the removal of the outer parts of a photo. Most photos benefit from cropping, whether to remove distractions from the frame, to straighten horizons, to improve the composition, to draw the viewer's eye to the subject, to fit a specific paper or frame shape, or simply to zoom in closer on the subject, if you were unable to move closer at the time of shooting.

Any cropping you do within Lightroom is non-destructive. No pixels are deleted from the original files. They're just hidden. If you later change your mind, you can return to the Crop tool to adjust or reset the crop markings.

IN THIS SECTION, WE'LL CONSIDER:

• Some basic rules to help your composition.

• How to crop photos to specific aspect ratios, to fit standard print sizes or frames.

• How to straighten wonky horizons.

• How to rotate photos by 90°, if the camera didn't do it for you.

COMPOSITION BASICS

Entire books are written on the subject of composition, so we won't attempt to cover the subject in detail in this book. However, the principles learned from composition books apply to cropping photos in Lightroom, as much as they apply to framing the photo in the camera.

If you're new to photography, there are a few basic principles to bear in mind when learning to crop your photos. They're not hard and fast rules, and as you grow in experience, you can break them, but they're a good place to start.

COMPOSITION TIPS

Use the Rule of Thirds to help you decide where to place the subject in the frame

Straighten the horizon, and any other lines that should be vertical or horizontal, especially if they're near the edge of the frame

Crop to fill the frame, to simplify the image and remove distractions

© Deposit Photos / DmitryPoch

Avoid cropping at people's joints as it looks unnatural. Crop mid-way between joints wherever possible

Avoid putting the subject or horizon
dead center (unless there's symmetry)

If the subject is moving, leave space
for the viewer's eye to follow

If a person or animal isn't looking
at the camera, leave space to
follow the subject's gaze

The orientation can affect the
direction the viewer's eye travels,
so select a vertical or horizontal
crop with that in mind

Flip a photo if it helps the viewer's eye
travel more smoothly from left to right

UNDERSTANDING ASPECT RATIO

Images on screen can be any shape you like, but if you're printing or framing a photo, you'll need to match the photo's aspect ratio to the paper or frame. If you don't crop to the right ratio, you'll either end up with white paper showing along two edges, or the printer will cut off more of the photo than you intended.

The same principle applies to other aspect ratios, not just cropping to square. Imagine trying to fit a panoramic photo into a normal rectangular frame, and you'll have the same choices to make.

We'll learn how to crop to a specific ratio in the next lesson.

WHAT IS ASPECT RATIO?

The aspect ratio is simply the proportional relationship between the width and height of a photo, in other words, it's the shape of the photo. You'll often see it written with a colon (2:3) or with an x (2x3).

Some aspect ratios are long and thin, whereas others are closer to square. A square is 1x1, which means the height and width are equal, whereas a 16x9 widescreen shape is a long and thin rectangle.

CROPPING FOR PRINTS/FRAMES

Imagine you have a rectangular photo and a square frame. Clearly it's not going to fit, so what are your options?

1. Squash the photo to fit. This never looks good, so Lightroom doesn't let you do it.

2. Keep the rectangular shape, but add white borders along the other edges.

3. Crop the top and bottom (or sides), so that it will fit.

4. Buy another frame that's closer to the aspect ratio of the photo, so you don't need to crop as much.

STANDARD ASPECT RATIOS

The shape of standard print ratios varies. 4x5 is quite square, whereas 2x3/4x6 is longer and thinner

Screen sizes vary from traditional rectangular ratios to newer widescreen formats

CROPPING FOR PRINT

A rectangular photo and a square frame... how do you make the photo fit?

Squash it?   Add borders?   Crop it!

CROPPING & STRAIGHTENING PHOTOS

In the last couple of lessons, we've learned about composition and aspect ratios, but now let's focus on the practicalities of cropping using Lightroom.

To **select the Crop tool** and show the crop options, click the icon in the right panel bar (desktop/tablet) / Edit view toolbar (phone) or press the C key (desktop).

← Crop tool

Select the Crop tool

STRAIGHTENING WONKY HORIZONS

Logically, our eyes expect the horizon to be horizontal, but most photographers have trouble getting it perfectly level at the time of capture. The Crop tool allows you to correct the rotation in a few different ways:

To let Lightroom attempt to **automatically straighten the horizon**, click the *Auto* button (desktop) / *Straighten* button (mobile) in the Crop panel.

To **straighten the photo by eye** on the desktop, float the cursor outside the bounding box (the edge of the crop) so the cursor turns into a double-headed arrow, then click and drag to rotate the photo. A grid displays to help you judge the rotation. On a mobile device, drag your finger anywhere outside the bounding box.

As you rotate the crop, the photo remains level, so you don't have to turn your head to see how the photo will look once it's cropped.

To **manually draw the correct horizon line** on the desktop, hold down the Ctrl

key (Windows) / Cmd key (Mac), click on the horizon and drag further along the horizon, then release the mouse. Lightroom straightens the line, and in the process, straightens the photo too.

To **straighten the photo using the slider**, adjust the *Straighten* slider in the Crop panel (desktop) / under the photo (mobile). While you're dragging the slider, a grid overlay displays to help.

To **reset the rotation**, click on the slider label (desktop) / double-tap the curved slider under the photo (mobile). This only resets the rotation and doesn't expand the crop back to the edges of the original photo.

CROPPING PHOTOS

To **crop a photo**, drag the edges or corners of the bounding box (that's the edge of the crop). Occasionally, you'll try to drag the edge of the bounding box, but it won't move. This is because the photo is slightly rotated and it's bumping up against the edge. Move the crop boundary away from the edge of the photo or reset the *Straighten* slider to fix it.

To **crop a vertical rectangle out of a horizontal photo**, or vice versa, click/tap the *Rotate Crop Aspect* button or on the desktop, you can also press the X key. You can also drag the corner of the bounding box at a 45° angle.

To **move the photo** under the crop overlay, click (desktop) / hold (mobile) and drag within the crop boundary.

To completely **reset the crop**, click the main *Reset Crop* button at the top of the Crop panel (desktop) or double-tap on the photo (mobile).

SELECTING AN ASPECT RATIO

If you're planning to print your photo using a standard print size or put it in a standard shape frame, you'll need to crop the photo to the right ratio, as we learned in the previous lesson (page 156). Lightroom offers the most frequent ratios as presets in the *Aspect* pop-up. The first set are standard print ratios, and the second set are standard screen shapes.

The *Original* and *As Shot* options are identical for most photos. Some cameras (including Lightroom's own camera) allow you to crop the photos to a specific ratio at the time of shooting, or display crop lines on the screen. *As Shot* respects the in-camera crop setting, whereas *Original* uses the full sensor data (where available).

To **constrain your crop** to a specific aspect

CROP PANEL (WINDOWS/MAC)

Reset Crop

Set Aspect Ratio

Rotate Crop Aspect

Auto Straighten

Select the Crop tool

Straighten Slider (click label to reset)

Constrain Aspect Ratio

Rotate 90° CCW or CW

Flip Horizontally or Vertically

Drag handles on edges or corners of bounding box to resize crop

Drag the corner at a 45° angle to switch orientation or press X ratio, click/tap the *Constrain Aspect Ratio* lock icon so that the lock is closed (desktop/mobile), or hold down the Shift key while adjusting the crop (desktop).

To **allow a freeform crop**, click to unlock the lock icon.

ROTATING & FLIPPING PHOTOS

If your camera doesn't automatically rotate vertical photos, you can manually **rotate by 90°** using the circular arrow buttons.

You can also **rotate multiple photos by 90°** on the desktop by selecting the photos in Grid view and going to *Photo menu > Rotate Left/Right* or using the keyboard shortcuts Ctrl-[(Windows) / Cmd-[(Mac) to rotate counter-clockwise/left and Ctrl-] (Windows) / Cmd-] (Mac) to rotate clockwise/right.

Occasionally you may want to flip a photo horizontally or vertically, because we read photos from left to right. To **flip the photo**, click/tap the *Flip Horizontal* or *Flip Vertical* buttons.

CROP TOOL (IOS/ANDROID)

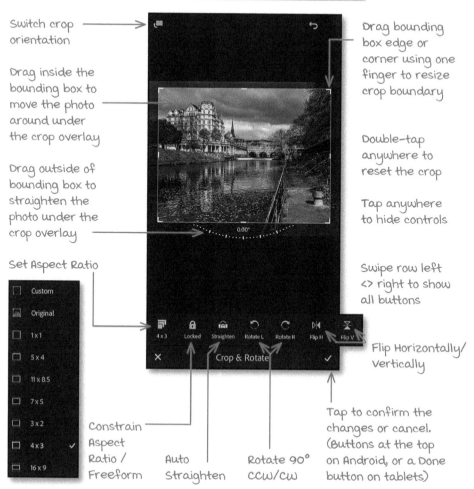

Switch crop orientation

Drag inside the bounding box to move the photo around under the crop overlay

Drag outside of bounding box to straighten the photo under the crop overlay

Set Aspect Ratio

Drag bounding box edge or corner using one finger to resize crop boundary

Double-tap anywhere to reset the crop

Tap anywhere to hide controls

Swipe row left <> right to show all buttons

Flip Horizontally/ Vertically

Constrain Aspect Ratio / Freeform

Auto Straighten

Rotate 90° CCW/CW

Tap to confirm the changes or cancel. (Buttons at the top on Android, or a Done button on tablets)

SELECTING YOUR LOOK

12

Over the last few years, presets and filters have become a popular way of editing photos. On page 115, we said that when used alone, they can be a bit of a blunt instrument. However, in combination with other editing skills, they can be a valuable addition to your workflow.

FILM STOCK

The idea of starting to build your photo from a base profile isn't a new concept. In the world of film photography, each film has its own characteristics, and a photographer chooses their film stock based on the kind of look they desire.

Kodak's Portra range is popular for portraits, with it's natural skin tones, realistic color saturation and fine grain, whereas their Ektar film offers much more vivid and highly saturated colors.

Slide films like Kodak's now-retired Kodachrome and Ektachrome, and Fuji's Provia and Velvia, have long been popular with landscape photographers for their vibrant, punchy colors and high contrast.

For B&W, the iconic Kodak Tri-X has lots of contrast and a distinctive grain, making it popular for street and documentary photography, whereas Kodak's T-Max had a finer grain for a cleaner look.

In the same way, you can build your photo edits from a specific base profile, depending on the look you desire.

PROFILES VS. PRESETS

Lightroom uses three different types of profiles and presets, each with their own advantages and disadvantages.

Camera-specific profiles only work on raw files and are designed to be a starting point for your own editing. They're found in the Profile panel, above the editing sliders.

Creative profiles can be applied to all sorts of photos to add a distinctive look, and they're designed to not need additional editing, beyond corrections for exposure, lens distortion, sharpening, etc. They can also be faded or exaggerated using an *Amount* slider, depending how strong an effect your prefer. These are also found in the Profile panel.

Presets, found in the Presets panel (opened using the button below the editing sliders), save sets of slider values to easily apply to other photos. They're ideal for saving your favorite vignette settings, or the sharpening settings you use for portraits, or the starting edits you apply to every photo.

The main differences are shown in the table overleaf, but in summary, they're slightly different tools for different jobs. Presets are best used for your own creations, and for modular systems (for example, to use one preset for sharpening and a different one for grain), whereas profiles are ideal for commercial developers to create special effects and film emulation.

WHEN TO APPLY PRESETS & PROFILES

You'll generally need to select your profile or preset before you start moving sliders, as profiles change the overall look, and presets move sliders, overwriting your changes.

The exception are presets that only move a few sliders, such as your favorite vignette settings.

IN THIS SECTION, WE'LL CONSIDER:

- The different types of profiles.

- How to preview and apply profiles.

- How to preview and apply presets.

- How to create your own presets.

DIFFERENCES BETWEEN PRESETS & PROFILES

Presets	Camera-Specific Raw Profiles	Creative Profiles
.lrtemplate or .xmp file extension	.dcp or .xmp file extension	.xmp file extension
Work on all photo formats, unless they call a raw-only profile	Work on raw files only (usually camera-specific)	Most work for all photo formats
Create them yourself using Lightroom	Mostly created by third-party developers using DNG Profile Editor (.dcp format) or Profiles SDK (.xmp format)	Mostly created by third-party developers using Profiles SDK
Moves sliders, so you can see how the adjustments were created	Separate layer of adjustments, which doesn't move visible sliders, so they're more difficult to learn from	Separate layer of adjustments, which don't move visible sliders, so they're more difficult to learn from
Can only adjust visible Lightroom tools such as sliders	Applies normal Lightroom edits behind the scenes, plus 3D LUT's for more advanced color adjustments	Applies normal Lightroom edits behind the scenes, plus 3D LUT's for more advanced color adjustments
Increase/decrease effect by moving the individual sliders	Can't be faded	Exaggerate/fade effect using *Amount* slider, then edit from there
Best for your own settings, to improve consistency and efficiency	Best as a starting point, like film stock	Best for special effects

BROWSING, APPLYING & IMPORTING PROFILES

Camera-specific and Creative profiles are found in the Profile panel, at the top of the Edit slider panels (desktop/tablet) or near the left of the Edit view toolbar (phone).

Profiles panel

To view the full range of profiles, click the **Browse** button, or on the desktop, use the shortcut Shift-B.

BROWSING & APPLYING PROFILES

When you first open the Profile Browser, you'll see a series of small thumbnails, grouped into sets. We'll come back to the difference between the sets on page 167.

To **apply a profile** on a desktop or tablet, click/tap on it and then click the *Back* button to return to the normal Edit sliders (or on the desktop, double-clicking on the profile will do both at once). On a mobile phone, tap on the profile and then tap the checkmark

to return to the normal Edit view.

If you change your mind, you can return to the Profile panel and select a different profile at any time.

On the desktop, the thumbnails may be a little small to preview properly, so float your cursor over the profile thumbnail or name to **preview the profile** on the larger image. To briefly stop previewing the profile, to compare it with your current profile, hold down the Alt key (Windows) / Opt key (Mac). You can change the thumbnail Grid view to a List view or Large thumbnail view by clicking the ... icon in the top right corner.

SETTING FAVORITES

Over the course of time, you're likely to use some profiles more than others. This is a good thing, because the profile becomes part of YOUR distinctive style. If you mix and match too many different profiles, your work will lack consistency.

To **mark/unmark a profile as a favorite** on the desktop, click the star icon in the

List view

Grid view →

Large view

THE PROFILE BROWSER (WINDOWS/MAC)

Show Profile Browser

Selected preset (and favorite presets in pop-up)

Back to sliders

Favorite Profiles

Show menu

Change thumbnail view

Filter profiles to show Color/B&W

Manage (Show/Hide) Profile Groups

Import Profiles

Favorite profile

Float over preset to preview effect

Click on preset to apply effect

Click to open/close preset group

THE PROFILE BROWSER (IOS/ANDROID)

Selective Healing Crop Profiles Auto Light Color Effects Detail Optics Geometry Presets Previous Versions Reset

⌐— Select the Profile Browser

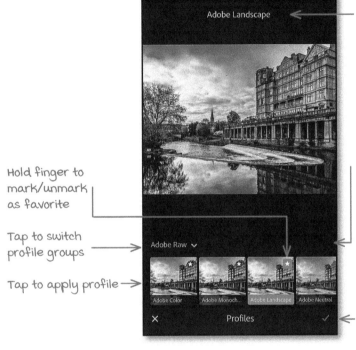

Name of selected profile

On Android, tap on the ... menu (not shown here) to show only color or only B&W profiles and show/hide profile sets.

Hold finger to mark/unmark as favorite

Tap to switch profile groups

Tap to apply profile →

Tap to confirm the changes or cancel. (Buttons at the top on Android, or a Back button on tablets)

corner of the thumbnail, or to the right in List view. On mobile, hold your finger on the thumbnail.

←— Favorite profile

←— Profile name

These profiles then show in the Favorites set at the top of the Profile Browser. On the desktop, they also show in the pop-up, so you don't have to open the Profile Browser every time you want to switch profiles.

MANAGING PROFILES

If you know you want to create a color or B&W photo, you can **temporarily filter the profiles** on Windows, Mac or Android by clicking/tapping the ... button and selecting *Color* or *B&W* from the menu. Select *All* to show all of the profiles again. (This filtering is not currently available on iOS.)

There will likely be some profiles that you don't use, and the number of profiles will grow over time as you download new ones, so Lightroom allows you to hide entire sets of profiles.

To **show and hide profiles** on the desktop, click the ... icon at the top of the Profile Browser panel and select *Manage Profiles*. Check or uncheck profile sets, and then click the *Back* button to return. If you right-click on a profile set in the Profile Browser, there's quick access to the *Hide* and *Reset Hidden Items* commands.

On Android, tap the ... menu in the Profile Browser and select *Manage Profiles* to check/uncheck profile sets. (This isn't currently available on iOS.)

INSTALLING & SYNCING PROFILES

Some third-party profiles are available for purchase and download.

To **install downloaded profiles** on the desktop, go to *File menu > Import Profiles and Presets* or click the ... icon at the top of the Profile Browser and select *Import Profiles*. Navigate to the folder or zip file containing the presets and click *Import*.

To **install profiles on Android**, tap the ... button in the Profile Browser and select *Import Profiles*. You can import profiles from your device's storage (such as the Downloads folder) or Google Drive. Select the individual profiles, or a whole zip file containing multiple profiles, to start the import.

Profile import is not yet available on iOS or Web, but once profiles are imported into the desktop app, they sync to your other devices.

MISSING PROFILES

If you've used other versions of Lightroom (such as Lightroom Classic), or you've used Adobe Camera Raw in Photoshop, you may

have used camera-specific profiles (DCP format) without realizing. For example, VSCO presets automatically select a camera-specific profile. These camera-specific profiles need to be imported into Lightroom, so they can be stored safely and synced to your other devices.

On first launch, Lightroom automatically imports any camera-specific (DCP format) profiles installed on your computer. However, if the profiles can't be automatically imported into Lightroom, it displays a missing profile warning on affected photos, to remind you to import the profile or select a different one.

SETS OF PROFILES

When you open the Profile Browser, you'll notice that the profiles are grouped into sections with a line between (called clusters), and into folders (called sets) too.

BASIC

The Basic set appears for rendered photos (JPEG/TIFF/PSD/PNG format), as they don't have Adobe Raw profiles. There are simple *Color* and *Monochrome* profiles for these file types.

ADOBE RAW

The Adobe Raw profiles aim to make photos from different cameras look as similar as possible, so if you change your camera or shoot an event with multiple camera brands, they'll blend well. They're available for raw photos from most (but not all) supported cameras.

Adobe Color is Adobe's default profile. The aim is to look great on a wide range of photos, so it adds a little contrast and saturation, while attempting to protect the skin tones.

Adobe Portrait is optimized for a wide range of skin tones, including very pale skin and very dark skin, so it's ideal for portraits and family shots. It has a little less contrast than *Adobe Color*, but you can add contrast if you prefer a bit more punch.

Adobe Landscape automatically compresses the tones to give a little more headroom for outdoor photos which often have a wide dynamic range, and the blues and greens are enhanced.

Adobe Vivid has a very punchy and saturated

effect. It's great for sunsets and other very colorful photos, but may be a little over the top for portraits.

Adobe Neutral is a very flat starting point, ready for you to edit in your own way. It's ideal for photos with very tricky colors and gradients that just don't quite work with the other profiles.

Adobe Standard is an older profile that all of the other Adobe Raw profiles are based on. It's similar to *Adobe Color*, but it has a little less contrast and saturation.

Adobe Monochrome is the default profile for B&W photos, and is automatically assigned when you click the *B&W* button in the Color panel.

CAMERA MATCHING

The camera matching profiles are designed to mimic your camera JPEG, so your raw files more closely match the image you saw on the back of the camera. In addition to the *Camera Default* or *Camera Standard* profiles, these profiles also try to emulate the other picture styles that your camera manufacturers offers. The names of these vary by manufacturer, for example, Canon calls them Picture Styles, Nikon names them Picture Control, Fuji has Simulation Modes, Olympus has Picture Modes and Sony calls them Creative Styles. These camera matching profiles are available for most current DSLR's, but may be missing from compact or older cameras, and they won't be available for rendered files.

PROFILES

If you've created camera-specific DCP

Camera-Specific Profiles

Creative Profiles

format profiles using Adobe's DNG Profile Editor tool or the X-Rite ColorChecker Passport plug-in for Lightroom Classic, or installed camera-specific profiles created by third-parties such as VSCO or RNI Films, they'll be found in a Profiles set.

LEGACY PROFILES

The Legacy Profiles set contains B&W versions of some camera-specific profiles. As the set name suggests, these are just to maintain compatibility with edits applied using previous Lightroom versions.

CREATIVE PROFILES

The next cluster of sets contain a selection of creative profiles. These are primarily designed to apply special effects or a specific "look" to your photo, and they'll work for rendered files (JPEG/TIFF/PSD/PNG) as well as raw photos.

The **Modern** profiles represent current fashions in photography, while the **Vintage** profiles are designed to look more like film photos. The **Artistic** profiles are designed to be more edgy, with stronger color shifts.

The **B&W** profiles are optimized for high impact black and white work, offering a range of color channel mixes and tonal adjustments. In addition to the selection of numbered B&W profiles, there are profiles to imitate the effect of adding a red, orange, yellow, green or blue filter. These are traditionally used at the time of capture when shooting B&W on film. The B&W profiles are a great starting point for B&W editing.

The effect of the Creative profiles can be faded or exaggerated using the **Amount** slider that appears immediately below

the profile thumbnail, or in the main Profile panel. 100 applies the effect as the developer intended, moving the slider to the left reduces the effect of the profile, and moving it to the right exaggerates the effect.

Creative Profiles can contain any normal slider adjustments to be applied "behind the scenes," but they can also include LUT's (Look Up Tables) for much more advanced color adjustments. 3D LUT's can, for example, tell Lightroom to make this shade of blue yellower and make this shade of blue more saturated and another shade of blue lighter. The tables allow profile developers to apply specific adjustments in very precise, targeted ways that are not possible through any of Lightroom's sliders.

Creative profiles created by third-party profiles are added as additional sets at the bottom of the Profile Browser.

SAVING SETTINGS AS PRESETS

Whereas profiles are created by third-party developers, you can create presets yourself. They can help you to:

Improve Efficiency—For example, perhaps you find yourself selecting a camera matching profile, decreasing *Highlights*, increasing *Shadows* and adding a little *Clarity* and *Vibrance* to most photos. Rather than having to move multiple sliders, you can select a single preset.

Improve Consistency—Presets (especially those you've created yourself) can help to ensure consistency over a group of photos, or over your entire portfolio by saving and applying the same settings.

Presets move visible sliders, so unlike profiles, you can apply multiple presets that do different things. For example, you may apply a preset that you use as a starting point, and another one that applies a vignette to some photos, and another that applies your landscape sharpening settings.

PREVIEWING & APPLYING PRESETS

To **show the Presets panel** on the desktop, select the Edit view then click the *Presets* button in the bottom right corner or use the shortcut Shift-P. On mobile, tap the Presets button in the toolbar.

Presets panel

To **show the individual presets** on a desktop or tablet, click/tap the arrows to open/close the preset groups. On a phone, select the preset group from the pop-up to

switch sets.

Some presets may be hidden from view, depending on the type of photo that is selected. For example, by default, a preset that includes an Adobe Raw profile does not show for a JPEG image, because the Adobe Raw profile is not available for JPEG images and would create a different result. To **show the partially compatible presets**, click/tap the ... button at the top of the Presets panel and toggle *Hide Partially Compatible Presets* (desktop) / *Show Partially Compatible Presets* (mobile).

To **preview a preset** on the desktop, float the cursor over the preset name. The effect is previewed on the photo in the main preview area, and the sliders move temporarily to their preset positions. On mobile, tap on the preset thumbnail (as the preset isn't applied on mobile until you confirm).

To **apply a preset to the selected photo** on the desktop, click on the preset name. On mobile, tap on the preset and then tap the checkmark/*Done* button.

To **close the Presets panel** on the desktop, click the X in the corner or the *Presets* button again.

CREATING PRESETS

As you start to find combinations of sliders that you like or use frequently, you can create your own presets.

To **create a preset**, click/tap the ... button at the top of the Presets panel and select *Create Preset*, then give the preset a name. If there's already another preset by that name in the same group, Lightroom asks whether to replace the existing preset or keep both, adding an extra number to your chosen preset name.

In the *Group* pop-up, select an existing preset group or select *New Group* to create a new one.

Check the panels or individual slider values you want to include in your preset and click *Save*.

If you frequently save the same sliders in presets, click the ... button in the Create Preset dialog (desktop only) and select **Set as Defaults** to automatically check those sliders in future.

If you later change the sliders and want to **update the preset**, you can right-click on the preset (desktop) / tap on the ... menu to the right of the preset (mobile) and select *Update with Current Settings*.

INSTALLING & SYNCING PRESETS

A large cottage industry has grown up around Lightroom, with a huge number of free and paid presets and profiles available.

Presets designed for Lightroom 4 or later work with Lightroom. These may be marked PV2012/PV2017 or PV3/PV4/PV5.

To **install presets on the desktop**, go to *File menu > Import Profiles and Presets* or click the ... icon at the top of the Presets panel and select *Import Presets*. Navigate to the folder or zip file containing the presets and click *Import*.

To **install presets on Android**, tap the ... button at the top of the Presets panel and select **Import Presets**. You can import presets from your device's storage (such as the Downloads folder) or Google Drive.

Select the individual presets, or a whole zip file containing multiple presets, to start the import.

Preset import is not yet available on iOS or Web, but any profiles or presets you import on the desktop (or create on any of your devices), are automatically synced to the cloud, so they're available everywhere.

ORGANIZING PRESETS

Over time, your collection of presets will grow, so you'll need to organize them. It's easy to end up with too many presets, and then you can't see the wood for trees.

To **rename a preset**, right-click on it (desktop) / tap on the ... menu to the right of the preset (mobile) and select *Rename*.

To **delete a single preset**, right-click on it (desktop) / tap on the ... menu to the right of the preset (mobile) and select *Delete* (but take care as it will be deleted from all of your devices).

To **move a preset into another group**, right-click on the preset and select *Move to Group > [the name of the new group]* (desktop only). While you're moving or creating a preset, you can also **create a new group**.

To **rename an existing preset group**, right-click on it and select *Rename Group* (desktop only).

To **delete an entire preset group**, right-click on it and select *Delete Group* (but it will be deleted from all of your devices, and entire preset groups can only be deleted from the desktop, not mobile).

To **hide a preset group** without deleting it, click/tap the ... menu at the top of the Presets panel and select *Manage Presets*.

Uncheck the preset group and click the *Back/Done* button to return to the Presets panel. To show them again, repeat the process and check the preset group. On the desktop, you can also right-click on the preset group and select *Hide* or *Reset Hidden Presets*. This visibility status is local, so you can have all of your presets available on the desktop, but only your favorite groups visible on your smaller mobile screen.

As your preset creation skills improve, you may want to **share a preset** with other photographers. To do so (desktop only), right-click on a preset and select *Export*, then navigate to a folder on your hard drive.

PRESETS (WINDOWS/MAC)

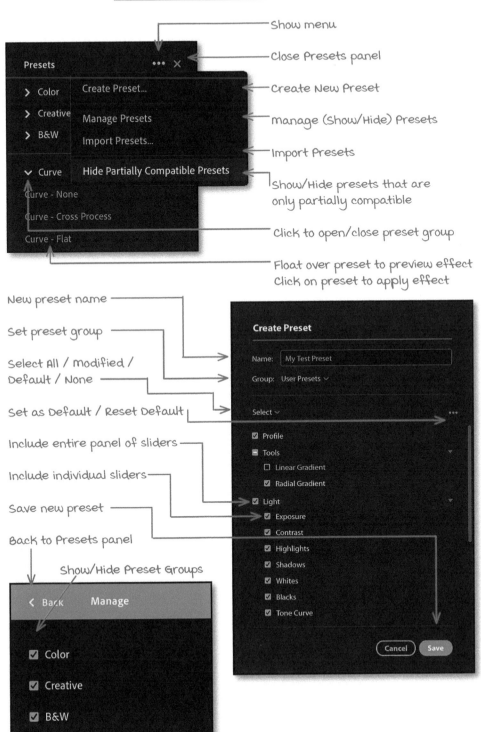

Show menu

Close Presets panel

Create New Preset

Manage (Show/Hide) Presets

Import Presets

Show/Hide presets that are only partially compatible

Click to open/close preset group

Float over preset to preview effect
Click on preset to apply effect

New preset name

Set preset group

Select All / Modified / Default / None

Set as Default / Reset Default

Include entire panel of sliders

Include individual sliders

Save new preset

Back to Presets panel

Show/Hide Preset Groups

PRESETS (IOS/ANDROID)

Tap to select preset group from menu

Tap to preview preset on photo

Tap ... at the top to create new presets, show/hide preset groups and on Android, Show/Hide Partially Compatible Presets

Tap ... to rename, update or delete preset. On Android, you can also move to a new preset group.

Tap to apply the preset or cancel (Buttons at the top on Android, or a Done button on tablets)

Save new preset

New preset name

Set preset group

Select All / None

Select Modified / Default also available on Android

Include entire panel of sliders

View checkboxes for individual sliders

Back to Presets panel

Show/Hide Preset Groups

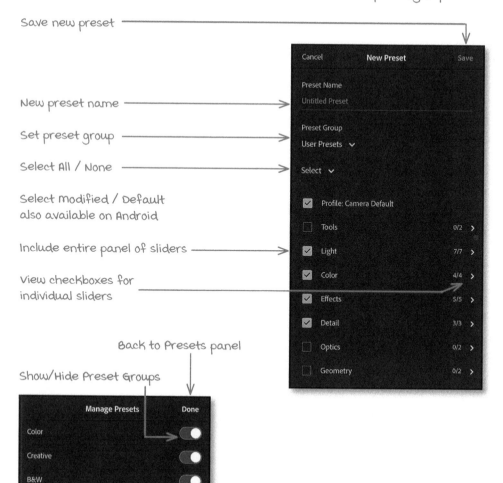

SETTING DEFAULTS

If you usually use the same profile or preset on your photos, or you like to switch between different camera styles on your camera, then you might want to change the default settings that are applied to new raw photos when you import them.

SETTING DEFAULTS

To **set your defaults**, go to *Preferences (desktop) / Settings (mobile) > Import* and select your chosen default from the *Raw Default* pop-up. Your new defaults automatically sync to your other devices. These are the choices:

Adobe Default is Adobe's own default setting, which uses the *Adobe Color* profile, with most sliders set to 0.

Camera Settings recognizes the picture style you selected in the camera and applies the camera matching profile, if it's available. This is particularly useful if you use a compact or mirrorless camera, since the picture style is what you see in the viewfinder or screen. Some recent cameras write additional Lightroom settings (such as custom sharpening) into the image metadata, so these settings are also applied.

Preset applies the preset of your choice (page 170). This is useful if, for example, you frequently apply the same settings to your photos. If any sliders are unchecked when creating the preset, Lightroom falls back on the Camera Settings as a default for these sliders. Adobe has provided a few default presets to get you started, including presets that apply specific profiles and enable lens corrections and noise reduction.

APPLYING DEFAULTS

The settings apply to any unedited raw files you import. They don't overwrite edit settings already stored with the file by Lightroom or Camera Raw. The defaults also apply when you reset a slider, panel or whole photo back to default settings (page 146).

BALANCING LIGHT & CONTRAST

13

Photography is all about balancing light, shade and the contrast between them. These adjustments are made using the sliders in the Light and Effects panels, and are the focus for this section.

IN THIS SECTION, WE'LL CONSIDER:

• How to set the *Exposure* slider to optimize the overall image brightness.

• How the *Contrast* slider increases or decreases the overall (or global) contrast.

• When to use *Highlights* & *Shadows* to lighten or darken the highlight or shadow tones in your photo.

• How the *Whites* & *Blacks* sliders can be used to increase the dynamic range or clip the highlight and shadow tones.

• How to use *Clarity* to add local contrast, giving the photo punch without compressing the highlight or shadow detail.

• How to use *Dehaze* to reduce or emulate atmospheric haze.

• When to use the Tone Curve instead of, or along with, the Light panel sliders.

• The best order to adjust the Light panel sliders.

ADJUST FROM THE TOP... MOSTLY

You may have read articles and watched videos by numerous Lightroom users on editing photos, and they all have different opinions.

Some will tell you to start at the top and always work down. Others will tell you to always set *Whites* and *Blacks* first. Some will tell you skip the Light panel (a.k.a. the Basic panel in Lightroom Classic) and use a Tone Curve instead. So who is right?

They're all right—and they're all wrong. It's impossible to set hard and fast rules because Lightroom's Light sliders are image-adaptive (intelligent). The range and effect of the sliders change based on the content of the photo and the values of the other Light panel sliders.

In this book, we'll discuss how the sliders were *designed* to work, as explained by the engineers who created them, because they know the tools better than anyone.

WORK TOP DOWN... SORT OF

The Light sliders were designed to be used top down, because the first few Light sliders affect the range of the lower Light sliders. For example, if you change *Highlights* and *Shadows* before *Exposure*, the sliders won't move far enough. It'll be ok for little tweaks, but you'll want to get *Exposure* in the right ballpark first.

The *Contrast* slider is the exception. It can be used at any time as it doesn't affect slider range, and it's usually easiest to set it after you've set the other Light sliders.

SKIPPING SOME SLIDERS

The top-down principle doesn't mean you have to adjust every slider. For example, a photo with a low dynamic range (one that doesn't stretch to pure white/black but should do so) is still best adjusted from top to bottom, but skip the *Highlights/Shadows* and go straight from *Exposure* to *Whites/Blacks*.

In the following lessons, we're going to look at the principles behind the "normal" use of each slider, as well as examples of when you might want to do things slightly differently, for example, if specific tonal ranges are more important than others, or where you want a softer look (without adding local contrast).

APPLYING AUTO ADJUSTMENTS

If you just need a quick way to improve photos, try the **Auto** button. You'll find it near the Light panel, depending on which device you're using. On the desktop, the shortcut Shift-A applies the *Auto* adjustments, and if you hold down the Shift key while floating over the slider label, you can apply *Auto* settings to that single slider.

Like your camera's exposure meter, it's not as intelligent as you, so it doesn't know what's in the photo or how it's meant to look. Sometimes it works great, sometimes it's a reasonable starting point for adjusting sliders further, and sometimes the result is awful.

LIGHT PANEL WORKFLOW

High or Normal
Dynamic Range

Exposure always goes
first as other sliders
won't work well with
incorrect Exposure

If the White Balance
is way off, you may
need to roughly fix
it before continuing

Low Dynamic
Range

− Highlights
+ Shadows
to pull back
highlight and
shadow detail

+ Whites
− Blacks to
extend tonal
range

+ Whites
− Blacks to bring
back contrast lost
by the Highlights/
Shadows
adjustments

Ignore
Highlights
and Shadows,
as they won't
work well

Exception: Highlights/
Shadows add local
contrast. In some
cases, you might
want the softer
look of a tone
curve instead of
Highlights/Shadows

Texture to
enhance
microcontrast

+ Clarity and/or
+ Contrast to bring
back midtone
contrast if needed

Exception: In some
cases, you might
want to use +
Highlights and/
or − Shadows to
brighten highlights
or crush shadows

White Balance

Adjust Vibrance
/ Saturation

SETTING OVERALL EXPOSURE

At the top of the Light panel, the **Exposure** slider sets the overall image brightness, and it uses the same f-stop increments as your camera, so +2.0 of *Exposure* is the equivalent of opening the aperture on your camera by 2 stops.

The *Exposure* slider attempts to maintain a gentle transition to pure white to avoid harsh digital clipping.

Clipped   Gentle Transition

It's important to get the *Exposure* setting about right before moving on to the other Light panel sliders, as the range of other sliders are affected and they won't work well if your *Exposure* slider is set incorrectly.

SETTING EXPOSURE

So how do you know where to set the *Exposure* slider? Try these tips:

Squint Your Eyes—If you screw your eyes up, you won't be able to see the detail in the photo, and you'll be left with the overall impression of how bright it is. You're aiming for a mid-gray.

The Only Slider—Pretend it's the only control you have available. If there weren't any other sliders, how bright would you make the photo?

Confuse Your Brain—Your eyes adjust to the original camera exposure, making it difficult to judge the correct exposure. It can help to confuse your brain by swinging the *Exposure* slider to the left and right like a pendulum and then settle somewhere in the middle, wherever it looks right.

Focus on the Midtones—Don't worry if the highlights are a bit bright or the shadows a bit dark, or if there are clipped highlights or shadows at this stage (white/black areas with no detail), as you'll pull them back using the *Highlights* and *Shadows* sliders.

You can hold down the Alt key (Windows) / Opt key (Mac) / two fingers (mobile) to view the clipping warnings, but don't worry about them at this stage.

To illustrate the effect of the Exposure slider, let's start with a photo set to 0. It's a little dark

Set to Exposure –2.5, we can see there's loads of detail available even in the brightest clouds, which can be pulled back using the Highlights slider, but it's way too dark overall

Set to Exposure +2.5, it's way too bright and we've lost all the detail in the clouds, but we can see there's loads of detail in the dark areas, which can be pulled back using the Shadows slider

I've settled on +0.43 as a good overall exposure value, and I'll pull the clouds back later using the Highlights slider

GLOBAL VS. LOCAL CONTRAST

Contrast is defined as the difference in tone or color that makes an object distinguishable from its surroundings. In real terms, this means that all of the detail we see in the world around us—or in a photo—depends on contrast.

Contrast also affects the feel of a photo, with high contrast adding drama and excitement, commanding your attention. Since our eyes are drawn to the highest contrast, you can use it to draw the viewers eye away from distractions and toward the subject.

Enhancing these contrasts is, therefore, one of the most important things we can do when editing photos.

The second slider in the Light panel is called **Contrast**, so it would be an obvious choice, but it's a bit of a blunt instrument, and there are better tools to use. Why?

INCREASING MIDTONE CONTRAST

Normally, to increase midtone contrast, you have to make light pixels lighter and dark pixels darker. This is called global contrast, and it's what the *Contrast* slider does. The problem is, you lose highlight and shadow detail in the process.

Fortunately, our eyes are more interested in local contrast—small contrasts in similar

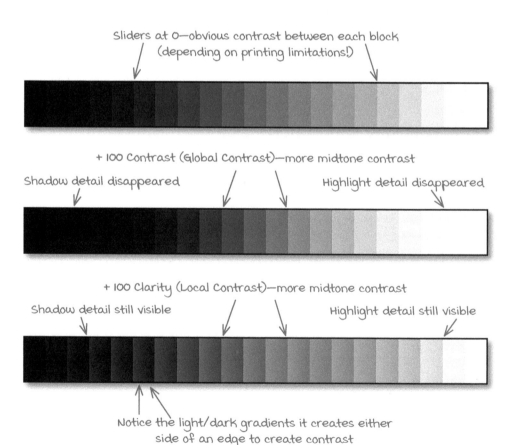

Sliders at 0—obvious contrast between each block
(depending on printing limitations!)

+ 100 Contrast (Global Contrast)—more midtone contrast
Shadow detail disappeared
Highlight detail disappeared

+ 100 Clarity (Local Contrast)—more midtone contrast
Shadow detail still visible
Highlight detail still visible

Notice the light/dark gradients it creates either
side of an edge to create contrast

Adding midtone contrast using the Contrast slider loses the highlight and shadow detail

Adding local contrast using the Clarity slider, enhances the highlight and shadow detail

Reducing contrast using the Contrast slider recovers the highlight and shadow detail, but the whole photo ends up really dull and flat

– Highlight brings back the cloud detail and + Shadows brings back the shadow details, but the photo still retains its punch thanks to the local contrast it applies

tones—than they are in big global contrast. Local contrast adjustments look for small changes in contrast and enhances them. This adds contrast without sacrificing as much detail in the highlights and shadows. Lightroom mainly adjusts local contrast using the *Clarity* slider, but it's also affected by the *Highlights*, *Shadows* and *Dehaze* sliders.

It can sound complicated, so let's illustrate the difference using the step wedges, and photos. (The step wedge is just an image created in Photoshop, with 21 blocks of gray in different shades, ranging from pure black to pure white, which makes it easier to see the differences.)

Once you've adjusted all of the other Light panels sliders, you can tweak the midtone contrast using the *Contrast* slider, but in many cases, it won't need adjusting at all.

DECREASING GLOBAL CONTRAST

But what if you have the opposite problem? If a photo has too much contrast (too wide a dynamic range), you can darken highlights and lighten the shadows using -*Contrast* to see more detail in those tones, but then you lose midtone contrast, making the photo look really flat. The *Highlights/Shadows* sliders are usually better at reducing dynamic range as they add local contrast at the same time, so it's often best to skip the *Contrast* slider altogether if you have too much contrast.

There may be exceptions, however. On a soft dreamy image, the extra local contrast may not be desirable, so you might want to use a negative *Contrast* adjustment in that case. Or if the *Highlights/Shadows* sliders don't go far enough, some negative *Contrast* can be useful to compress the tones.

CONTRAST VS. TONE CURVE

If you want to add or reduce global contrast, a Tone Curve is a better choice than the *Contrast* slider, because it allows you to control which tones gain or sacrifice contrast. To learn how to use curves to add or reduce contrast, turn to page 191.

RECOVERING HIGHLIGHT & SHADOW DETAIL

After setting *Exposure*, the *Highlights* and *Shadows* sliders are next in line for adjustment.

The **Highlights** slider mainly adjusts the brighter tones in the photo and barely touches the darker tones. It's generally intended to be dragged to the left (-) to recover highlight details, such as fluffy clouds in the sky or detail on a bride's dress.

Shadows does the opposite, mainly affecting the darker tones in the photo. It's generally intended to be moved to the right (+) to lighten shadow details, such as shadowed areas on people's faces or detail in a groom's suit.

Brightening shadows and darkening highlights usually comes at the cost of midtone contrast, making the photo look flat. Unlike a simple highlights or shadows control, Lightroom's *Highlights* and *Shadows* also add local contrast (page 182) and saturation to help to compensate for the loss of global contrast.

In most cases, the additional local contrast is beneficial, but you don't have any control over how much is added. For average

− Highlights brings back cloud detail without darkening the shadows

+ Highlights lightens the highlight tones without affecting the shadows

− Shadows darkens the shadows without affecting the highlights

+ Shadows lightens the shadow tones without lightening the highlights

photos, that's not a problem, but for some photos you may want a softer look, so you might prefer to use the Tone Curve to reduce the contrast in those cases.

SETTING HIGHLIGHTS/SHADOWS

So how do you know where to set the *Highlights* and *Shadows* sliders?

Amount—How much highlight and shadow detail you choose to recover will depend on the results of your photo analysis. For example, if the photo is of a stormy beach, the detail in the clouds will be essential, so you'll use more highlight recovery. Likewise, if the photo is a woodland scene, you'll need more shadow detail in the leaves and bark. In contrast, you won't need as much shadow recovery if the shadow detail is unimportant, such as the bushes in the background of a portrait.

Clipping—While you're moving the *Highlights* slider, hold down the Alt key (Windows) / Opt key (Mac) / two fingers (mobile) to see the clipping warnings, to ensure your adjustment is recovering any clipped highlights.

Keep It Natural—The effect on local contrast gets stronger as you move the sliders further. Both sliders look fairly natural up to 50, but beyond that, the effect becomes more surreal and halos can become noticeable, which can make photos look over-processed if not used carefully.

Slider Direction—Due to the local contrast and saturation changes applied by the *Highlights/Shadows* sliders, they usually work best when they're fairly symmetrical, for example, -50 *Highlights* and +50 *Shadows*. There are always exceptions, for example, you may only want local contrast in the clouds but softer shadows.

If you need to swing both sliders in the same direction, it's usually (but not always) a sign that the *Exposure* slider needs moving in that direction.

Follow with Whites/Blacks—Darkening highlights and lightening shadows decreases the midtone (global) contrast, so you'll usually need to adjust the *Whites/Blacks* sliders after *Highlights/Shadows*. We'll look at these sliders in the next lesson.

CONTROLLING WHITE & BLACK CLIPPING

The **Whites** and **Blacks** sliders affect the clipping point and roll off at the extreme ends of the tonal range. If you've used other image editing software, they're similar to the black and white points in Levels.

In most cases, the *Whites* slider is pulled to the right (+) and *Blacks* is pulled to the left (-) to expand the tonal range.

If a photo was captured in flat light, and therefore has a low dynamic range, use +*Whites* and -*Blacks* to stretch image data to fill the entire histogram, making a few pixels black and a few pure white.

The sliders adapt to the range of the photo, so even a foggy white photo can be stretched to fill the entire tonal range. This becomes even more useful when working with scans of old faded photos, as it allows you to create a bright white and deep black point in even the lowest contrast photos if you need to do so.

Use + Whites and - Blacks to stretch the histogram to the ends to fill the whole dynamic range

SETTING WHITES & BLACKS

So how do you know where to set the *Whites* and *Blacks* sliders?

Auto Adjust—On the desktop, hold down the Shift key and click on the slider name to automatically set the clipping points. This is an automatic setting that Lightroom often calculates correctly.

Check the Clipping Warnings—Hold down the Alt key (Windows) / Opt key (Mac) / two

+ Whites clips light pixels to pure white, but we've pushed it too far and lost detail in the clouds. Try to only clip small specular highlights like the shiny mudguard

- Blacks clips dark pixels to pure black. We've pushed it way too far and lost too much detail in the shadows. It's ok to clip dark pixels to black, but avoid creating large areas of solid black like this fingers (mobile) while dragging the *Whites* or *Blacks* sliders to view the clipping warnings, so you can check you're not clipping important details (making large areas pure white or pure black). The colored overlay shows whether the clipping only affects one channel, multiple channels, or all channels.

What to Clip—Turn back to page 125 for a reminder of what's ok to clip and what to avoid.

Deep Blacks—Deep blacks, caused by clipping larger numbers of dark pixels, is a popular choice to enhance contrast. Just be careful not clip too far and lose important shadow detail. This is more frequently done with a tone curve (page 191), as it compresses the dark tones with gentler transitions.

Clipping Studio Backgrounds—If you're shooting against a white studio background, which you want to keep pure white, the *Whites* slider allows you to clip highlights that would otherwise be protected by the *Exposure* slider's gentle roll off. If the photo was correctly exposed, with the whites close to clipping, a small value such as +15-25 is enough to blow the white background without having a noticeable impact on the overall exposure. The same principle applies using the *Blacks* slider with a black studio background.

After –100 Highlights and + 100 Shadows, the full range of detail is back but the photo looks very flat

If we use +21 Whites and –61 Blacks (below left), we can add back contrast without losing it anywhere important

On the Blacks clipping warning we can see we're just clipping the blacks in areas where the detail doesn't matter

ADDING 'POP' USING CLARITY

The **Clarity** slider is found in the Effects panel, but it affects brightness and contrast, so we're including it in this section.

As we learned on page 182, *Clarity* creates local contrast in the midtones by searching for edges and other areas of local contrast and enhancing that contrast. You might also use words like definition, punch or pop.

The *Texture* slider, which we'll come back to on page 232, does something similar on smaller details.

Wrinkles on faces create local contrast, so avoid adding more using the Clarity slider. I know of very few women who appreciate having their wrinkles exaggerated!

SETTING CLARITY

Positive Clarity is very good at emphasizing large details, so it works well on architecture and landscapes, adding a distinctive crisp feel, and it can also look great on high contrast B&W photos.

Use a very low setting for portraits, if you use it at all, as it can accentuate lines and wrinkles.

The Clarity slider helps to add 'pop' to buildings, landscapes and other textured scenes, which naturally have small contrasts between similar tones

Although the slider goes to 100, that's almost always too strong, as it can create wide halos. *Clarity* can quickly make your photos look over-processed, so be conservative with the amount you apply.

It doesn't increase saturation, so you may find that the colors start to look a little muted. Adding a little *Vibrance* or *Saturation* (page 208) can make the effect look more natural.

Negative Clarity creates a diffuse, soft-focus, dreamy effect. It adds a gentle glow to the photo, similar to the well known Orton effect, so it can look good on B&W, vintage style or infrared photos.

In the past, negative *Clarity* has been used for softening faces, but the *Texture* slider gives a more realistic effect.

REMOVING HAZE USING DEHAZE

Like *Clarity*, the **Dehaze** slider is found in the Effects panel. It's designed to remove (or add) haze, for example, atmospheric haze over a landscape or city smog. It also works well on photos of the night sky, backlit photos, underwater photos, reflections, scans/photographs of old faded photos, and more. It's also brilliant for adding a high contrast gritty feel to B&W photos.

It runs complex calculations to try to estimate the light lost as it passes through the atmosphere, adapting to the content of each photo to get a good result as quickly as possible.

SETTING DEHAZE

To get the best result, adjust the white balance first (page 204), as it uses the color of the light in its calculations, then adjust the *Dehaze* slider until your photo looks great.

It's best used in combination with the normal adjustment sliders. Use *Dehaze* to remove the worst of the haze, and then use the other sliders as normal to finish editing the photo.

Dehaze is a magical slider, but it can have negative side effects such as unwanted color shifts and halos, stronger noise, and more noticeable sensor dust and lens defects. As a result, you may need to adjust the Light panel sliders, *Vibrance* or *Saturation*, *Noise Reduction*, *Vignette* and remove additional sensor dust spots after applying the *Dehaze* slider. It has fewer side effects when applied to a localized area using the selective editing tools (page 241).

Because *Dehaze* adapts to the content of each photo, it's best avoided when doing timelapse photography.

Atmospheric haze can be reduced using the other Light and Color sliders, but it's far easier with Dehaze!

USING TONE CURVES

Tone curves are primarily used for controlling brightness and contrast in specific tonal ranges, but you can do that with the Light panel sliders, so why use a tone curve?

In the Contrast lesson (page 182), we said that when you add contrast in one tonal range (e.g., the midtones), you lose contrast in other tonal ranges (e.g., the highlights and shadows). There's always a trade-off.

The Light panel sliders adjust broad ranges of tones, whereas a tone curve allows you to carefully control where you're willing to sacrifice contrast to gain it in other areas. For example, the *Contrast* slider adds contrast using a simple S curve, with almost equal compression in the highlights and shadows. However, you may decide that you're willing to lose more shadow detail in the deepest shadows but you want to keep more contrast in the highlights.

Likewise, if you have a photo with too much contrast, if you lighten the shadows and darken the highlights to see more detail, you lose contrast in the midtones. The *Highlights* and *Shadows* sliders compensate by adding local contrast, but the resulting halos can be too strong, especially on photos that benefit from a softer look. The tone curve doesn't add local contrast or saturation, leaving you to decide whether to add it yourself.

As a rule of thumb, the Light and Color panel sliders are designed for the heavy-lifting—the major adjustments—and the Tone Curve is usually used for fine tuning, but rules are made to be broken, so feel free to experiment!

READING A TONE CURVE

Straight 45° diagonal line = no changes applied to pixel brightness/contrast

moving a point up/left makes tones lighter

moving a point down/right makes tones darker

Before/After Swatches

100% (white) didn't change

75% values now lighter

Steeper line = more contrast between these tones

50% values didn't change

25% values now darker

Flatter line = less contrast between these tones

0% (black) didn't change

Y axis = Output

X axis = Input

CURVES VS. SLIDERS

Highlights and Shadows (left) add local contrast, which may not be desirable in a photo shot in lovely soft light, whereas the Tone Curve (right) allows you to reduce excessive contrast without adding local contrast

READING A TONE CURVE

Along each axis are all the possible tones, with pure black (0%) in the bottom left and pure white (100%) in the top right. The tone curve starts as a straight 45° diagonal line, with no changes being applied to the photo. Moving the line up/left makes the tones lighter, and moving down/right makes the tones darker. The line getting steeper means contrast is increased, and getting flatter means contrast is reduced.

PARAMETRIC VS. POINT CURVES

To display the Tone Curve in Lightroom, click/tap the button in the Light panel.

Lightroom offers two different types of tone curve: a parametric curve and a series of point curves. These are toggled using the circles above (desktop) / below (mobile) the curve grid.

Parametric RGB Red Green Blue

The parametric tone curve is the default view, and it allows you to adjust four different regions of the curve called *Highlights*, *Lights*, *Darks* and *Shadows*, rather than individual points. This protects the photo from extreme adjustments, so it's a great way to start experimenting with curves.

The point curve interface, represented by the colored circles, is usually used by more advanced users or those familiar with Photoshop's curves dialog. It gives you full control over the curve, including the individual RGB channels.

Point curves aren't necessarily an alternative to the parametric curves. You may be more comfortable with one or the other, but both types of curves are active at the same time and the effect is cumulative.

USING THE PARAMETRIC CURVE

Let's start experimenting with the parametric curve by selecting the parametric tone curve icon.

The most frequently used curve is a basic contrast curve which is an S shape. Click/ tap on the white line in the *Shadows* or *Darks* regions and **drag down to darken** the shadow tones, then click/tap on the white line in the *Lights* or *Highlights* section and **drag upwards to lighten** the highlight tones.

How far you drag away from the center line controls how much you brighten or darken

those tones. As you drag, the highlighted section shows the **maximum range of movement** for that region of the curve. It's limited in order to maintain smooth transitions between tones and protect your photo from banding/posterization.

If you change your mind, double-click on the line to **reset a section** of the curve (desktop only), or right-click and select *Reset* to **reset the whole parametric curve** (desktop only). For some unknown reason, there isn't currently a way to reset the parametric curve on mobile! To **reset both the parametric and point curves** at once, hold down the Alt key (Windows) / Opt key (Mac) and click on the Tone Curve label.

You can **fine tune the curve using the split point markers** at the bottom.

Shadows   Darks   Lights   Highlights

They define the tonal range for the regions. For example, if you've used the *Shadows* and *Highlights* regions to create strong midtone contrast, you may move the 25% and 75% split points out to restrict the flattened contrast to the lightest highlights and the deepest shadows. They're also useful if you've got the shape of the curve about right, but it's a little light or dark overall. There are some examples on page 198. On the desktop, double-clicking on any of those split points resets it to the default position at 25%/50%/75%.

USING THE TARGETED ADJUSTMENT TOOL

When adjusting the tone curve itself, you

PARAMETRIC TONE CURVE (WINDOWS/MAC)

Select parametric curve

Enable/disable tone curve

Targeted Adjustment Tool

Drag line to adjust curve

Highlighted area shows maximum range of movement

Alt-click / Opt-click on Tone Curve label to reset all curves

Double-click or right-click on line to reset single region. Right-click on curve to reset parametric curves

Split points control the range of each adjustment

Shadows   Darks   Lights   Highlights

PARAMETRIC TONE CURVE (IOS/ANDROID)

Drag line to adjust curve

Highlighted area shows maximum range of movement

Split points control the range of each adjustment

Tap Done to return to the Light sliders

Select parametric curve

PARAMETRIC SPLIT POINTS

The shape of the curve changes depending on whether the split points are at their defaults (left), far apart (center) or close together (right), so you can use it to fine tune the curve

Dragging all of the split points to the left or right can change the overall brightness without changing the relative shape of the curve

have to guess the right spot on the line, and this takes some experience. On the desktop, there's a handy tool called the Targeted Adjustment Tool (TAT tool), which removes this guesswork.

To **activate the TAT tool**, click the icon in the Tone Curve panel or use the keyboard shortcut Ctrl-Alt-Shift-T (Windows) / Cmd-Opt-Shift-T (Mac).

Targeted Adjustment Tool

As you float the cursor over the photo, the circle moves along the Tone Curve line, showing the affected tonal range.

Click and **drag left <> right on the photo to lighten or darken** the selected tonal range. For example, to darken the shadows, click and drag to the left on a shadowy area of the photo until you're happy with the result. A slider displays on the photo as you drag, and you'll see the tone curve update too.

Adjusted value   Starting value

<-- Darken   Lighten -->

For greater control, float the cursor over the

tones you want to change and tap the up/down arrow keys on your keyboard. Holding the Shift key moves in larger increments, or holding the Alt key (Windows) / Opt key (Mac) moves in tiny increments.

To **switch the TAT tool** from the Parametric Curve to an RGB, Red, Green or Blue Point Curve, click the circles in the Tone Curve panel or the floating TAT panel.

Drag here to move floating panel

Switch TAT to HSL/B&W   Switch tone curve type   Close TAT tool

USING THE POINT CURVE

If you need greater control, click the gray circle to display the RGB point curve. Click/tap anywhere on the curve line to **add a control point**, and then drag it up or down to adjust the curve. Control points can make adjustments or lock the curve in position, so you can adjust other tonal ranges without those changing.

You'll usually want to keep the curve to a smooth line, without any sharp bends, otherwise you may introduce posterization (banding).

On the desktop, holding down the Alt key (Windows) / Opt key (Mac) slows down the movement for greater accuracy, or holding the Shift key constrains the movement to vertical only. If you're a little OCD and like everything perfectly

lined up, there's also a **Snap to Grid** option in the right-click menu, which locks the control points to the intersections of a 20x20 grid, rather than the standard 4x4 grid.

If you change your mind, you can **delete a control point** by double-clicking/double-tapping on it. To **reset the selected channel** or **reset the whole point curve**, right-click on the curve (desktop only).

The point curve interface also gives you access to the red, green and blue channels that make up your photo. These are often used for cross processing effects, or for correcting scans or other tricky white balance situations. For example, where color casts differ between the highlights and shadows—perhaps where the overall color is correct but the shadows have a magenta tinge—normal white balance adjustments would be unable to fix it, but RGB curves allow you detailed control over each channel.

There are some example point curves on page 198 to give you some ideas of how they can be useful.

Be careful not to place too many points as extreme twists and turns in the curve can create posterization (banding) in the photo

POINT TONE CURVE (WINDOWS/MAC)

Enable/disable tone curve

Select RGB, Red, Green or Blue

Targeted Adjustment Tool

Click on the line to add control point. Drag to adjust the curve. Hold Alt / Opt to slow the cursor for greater control. Hold Shift to constrain to vertical movement

Double-click on point to reset it

Alt-click / Opt-click on Tone Curve label to reset all curves

Input/Output value for selected point

65.9 76.9

Right-click to show menu...

Delete Control Point
Reset Channel
Reset All Channels
Copy Channel Settings
Paste Channel Settings
Snap To Grid
✓ Show All Curves

To show/hide other color channel lines, select Show All Curves from right-click menu

POINT TONE CURVE (IOS/ANDROID)

Tap on line to add control point, drag to adjust curve

Double-tap point on curve to reset it

Tap Done to return to the Light sliders

Select RGB, Red, Green or Blue

SAMPLE POINT CURVES

A standard S-curve adds midtone contrast, like the Contrast slider

To roughly correct color casts in scans, move the ends of the point curve to the ends of the histogram on each color channel

Locking most of the curve in place and then lifting the deepest shadows creates the flat shadows effect popular in film-effect presets

Reversing the tone curve inverts scanned negatives, although it doesn't remove the orange mask of color film, and the Light panel sliders go "the wrong way"

RGB point curves are used for cross-processing effects, creating a different result to the split toning sliders

CURVES FOR ILLUSTRATING SLIDERS

Once you're familiar with reading tone curves, they're also useful to illustrate and compare the effect of different Light panel sliders on the brightness and contrast of different image tones.

CURVES ILLUSTRATING LIGHT PANEL SLIDERS

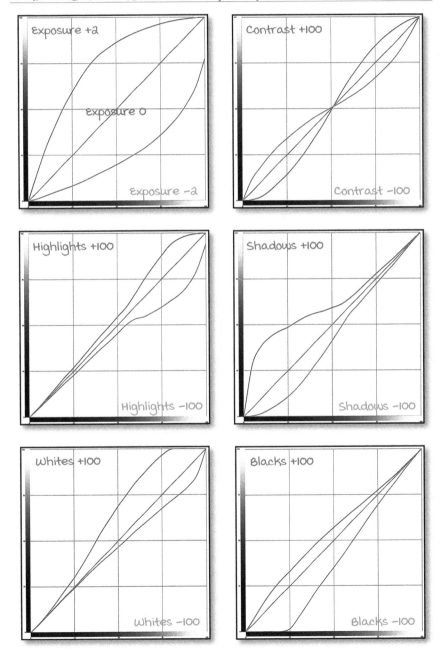

MERGING HDR IMAGES

Many photographers use the term HDR to describe a specific surreal style of editing, but think about the letters HDR... they stand for high dynamic range. (We discussed dynamic range while analyzing our images on page 124.)

WHY USE HDR?

Camera sensors have difficulty capturing the full range of detail in **very high contrast scenes**. If you expose for the highlights, the shadows become very noisy, but if you expose for the midtones or shadows, the highlights burn out.

To solve this problem, you can take a series of identical shots with **bracketed exposures** and merge them using Lightroom. The result is a high dynamic range (HDR) file which retains detail in both the lightest and darkest tones. It's currently only available on the Windows/Mac apps.

If the source photos are raw files, the resulting 16-bit floating point HDR data is stored using the linear DNG format. This

Expose for the highlights and for the shadows...

And then merge them using Lightroom

simply means that the raw data is partially processed (demosaiced), but that it retains the editing flexibility of a raw file. This is a big advantage over other HDR software, which has to convert the raw data before merging, limiting the dynamic range and white balance flexibility.

Having created the high dynamic range file, you can then use Lightroom's editing tools to tone map the image, compressing it into a lower dynamic range suitable for viewing on a screen or print.

SHOOTING FOR HDR

The **source photos** must all be the same file type, captured on the same camera. For the best quality, shoot in your camera's raw file format. In an ideal world, it's best to use a tripod to ensure the photos are correctly aligned.

Many DSLR, mirrorless and advanced compact cameras have a built-in **automatic exposure bracketing** (AEB) mode which automatically adjusts the exposure and captures the photos in a quick burst to minimize movement.

SELECTING THE SOURCE IMAGES

Unlike most HDR software, Lightroom works best with **as few source images as possible**. In most cases, this is only two raw files—one correctly exposed for the highlights and one correctly exposed for the shadows. As Lightroom's working with the raw data, it doesn't need the exposures in between. Additional photos actually increase the risk of misalignment that can result in a double image (known as ghosting).

If the photos are **more than 3 stops apart**, add one or more additional photos in

between to reduce noise, for example:

-1.5 to 1.5 = 2 photos (-1.5, 1.5)
-3.0 to 3.0 = 3 photos (-3, 0, 3)
-4.5 to 4.5 = 4 photos (-4.5, -1.5, 1.5, 4.5)
-6.0 to 6.0 = 5 photos (-6, -3, 0, 3, 6)

PREPARING TO MERGE

There's **no need to edit the photos** before you merge them, but if you've already been experimenting, Lightroom automatically copies some of the edits from a source photo onto the merged photo. It skips things like the Light panel adjustments, crop, perspective corrections, spot healing and selective edits, as they may not line up correctly on the merged photo.

MERGING PHOTOS

To **merge your photos**, select them, right-click on one and choose *Photo Merge > HDR Merge*. You'll also find it under the Photo menu. Lightroom automatically downloads the originals from the cloud. If the originals are unavailable, perhaps because you're offline, then Smart Previews will be used to create a smaller (2560px) HDR image.

The preview shows how the photo will look after merging. It's a low resolution preview so it updates quickly as you adjust the settings.

The *Auto Align* checkbox is worth checking if the photos were shot handheld and may not be perfectly aligned. If the photos were shot using a tripod and remote release, with no risk of movement, you can leave it unchecked.

Auto Settings can be applied to the preview to give you an idea of the tonal range before merging. Once the photo's merged, you can edit it using Lightroom's editing tools.

The **Deghost** options are needed if there's a moving subject in the photo, for example, water or trees, as these can creates ghosts (double images) or softness when photos are merged. There are three levels to choose from—*Low*, *Medium* or *High*—and they control how sensitive Lightroom is to movement in the photo. The *High* setting is much more aggressive, whereas *Low* just picks up significant ghosting. Because deghosting uses the image detail from a single photo, it can introduce noise or sharp edges, so use the lowest setting possible.

Check the **Show Deghost Overlay** checkbox to see which areas are affected by the deghosting (highlighted in red). Remember to check these areas in the finished photo to ensure you're happy with the resulting image detail.

When you press **Merge**, the merge happens in the background so you can continue working on other photos. If your computer is of a high enough specification, you can run multiple merges at the same time, however it's very memory intensive. The **Cancel** button cancels without merging, of course.

EDITING THE RESULTING HDR PHOTO

Once the merge completes, you'll **find the HDR file** next to the originals. The filename ends in -HDR, and there's a badge on the thumbnail to help you identify it. If you were viewing an album, the source photos are automatically stacked.

To edit the photo, switch to the editing tools and edit as normal. You'll notice that the *Exposure* slider runs from +10 to -10 (usually +5/-5), and the *Highlights* and *Shadows* sliders have a stronger effect.

STEP-BY-STEP

There's a pair of bracketed photos in the demo images download in the Members Area, so let's give it a try:

1. Select a series of bracketed photos. In most cases, select just two photos—one for the highlights and one for the shadows.

2. Right-click on the photos and select *Photo Merge > HDR Merge*.

3. Check the *Auto Align* and *Auto Settings* checkboxes.

4. If there's movement in the photo (e.g. water), try the *Deghost* options until you find the one that gets the best result. If there's no movement, leave it set to *None*.

5. Press *Merge*.

6. Switch to the Edit sliders and edit the photo as normal.

PERFECTING COLOR

14

We see the world around us in color, and since the advent of color film, it's been an important part of photography. The Color panel allows us to correct colors to match the scene we remember, or to make more creative artistic choices.

IN THIS SECTION, WE'LL CONSIDER:

• How to use the White Balance sliders to correct color casts, which can cause the photo to look dull and muddy.

• How to adjust the saturation of the colors throughout the whole photo to influence the viewer's mood.

• How to use the Color Mixer to optimize the brightness and saturation of specific color ranges, to draw the eye.

• How to shift the hue of specific color ranges, for example, reducing ruddy cheeks or tweaking memory colors.

• How to use color grading to paint a particular mood.

∨ Color		
White Balance As Shot ∨		🖋
Temp	—O———	4850
Tint	———O—	+ 12
Vibrance	———O—	0
Saturation	———O—	0
○ Color Mixer		
⚬ Color Grading		

PERFECTING WHITE BALANCE

The color of light varies depending on its source. It can range from cool (blue sky) to warm (candlelight or tungsten), and the color temperature is measured using the Kelvin scale.

Our eyes and brain automatically compensate for different lighting conditions, which is why a white object looks white to us whether it's viewed in sunlight, shade or indoors using artificial lighting.

Cameras aren't quite so smart. A camera's auto white balance works fairly well in a narrow range of daylight with "average" image content, but it doesn't take much to confuse it. Capture a scene of autumn leaves, and the camera's likely to make the photo a little cold and blue. Shoot a snow scene, and the camera will probably try to warm it up.

Lightroom's White Balance sliders are designed to compensate for the color of the light in which the photo was taken. When you get the white tones right, everything else falls into place.

Most of the time, you'll want the colors in the scene to be rendered as accurately as possible, but sometimes you'll want to warm or cool the scene to suit the mood of the photo.

If you look outside on a cold winters day, the light is cool and blue, but during a beautiful sunset, it may be warm and orange. If you neutralize these colors, you lose the atmosphere.

WHITE BALANCE

- Temp makes the photo cooler/bluer

- Tint makes the photo greener

The camera's auto white balance did pretty well on this photo!

+ Temp makes the photo warmer/yellower

+ Tint makes the photo more magenta (pinker)

SETTING WHITE BALANCE

White balance adjustments are made using the **Temp** *(Temperature)* and **Tint** sliders in the Color panel, but there are a few ways of deciding on the best values.

Auto—In the *White Balance* pop-up, select *Auto*. It attempts to neutralize the photo, but like the camera's auto white balance, it's not as intelligent as your eyes, so the results may not be perfect.

Presets—If you're working on a raw file, the **White Balance** pop-up includes presets for standard lighting conditions. They include *As Shot, Daylight, Cloudy, Shade, Tungsten, Fluorescent* and *Flash* settings. Select the right preset for the lighting conditions, for example, if the photo was captured on a cloudy day, select the *Cloudy* preset.

Eyedropper—For more control, the White Balance Selector allows you to click in the photo to automatically neutralize any color cast.

 ⟵ White Balance Selector

On the desktop, click the eyedropper icon in the Color panel or press the W key, then click on something in the photo that *should be* neutral, for example, the shadows on a white t-shirt.

On a mobile device, tap the eyedropper icon in the Color panel, then drag the eyedropper to something that should be neutral, such as this lighthouse, and tap the checkmark to confirm your selection. On a small screen, it may help to zoom in before selecting the eyedropper.

Using white or light gray subjects gives a more accurate result than darker shades, but avoid whites that are too bright, as some of the color data may be clipped.

When you click with the eyedropper, the pop-up changes to *Custom* and the sliders automatically adjust. If it still doesn't look right, click somewhere else to try again or tweak the sliders by eye. The eyedropper's often a good way to get the white balance in the right ballpark before fine-tuning the sliders.

If you regularly shoot in difficult lighting or you struggle to select the right white balance, a WhiBal, ColorChecker or other calibrated neutral light gray card is an easy way to guarantee correct white balance. Simply shoot a photo of the card in the same lighting conditions as the subject and click the eyedropper on that photo to get an accurate white balance setting. You can

SETTING WHITE BALANCE USING THE EYEDROPPER

Select the White Balance eyedropper and click on something that SHOULD be white or light gray, like this lighthouse

Ooops, clicking on the stone path turned the photo too blue

Clicking on the window made it a bit too warm and pink because it's reflecting the surroundings

What else might be neutral in this picture?

Darker areas of clouds may work if they weren't partially clipped (white with no detail), but results can vary depending on where you click

The satellite dish gave the best result, but it's still a bit cold, so try an extra 200K-400K on Temp

Paintwork and white fabrics often yellow over time

Shiny objects are no good, as they'll reflect surroundings

Stone sometimes works, but it's rarely perfectly neutral

then copy these values to other photos shot in the same conditions.

Adjust Sliders By Eye—As you gain experience, you can go straight to the *Temp* and *Tint* sliders. If the photo's too yellow or warm, move the *Temp* slider to the left to compensate, and if it's too blue or cold, move the slider to the right. Likewise, the *Tint* slider adjusts from green on the left to magenta on the right.

If you're working on a raw file, the *Temp* slider uses the Kelvin scale to measure the color of the light. For JPEGs and other image formats, the scale runs from -100 to 100, because the white balance compensation has already been applied to the image data (e.g., by the camera), and now you're simply warming or cooling the photo.

ADJUSTING FOR MOOD

Once you've made the photo neutral, you can tweak the white balance to enhance the mood. For example, indoor photos often look better with a *Temperature* value 200-400K higher than neutral, to bring back a pleasant warmth. Or a sunset shot may need warming up to reflect the lovely warm light usually seen at that time of day.

HANDLING MIXED LIGHTING

Sometimes your photos will be shot with light from two or more sources. For example, a photo shot at night may have moonlight and street lighting, a photo shot near a window may have warm tungsten light and cooler daylight, or a photo shot outdoors may have bright sunlight and shade.

In this case, you have three choices:

• Pick a white balance in the middle that

Candlelit photos look better warm. Some photos just aren't meant to be perfectly neutral!

Photos shot in mixed lighting can be tricky to correct

looks ok for both.

• Get the lighting right for one light source and don't worry about the other.

• Use Lightroom's Selective Editing tools to apply a different white balance to each area of the photo (page 255).

VIBRANCE VS. SATURATION

Saturation describes the intensity or purity of a color. Lightroom offers two different global saturation controls, with slightly different behaviors:

Saturation is quite a blunt instrument which adjusts the saturation of all colors equally. This can result in some colors clipping as they reach full saturation.

Vibrance is more intelligent as it adjusts the saturation on a non-linear scale, increasing the saturation of lower-saturated colors more than highly saturated colors. It also aims to protect skin tones from becoming over-saturated.

SETTING VIBRANCE OR SATURATION

Our eyes are drawn to vivid saturated colors, but if you go too far, it becomes garish and cartoon-like. This is particularly true on skin tones, which look ridiculous when heavily saturated.

The saturation of colors affects the mood of the photo. For example, you may want bright, saturated colors for a kid's party, but calm, muted colors may be better suited to a newborn photo.

In practice, you may use a little of both sliders, or just stick to the *Vibrance* slider for more natural colors.

If you need even more control over the saturation of specific tones, you can use the Color Mixer tool (page 209) or selective editing (page 241).

+ Vibrance enhances the blue tones (sky!) more than Saturation

+ Vibrance keeps reds/oranges (skin!) looking more natural than Saturation

− Saturation completely desaturates to B&W (but there are better B&W tools)

− Vibrance is much more gentle, fading colors to pastel tones

ADJUSTING COLOR RANGES USING THE COLOR MIXER

When your white balance is perfect, you can enhance specific colors using the Color Mixer. The sliders are hidden by default, but appear when you click the color wheel icon in the Color panel.

SETTING THE HSL SLIDERS

The Color Mixer panel can look slightly daunting to start with, as there's a multitude of sliders covering different color ranges. You may also hear these referred to as HSL sliders:

H stands for **Hue**, which is the shade of a color, for example, a red jumper may lean towards orange or pink.

S stands for **Saturation**, which is the purity or intensity of the color.

L stands for **Luminance**, which is the brightness of the color.

The default view is *Color*, which displays circles for each color range, and the *Hue*, *Saturation* and *Luminance* sliders for the selected color range below.

If you prefer, you can select *Hue, Saturation* or *Luminance* in the **Adjust** pop-up. They're exactly the same sliders, just presented in a different format.

The sliders are tinted to help you remember how the color will change, for example, moving the *Red Saturation* slider to the left reduces the saturation of the reds in the photo. There are some examples to follow.

The Color mixer can be displayed in two different ways

USING THE TARGETED ADJUSTMENT TOOL

Rather than trying to guess which colors make up a particular shade of turquoise, there's a handy tool called the Targeted Adjustment Tool (TAT tool). It allows you to adjust the Color Mix visually by dragging directly on the photo, while it figures out which sliders to move.

To **activate the TAT tool on the desktop**, click the icon in the Color Mix panel.

As you float the cursor over the photo, small circles show the color ranges that will be affected by your adjustment, and in what kind of proportions. For example, this bush is mainly yellow with some green.

Click and **drag left <> right on the photo to adjust** the selected color range. For example, to make these bushes more saturated, switch to *Saturation* mode, click and drag to the right on the bushes until you're happy with the result. A slider displays on the photo as you drag, and you'll see the tone curve update too.

For greater control, float the cursor over the tones you want to change and tap the up/down arrow keys on your keyboard. Holding the Shift key moves in larger increments, or holding the Alt key (Windows) / Opt key (Mac) moves in tiny increments.

To **switch the TAT tool** to *Hue, Saturation* or *Luminance* mode, select from the pop-up in the Color Mix panel or click the buttons in the floating TAT panel.

To **use the TAT tool on mobile**, tap the icon above the colored dots. Hold your finger on the tone you wish to adjust (e.g. the blue sky) and drag up/down to move in large increments or left/right to move in smaller increments.

On mobile, select the TAT tool and drag on the photo itself to adjust the HSL sliders

EXAMPLE COLOR MIX IMAGES

memories—Imagine you've been shooting on the coast, but in your photos, the sea's just not as turquoise as you remember. Try moving the Aqua Hue slider to the right, and perhaps add a little Aqua Saturation

Blue Skies—Unless it's truly overcast, there's often some blue sky hidden among the clouds. Try reducing the Blue Luminance and increasing the Blue Saturation to enhance it. Don't go too far on either slider, as you'll start to introduce noise

© David Bampton

Fix Colors—Due to allergies, Charlie isn't quite as white as he should be. Reducing the Saturation and increasing the Luminance of the orange tones reduces the brown tones without losing the color in his tongue

Changing Colors—The Hue slider allows you to shift the colors toward a nearby color, for example, from red toward pink or orange. If you need to completely change colors, you'll need the Brush tool (page 255)

Sunsets—If the sunset isn't quite the color you need for your room's color scheme, shifting the Hue and Saturation of colors can create a whole new look

COLOR GRADING

Whereas the White Balance and HSL tools are primarily used for color correction, Color Grading is designed for color effects.

It can be used for toning monochrome photos (page 226) but it also works well for influencing the mood of the viewer, applying cross-processed color effects, or simply enhancing the lighting.

COLOR GRADING CONTROLS

The Color Grading controls are hidden by default, but appear when you click the Color Grading icon in the Color panel.

There are a number of color wheel views, selected using the circle icons at the top of the panel.

The **Global** wheel applies a single tint to the entire photo, for example, adding a golden hour feel to the photo.

Shadows, **Midtones** and **Highlights** wheels apply the tint to individual tonal ranges. The **3 Way** view shows a smaller version of the Shadows, Midtones and Highlights color wheels. It's useful for seeing existing settings, but they're a bit small to make fine adjustments.

The inner and outer handles are used to adjust the **Hue** and **Saturation**. It's often easiest to pull the inner handle to the edge for maximum Saturation, and use the outer handle to select just the right Hue. Then hold down the Shift key (desktop) while using the inner handle to reduce the Saturation to taste. The Shift key constrains the movement so the Hue doesn't change.

The numeric Hue and Saturation values show beneath the color wheels (except in 3 Way view), and you can click and type directly in these fields. If you prefer to adjust the Hue and Saturation using sliders, click the disclosure triangle to show the sliders.

COLOR GRADING (WINDOWS/MAC)

Hold Alt/Opt to reset all

Combined view

Individual Shadows, midtones and Highlights wheels

Inner Handle adjusts Hue & Saturation. Hold Shift to constrain to Saturation. Hold Ctrl/Cmd to constrain to Hue. Double click to reset

Outer Handle adjusts Saturation only

Click to type in numerical Hue and Saturation values

Enable/disable color grading

Global tone

Hold Alt/Opt to reset selected wheel

Switch to next wheel

Right-click to show menu to reset or copy/paste

Show full Hue and Saturation sliders

Luminance

Blending

Balance

You can also adjust the **Luminance** (or brightness) of the tint using the slider below the color wheel.

The **Blending** slider controls how much the highlight and shadow tones blend into each other. To illustate, if we give the shadows a blue tint and the highlights a red tint, you can see that the midtones remain neutral at 0 (unless there's a midtone tint, of course), whereas red and blue blend into purple at 100.

If there is a midtone tint applied, such as the green applied here, that tint is also blended into the highlight and shadow tints.

This can be useful, for example, if you only want a tint to apply to the highlights but you don't want it to affect the midtones too much. Imagine you're adding a tint to sunset, but you don't want to significantly affect the building in the foreground. Depending on the range of tones in a photo, the effect may be more or less noticeable.

COLOR GRADING (IOS/ANDROID)

Done to return to Edit sliders

Individual Shadows, midtones and Highlights wheels

Combined view

Show menu

Inner Handle adjusts Hue & Saturation

Outer Handle adjusts Saturation only

Show full Hue and Saturation sliders

Luminance

Blending

Double-tap to reset sliders

Balance

Holding down the Alt (Windows) / Opt (Mac) key while moving both the *Blending* and *Balance* sliders temporarily sets the *Saturation* of the tints to 100, making it easier to see the effect.

The **Balance** slider defines the range of tones affected by each color wheel. To illustrate, if we set the shadows to blue, the midtones to green and the highlights to red, you can see that at the default of 0, each color wheel affects approximately 1/3 of the tonal range. Moving to -100 results in the shadow tone affecting the majority of the tonal range, with just a small amount of midtones, and moving to +100 primarily

applies the highlight tint.

SPLIT TONING REPLACEMENT

Color Grading replaces the older Split Toning controls, but it's fully compatible, and just extends what is possible.

To reproduce older split toning adjustments, simply set the *Blending* slider to 100 and leave the other controls at their defaults. You can then select the tint for the *Shadows* and *Highlights* and adjust the *Balance* slider, as you would have using the old interface.

COLOR COMBINATIONS FOR COLOR PHOTOS

So how do you know which colors to use? There are no set rules, but some combinations typically go well together.

Pairs of complementary colors—those opposite each other in the color wheel—look great together. Other traditional color schemes also work well.

While there can be exceptions, you generally want warm tones in the highlights and cool tones in the shadows, as this reflects the way we see the world around us.

Usually the midtones are assigned the same color as the shadows, but you're free to do it differently as long as you keep in mind the Color Theory as a guideline.

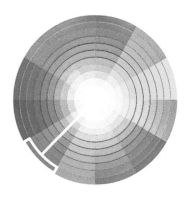

monochromatic schemes use a single dominant color across the range of tones. These are popular for tinting B&W photos

Complementary color schemes use colors directly opposite each other on the color wheel, such as warm vs. cool

Triadic color schemes use three equally spaced colors

Split complementary color schemes use the two colors adjacent to the exact complementary color, for a more subtle effect

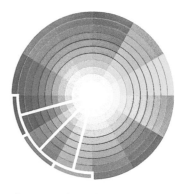

Analogous color schemes use colors adjacent to each other. It looks much like the monochromatic color scheme but with more colors

Yellow highlights and blue shadows is also flattering to a range of photos if not overdone, or a softer combination of sepia (brown) and selenium (blue) can add a little color contrast without being obvious.

Watch out for memory tones in the images and ensure these remain natural. We're particularly quick at spotting unnatural skin tones.

CINEMATIC COLOR GRADING

Do you have a specific color palette in mind? You may have heard of cinematic color grading, which is often used by movie editors to convey a specific look or mood. Next time you're watching a movie, especially summer blockbuster movies, look out for the color palette they've used and how it makes you feel, or Google *movie color palettes* to see some examples.

Orange and teal/blue is popular in Hollywood, because the teal shadows contrast with people's skin tone, making the actors stand out from the background. This is an effect you can replicate on your own photos, but you have to be quite subtle with the orange saturation if there are people in the photos, or you'll make them look seriously ill.

ENHANCING COLORS USING COLOR GRADING

The Color Grading controls can also be used to enhance the tones in a photo to tell your story.

As a simple example, adding yellow to the highlights and blue to the shadows can give an "golden hour" feel to photos that weren't shot in ideal lighting.

Slightly warming the highlights on a portrait can make it feel like your person has the sun on their face, without the overall warming of a white balance adjustment.

Likewise, adding blues and purples to the shadows can make your nighttime photos crisp and clean.

You can also use Color Grading to play with the colors of a sunset.

Color Grading can also be helpful when mimicking certain film styles, for example, Kodak Portra has blue shadows and yellow highlights, whereas expired film has red shadows and blue highlights.

BE SUBTLE

Although I've exaggerated the effects in this book so you can see the difference, the key in real life is to be subtle, enhancing the existing colors rather than blowing them away, unless you're aiming for a quirky cross-processed effect.

For the shadows, try a *Saturation* value between 10 and 25, regardless of the *Hue*. This because the darker you go, the more intense and saturated the colors will look.

If you're setting a midtone tint (you often may not need to), try a *Saturation* value of between 15 and 30, and for the highlights, aim for between 20 and 35.

Of course, rules are made to be broken, but as we said in the Developing Your Own Style lesson on page 135, it's best to be consistent.

STEP-BY-STEP

1. Click/tap the Color Grading icon in the Color panel to open the Color Grading panel.

2. Select the *Highlights* color wheel and drag the central handle to your chosen color.

3. Repeat for the *Shadows* color wheel, but don't overdo the saturation on the shadows.

4. Adjust the *Blending* and *Balance* sliders to suit the selected photo.

GREAT B&W CONVERSION

15

Black and white photography is an art in its own right. Some photographers consider it more creative than color photography, because it doesn't match the reality we see around us.

In the days of film, you generally had to make the decision at the time of capture, and add filters to change the appearance. For example, you'd use a red filter to create a dark dramatic sky. Today, you can make the decisions while editing the photos.

Lightroom offers great control over the contrast between light and dark, and between the different colors that made up the original scene.

HOW DO YOU DECIDE WHICH PHOTOS TO CONVERT TO B&W?

A good color photo usually also makes a good B&W photo, so how do you decide which photos to convert? Do you have to test a B&W conversion on every single photo?

If you're not sure, think back to the decisions you made when you were analyzing the photo, and ask yourself...

• Does the color add anything to the photo? For example, if the photo's of a sunset, the answer's probably yes, but in bad weather, the photo may be better without color.

• Is the color distracting? For example, is the color drawing your eye to the wrong spot?

• How would conversion to B&W affect the story and mood of the photo? The way we respond emotionally to color may conflict with the story we're trying to tell.

Also look out for a few features that make particularly good B&W photos, including:

• Contrasts of brightness, especially the beams of light and strong shadows caused by directional light.

• Contrasts of color (light vs. dark, saturated vs. unsaturated, warm vs. cold.)

• Shapes, textures, patterns and compositional features like leading lines. By removing the color, your eye is drawn to these elements.

IN THIS SECTION, WE'LL CONSIDER:

• How to do a simple B&W conversion using pre-mixed Profiles.

• How to enhance contrasts between colors when converting to B&W.

• Which other tools you might want to use to optimize your B&W photo.

SOME REASONS YOU MIGHT CONVERT TO B&W

Photos that don't have much color often look more striking in B&W

The bright colors in this photo detract from the somber story of homelessness

Color can be a distraction, drawing your eye to the wrong spot, like the warm tones in this photo. By removing the color, we notice the lines and textures

UNDERSTANDING B&W CHANNEL MIX

Before you convert the photo to B&W, take a close look at the subtle contrasts between the different colors in your photo. These different shades become varying levels of brightness in the B&W photo, and by mixing the colors to make some colors lighter and others darker, you can control the contrast (or tonal separation) in your B&W photo.

In the color wheels below, you can see that the first B&W conversion makes all of the tones a similar brightness, and it lacks contrast as a result. You don't know where to look first. However, when adjusting the brightness of the different colors, we can create some interesting contrasts and start to control how the viewers eye travels around the photo.

Now let's put this into a simple real world situation. If you look at a landscape on a sunny day, the sky may be vibrant blue and the grass and bushes a vibrant green, so there's an interesting contrast, however the default conversion may make them a similar shade of gray. Instead, you might darken the blue sky to contrast with the white fluffy clouds, and lighten the greens and yellows to move these into the midtones, enhancing the texture and details. We'll take a look at how in the next lesson.

The way you mix the colors can add contrast and draw your eye to different areas of the photo

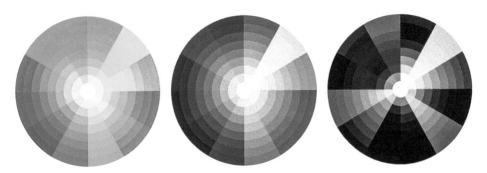

The default B&W conversion (center) lacks contrast, but adjusting the B&W mix (right) allows you to lighten some colors and darken others

CONVERTING TO B&W

Having discussed the theory, let's move on to the practicalities of B&W conversion using Lightroom.

CORRECT COLOR FIRST

Before you convert a photo to B&W, first adjust the photo in color. This removes any color cast or other problems, so you can accurately judge the best B&W settings. You may even want to create a copy (page 148), so you retain your color version as well as the B&W rendition.

CONVERSION OPTIONS

There are numerous ways to convert a photo to B&W, including:

• Shoot using the B&W mode on your camera with the JPEG file format. This isn't a great option as it limits your editing options later. (Shooting in B&W mode in raw, however, can be helpful in visualizing how a photo would look in B&W. As it's raw, it'll be imported into Lightroom as a color photo, ready for you to convert to B&W yourself.)

• Move the *Saturation* slider to -100. It's a very limited way of converting to B&W, because you can't control the ways the color channels are mixed.

• Select a B&W profile from the Profile panel, or a preset from the Presets panel. These profiles and presets are "pre-mixed," so you can pick one that suits your photo and tweak it from there.

• Click the B&W button in the Color panel and manually mix the color channels to suit the photo.

Let's take a closer look at two of these options that give you control over the look of the photo.

STEP-BY-STEP USING PROFILES

On page 161, we introduced the Profile panel. B&W film photographers select a specific film stock and filters, depending on the look they desire. Profiles allow you to do the same when editing your digital photos. Let's give it a try:

1. On a desktop or tablet, select *Browse* in the Profile panel to open view the available profiles. On a phone, select the Profiles view.

2. Open the B&W folder to view the B&W profiles. If you've installed third-party profiles, there may be more B&W profiles in other folders too. On Windows, Mac or Android, you can temporarily filter to show just the B&W profiles by clicking the ... button and selecting *B&W* from the menu. (This filtering is not currently available on iOS.)

3. Once you've found a profile that suits the photo, apply it on a desktop or tablet by clicking/tapping on it and then clicking the *Back* button to return to the normal Edit sliders. On a phone, tap on the profile and then tap the checkmark to return to the normal Edit view.

STEP-BY-STEP USING B&W MIX

If you prefer to "blend your own" B&W mix, you can use the B&W Mixer sliders to control how the color channels are mixed.

1. Click the ***B&W*** button above the Edit

There's a range of B&W
profiles built into Lightroom

sliders on the desktop, or in the Color panel on mobile. This automatically selects the default *Adobe Monochrome* profile for raw photos, or the default B&W profile for rendered (JPEG/TIFF/PSD/PNG) photos.

2. Open the B&W Mixer by clicking the color wheel icon in the Color panel.

3. There is an **Auto** button, and while the computer can't evaluate the scene as accurately as your eyes and brain, it can be a good starting point.

4. Adjust the sliders for each color range, for example, move the blue slider to darken the sky. As you move a slider to the left, the color channel is darkened, and as you move between different colors, which we discussed on page 221) and don't worry about the overall brightness and contrast initially. Ansel Adams, who is famous for his B&W photos, frequently used a dark sky to contrast with white fluffy clouds, and lightened the greens and yellows. On portraits, lightening the skin can make it seem smoother, whereas darkening it enhances wrinkles.

As with most things, moderation is key. Pushing the blue tones too far can introduce noise into your photo, and extreme adjustments between contrasting colors can create halos.

B&W MIX USING THE TARGETED ADJUSTMENT TOOL

Rather than trying to remember the exact shade of each object in your photo, there's a handy tool called the Targeted Adjustment Tool (TAT tool). You'll already be familiar with it, as we used it for the Tone Curve (page 193) and Color Mix sliders (page 209). When used with the B&W Mix sliders, it allows you to adjust the brightness of different color ranges by dragging directly on the photo.

To **activate the TAT tool on the desktop**, click the icon in the B&W Mixer panel.

Targeted Adjustment Tool

As you float the cursor over the photo, small circles show the color ranges that will be affected by your adjustment, and in what kind of proportions. For example, the sky under the cursor in this photo is almost entirely blue, but greenery is often a mix of

to the right, the color channel is lightened. The colors overlap, for example, adjusting the orange slider also affects red and yellow tones in the photo.

As you're adjusting the sliders, concentrate on increasing tonal separation (the contrast yellow and green.

Cursor
Affected sliders

Click and **drag left <> right on the photo to lighten or darken** the selected tonal range. For example, to darken the shadows, click and drag to the left on a shadowy area of the photo until you're happy with the result. A slider displays on the photo as you drag, and you'll see the tone curve update too.

Adjusted value   Starting value

<— Darken   Lighten —>

For greater control, float the cursor over the tones you want to change and tap the up/down arrow keys on your keyboard. Holding the Shift key moves in larger increments, or holding the Alt key (Windows) / Opt key (Mac) moves in tiny increments.

To **use the TAT tool on mobile**, tap the icon above the colored dots. Hold your finger on the tone you wish to adjust (e.g. the blue sky) and drag up/down to move in large increments or left/right to move in smaller increments.

Gray Mix   Done

Luminance   -9

Select the TAT tool and drag on the photo itself to adjust the B&W mix

FINE TUNING B&W

Most B&W photos need a full range of tones, from a deep black with detail to a bright white with detail, and all the shades in between, so once you've selected your profile or adjusted the B&W mix, you'll likely need to fine tune the overall contrast using the Light panel sliders (page 177) or the Tone Curve (page 191).

The Linear Gradient (page 249) can be useful for darkening the sky in a B&W photo, like an ND Grad filter, and you can add *Clarity* to bring out contrast in the clouds. A Radial Gradient can darken the edges of the photo to draw your eye into the center, especially if there are bright areas around the edge that draw the viewer's eye out of the photo.

You may also want to use the Brush tool (page 242) to dodge and burn to add emphasis, or add local contrast. Be careful not to go overboard, or the changes will stand out. You can also damp down the contrast in some areas to draw the viewer's eye away from distractions.

Many people love the grain inherent in many popular B&W film stocks, so turn to page 230 to learn to add grain to your B&W photos.

COLOR GRADING FOR B&W

We've already looked at Color Grading for color photos on page 213, but the same tool works well for toning monochrome photos.

COLOR COMBINATIONS FOR B&W PHOTOS

Traditionally, sepia (a brown tone) or selenium (a blue tone) were used to tone B&W photos to increase the longevity of the prints, and while this is no longer the aim, these tones are still popular choices, adding a soft warm look or a crisp cool look.

For a Sepia effect, set the *Shadow Hue* to around 40-50 and adjust the Saturation to taste.

For a Selenium effect, try a *Shadow Hue* of around 215-225 and adjust the *Saturation* sliders to increase or decrease the strength of the effect.

A mix of these tones can also look great, with sepia highlights and selenium shadows, or you can create your own combinations.

Sepia tone

Selenium tone

Split tone

ADDING EFFECTS 16

In previous sections, we've focused on correcting and optimizing the brightness, contrast and color of your photos. We also looked at Color Grading for color effects. In this section, we're concentrating on the Effects panel.

We've already discussed the *Clarity* and *Dehaze* sliders along with the Light panel sliders on page 189, as they affect the tone and contrast in the photos.

We'll come back to *Texture* in the Detail chapter on page 232, because it's similar to sharpening.

IN THIS SECTION, WE'LL CONSIDER:

• How to add a vignette to draw the viewer's eye into the photo.

• How to add grain for a film-like old-fashioned look.

ADDING A VIGNETTE

Vignetting is the darkening or lightening of the corners of a photo. It helps to draw your eye into a photo and focus on the main subject, rather than being distracted by the edges.

It may seem silly to remove the vignetting created by the lens and then add it back using the sliders in the Effects panel, but the Effects sliders are tied to the crop boundaries, whereas any lens vignetting may be partially cropped away.

VIGNETTE SLIDERS

The main **Vignette** slider controls how dark or light the vignette should be, with 0 not applying a vignette at all. Most photos look better with a dark vignette, rather than a white one.

For many photos, the main *Vignette* slider is the only one you'll need to adjust, but if you want more control, there some additional sliders. These are hidden behind a disclosure triangle on the desktop.

The **Midpoint** slider controls how close to the center of the photo the vignette affects. The vignette created by the Effects panel is always centered within the crop boundaries, but if you need an off-center vignette, you can use the Radial Gradient instead (page 249).

A vignette helps to draw the eye to the center of the photo

Vignette midpoint

The **Roundness** slider controls how round or square the vignette is. -100 is almost rectangular and barely visible whereas +100 is circular. Most vignettes look great with the default of 0, which matches the ratio of the photo.

Vignette Roundness

The **Feather** slider runs from 0 to 100, with 0 showing a hard edge, and 100 being so soft it almost disappears. The default of 50 is a great starting point, with most vignettes ranging from 35 to 65.

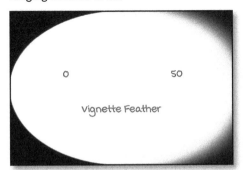

Vignette Feather

The **Highlights** slider runs from 0, which has no effect, to 100, which makes the highlights under a dark vignette brighter. This allows you to darken the edges without the photo becoming too flat and lacking in contrast.

STEP-BY-STEP

Ready to give it a try? You can use the sliders in any order, but this works well:

1. Move the *Amount* slider to -100, so you can easily see the effect of the other sliders.

2. Adjust the *Midpoint* slider, so the vignette doesn't cover important areas of the photo.

3. Adjust the *Feather* slider so the edge of the vignette disappears.

4. Move the *Vignette Amount* back towards the center, until you're drawn into the photo, but the vignette isn't immediately obvious.

5. Adjust the *Highlights* slider if the corners look too flat and lacking contrast.

ADDING GRAIN

We spend a lot of time trying to reduce the noise in our photos... and then put grain back! However, some photos look great with a little extra grain, particularly if they're B&W, toned, or have a film emulation preset applied. It can also help to hide the plasticky look that results from high noise reduction.

GRAIN SLIDERS

The main **Grain** slider in the Effects panel affects the amount of grain applied. The noise is applied equally across the photo, giving a much more film-like quality than digital noise, which tends to be heavier in the shadows.

There are additional sliders for fine-tuning the quality of the grain. These are hidden by a disclosure triangle on the desktop.

Size affects the size of the grain, just as grain on film came in different sizes, and it gets softer as it gets larger. More expensive film usually had smaller grain. (This may be hard to see in the paperback!)

Roughness affects the consistency of the grain, so 0 is uniform across the photo, whereas higher values become rougher and less "digital."

You'll need to zoom into 1:1 view to get an accurate preview. Grain is very sensitive to resizing, sharpening and compression, so if you're going to downsize the photo when saving it, you'll need stronger grain than looks right on screen.

OPTIMIZING DETAIL

17

Our eyes can see an incredible amount of detail in our surroundings (at least when we're young!) and adjust for very low-light conditions.

Cameras have made incredible progress, but they still can't match the human eye. A little editing is required to optimize the detail in a photo, allowing the viewer to focus on the content of the photo rather than being distracted by false detail (noise). These adjustments are made using the Detail panel.

IN THIS SECTION, WE'LL CONSIDER:

• How to enhance the texture in your photo to make it look three dimensional.

• How sharpening works.

• How to sharpen your photos effectively but without over-sharpening.

• How to reduce digital noise without creating a plastic effect.

ENHANCING TEXTURE OR 'STRUCTURE'

The **Texture** slider, found in the Effects panel, is designed to enhance mid-size details in your photo. You might describe the effect using words like structure, micro-contrast, bite, crispness, a 3D look or, of course, texture.

This might remind you of the *Clarity* slider (discussed on page 189), and for good reason, as there are similarities. Both increase local contrast along edges.

Clarity enhances larger details, and has a significant effect on overall contrast, whereas *Texture* primarily affects mid-size details and the effect is much more subtle.

Sharpening, which we'll discuss in the next lesson (page 234), targets even smaller details.

You can see these differences illustrated in the photo of the archway. This photo is available to download from the Members Area, as the effect is easier to compare at 1:1 view on your own screen.

The Texture slider enhances medium sized details without affecting the overall contrast

SETTING TEXTURE

Positive Texture can be used for a lot of different purposes, but it's particularly good for landscapes, nature photography, architecture and B&W photography. It adds a crispness without looking over-sharpened, and without adding unnatural levels of contrast.

Because the effect is subtle, you may need to zoom into 1:1 view (click/tap on the photo), especially on very high resolution photos. Artifacts are rare, even when pushed to 100, but watch out for small halos that can occasionally be created. It can make Chromatic Aberration (color fringing)

more obvious, but we'll learn how to fix this fringing on page 262.

As with *Clarity*, be careful adding texture to people's faces, as it will enhance wrinkles, but can be brushed over the eyes to define the eyelashes.

Negative Texture is ideal for softening skin. Because *Texture* primarily affects mid-size details and ignores the smallest details, it retains some of the skin texture, minimizing the smooth plastic appearance that can happen with skin smoothing. Rather than applying it globally, use the Selective Editing tools (starting on page 241) to apply only to the face.

Negative Texture is ideal for smoothing skin without making the person look like a plastic doll

SHARPENING VS. TEXTURE VS. CLARITY

Sharpening 150, others at default – While you can experiment with the settings, extreme sharpening just makes the photo look "crunchy" rather than defining structures in the image

Texture +100 – The archway stones are more defined and the rocks have greater depth, but the overall contrast remains the same and there's no sign of over-sharpening

Clarity +100 – While it's added punch and definition to the larger objects, notice the strong shift in overall contrast

SHARPENING PHOTOS

Most photos benefit from some sharpening, because it highlights the detail in the photo and makes edges look more defined by adding local contrast on a very small scale.

It's easy to get carried away and apply too much sharpening, especially if the photo is slightly out of focus. No amount of sharpening will recover the detail lost in a blurry photo. It can only enhance detail that has been captured.

Over-sharpening can often look worse than too little sharpening. In this lesson, we'll learn how to adjust the Sharpening sliders to get the balance just right.

TYPES OF SHARPENING

Digital image sharpening works in two ways:

USM, or unsharp mask, works by creating small halos along edges to make them appear sharper. On the dark side of an edge it creates a darker halo, and on the light side of an edge it makes a lighter halo.

Deconvolution sharpening attempts to calculate and reverse the cause of the blurring.

Lightroom uses both kinds of sharpening, balanced using the *Detail* slider.

SHARPENING SLIDERS

Lightroom has four sharpening sliders, three of which are hidden under the disclosure triangle on the desktop. Although most of the hidden sliders in Lightroom can remain hidden, these sliders are important.

The number of Sharpening sliders can look overwhelming to start with, but the principles are simple:

• Only sharpen real detail, not noise.

• Avoid making the sharpening halos obvious.

• Always judge sharpening at 1:1 zoom.

Let's take a closer look at how the individual sliders work, and then we'll put it into practice:

Sharpening works like a volume control, running from 0-150. The higher the value, the more sharpening is applied. If you're shooting JPEG, the photos are usually sharpened by the camera, so you'll need less sharpening than a raw file.

You won't usually want to use the slider at 150 unless you're combining it with the *Masking* or *Detail* sliders, which suppress the sharpening.

If you hold down the Alt key (Windows) / Opt key (Mac) / two fingers (mobile) while moving the *Sharpening* slider, you can see the amount of sharpening being applied without being distracted by color.

Radius affects the width of the sharpening halo. It runs from 0.5-3, with a default of 1.0. Photos with fine detail need a smaller radius, as do landscapes, but a slightly higher radius can look good on portraits.

Hold down the Alt key (Windows) / Opt key (Mac) / two fingers (mobile) while moving the *Radius* slider to see the width of the halos.

Detail and *Masking* are both dampening sliders, allowing you to control which areas of the photo get the most sharpening applied and which are protected, but there's a difference in the way they behave.

Detail is very good at controlling sharpening of textures. Under the hood, low values use the USM sharpening methods, and as you increase the slider, it gradually switches to deconvolution methods. In the real world, this means your *Detail* setting will depend on the content of the photo.

The default of 25 is a good general *Detail* setting for most raw files. A low value is ideal for large smooth areas, such as portraits (skin) or sky, where you don't want to sharpen pores or noise. A high value works well for landscapes or other shots with lots of fine detail, where you want to sharpen details like the leaves on the trees.

As you increase *Detail*, it also starts to amplify the noise in the image, so you may need to reduce the *Sharpening* slider and increase the *Masking* and *Luminance Noise Reduction* sliders (page 239) to compensate.

If you hold down the Alt key (Windows) / Opt key (Mac) / two fingers (mobile) while moving the *Detail* slider, you can preview the effect in more detail. The white areas of the mask will be sharpened and the gray areas will be protected. (It's much easier to see on screen than in print.)

The **Masking** slider creates a soft edge mask from the image, so that only the edge details are sharpened. Hold down the Alt key (Windows) / Opt key (Mac) / two fingers (mobile) while moving the *Masking* slider to see the mask it's creating.

The aim is to move the *Masking* slider until only the detail you want to sharpen is white, and everything else is black.

STEP-BY-STEP

That's all very interesting, but how do you know where to set the sliders to get a crisp result without over-sharpening? Try this:

1. Zoom out to Fit view so you can see the entire photo.

2. Hold down the Alt key (Windows) / Opt key (Mac) / two fingers (mobile) and drag the *Masking* slider to the right. You're aiming to make areas of low detail, such as the sky, turn black so the noise in these areas will be protected from your sharpening.

3. Zoom into 1:1 view to accurately preview your further adjustments. (On mobile, tap on the photo to zoom in, but remember it won't be a perfectly accurate 1:1 view if the original is not available/downloaded.)

4. Increase the main *Sharpening* slider to easily preview the effect of your adjustments. Try around 75-100 temporarily.

5. Hold down the Alt key (Windows) / Opt key (Mac) / two fingers (mobile) and drag the *Detail* slider to the left for portraits or to the right for detailed shots such as landscapes. The aim is to enhance the detail,

shown in white, without sharpening the noise, protected in gray.

6. Hold down the Alt key (Windows) / Opt key (Mac) / two fingers (mobile) and drag the *Radius* slider to the left for detailed shots such as landscapes or slightly to the right for portraits. Watch the size of the black and white halos you're creating along the edges, as you don't want them to overwhelm the image detail.

While viewing the *Radius* mask, take note of where the halos are most visible. You'll usually notice them most along high contrast edges.

7. Hold down the Alt key (Windows) / Opt key (Mac) / two fingers (mobile) and drag the *Sharpening* slider to the left until the halos almost disappear.

ENHANCING DETAIL ON SPECIAL PHOTOS

Most digital cameras use a color filter array over the sensor, made up of red, green and blue pixels in a mosaic pattern.

Bayer Sensor   Fuji X-Trans

The mosaic pattern must be converted into a full color image before it can be viewed, and this process is called demosaicing. When you're shooting JPEG, this is done in the camera, but when you're shooting in a raw file format, Lightroom looks after this demosaic process.

Lightroom's default demosaic happens silently in the background whenever you open a raw photo. It's fast and usually does an excellent job, however in some cases, there may be a little more detail in the file that can be extracted. This is where the Enhance Details tool comes into its own.

WHEN TO USE ENHANCE DETAILS

Enhance Details is not a tool you'll need or want to use on every photo, as the resulting DNG files are huge and it takes extra time to run. It's handy to have in your toolbox for special occasions, for example:

• You're affectionately known as a pixel peeper because you like to view your photos at 1:1 view or greater and eek out every last bit of detail.

• You're creating very large prints.

• You're a Fuji X-Trans photographer who notices "worm" artifacts when sharpening your photos.

• You're shooting with a high quality Bayer

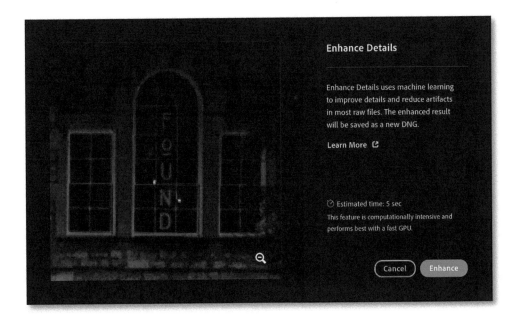

Enhance Details

Enhance Details uses machine learning to improve details and reduce artifacts in most raw files. The enhanced result will be saved as a new DNG.

Learn More ⏷

⏱ Estimated time: 5 sec
This feature is computationally intensive and performs best with a fast GPU.

Cancel   Enhance

sensor without a low pass filter and you're using a very sharp lens.

HOW TO ENHANCE DETAILS

To use Enhance Details, you must be running Windows 10 October 2018 release (or later) or macOS 10.13 (or later), because it uses operating system components that aren't in earlier versions.

Select one or more original raw photos, right-click and select **Enhance Details**. You'll also find it under the Photo menu.

If only one photo is selected, the Enhance Details dialog includes a small preview window, so you can check that the extra processing will make a difference before running the conversion.

THE RESULTING FILE

This advanced demosaic is much slower than the standard demosaic, so the Enhance Details tool saves the result as a separate linear DNG file, rather than running the demosaic every time you view the file. (If you find that you're using it frequently, a fast GPU can significantly improve processing times.)

The resulting DNG file appears next to the original, with -enhanced added to the file name. Lightroom automatically copies all of the metadata and Develop edits already applied from the original to the new enhanced file, and stacks the two photos. You can edit it as normal.

The original mosaic data is also stored within the DNG file, so even if you delete the original file, you can run Enhance Details again in future when it improves further.

SPOT THE DIFFERENCE

To see any changes, you'll need to zoom into 1:1 or greater, and you'll probably need to flick back and forth a few times.

If the standard demosaic is already extracting all of the available detail, you won't be able to see a difference.

In most cases, the changes will be tiny details, so it helps to know where to look for improvements. Look out for:

• **Very fine details**, less than 1px wide, especially if they're diagonals or curves, for example, hair or fur.

• **Edges of different colors** (especially orange against blue), such as a field of flowers, autumn leaves against the sky or neon signs.

• **Moiré patterns** that may be reduced.

I'd love to include some examples, but you wouldn't be able to see them in screenshots of this size!

REDUCING NOISE

Noise in your photos can be distracting. You'll particularly notice it in photos shot at a high ISO, for example, shot without flash in a darkened room, or photos shot using a small sensor. If you've increased the exposure considerably within Lightroom, that can also increase the appearance of noise. Fortunately, Lightroom's Noise Reduction tools are excellent.

NOISE REDUCTION SLIDERS

There's an array of noise reduction sliders, but just because they exist doesn't mean you need to use them on every photo. Most photos only require the main *Noise Reduction* and *Color Noise Reduction* sliders. Additional sliders are available for more extreme cases, and can be left at their default settings most of the time. They're hidden under a disclosure triangle on the desktop.

The **Noise (Noise Reduction)** slider controls the amount of luminance noise reduction applied. 0 doesn't apply any noise reduction, but at 100, the photo has a soft, almost painted effect.

If you hold down the Alt key (Windows) / Opt key (Mac) / two fingers (mobile) while moving the *Noise Reduction* slider, you can see the amount of noise reduction being applied without being distracted by color.

The aim is to reduce the noise, without losing the detail or making the subject look like plastic, so don't push it too far.

The **Color Noise (Color Noise Reduction)** slider tries to suppress single pixels of random noise without losing the edge detail. I've zoomed in on Charlie's eye to make the small colored pixels more visible, but you'll see them more clearly at 1:1 view in your own photos.

EXTREME NOISE REDUCTION

The other noise reduction sliders only make a noticeable difference to extremely noisy images, such as those produced by the highest ISO rating that your camera offers, or where a high ISO file is extremely underexposed. You're unlikely to see a difference at lower ISO ratings, for better or for worse, so in most cases you won't need to change these settings from their defaults. I haven't included screenshots, because the difference is so small, you wouldn't be able to see it. Like the main *Noise Reduction* slider, holding down the Alt key (Windows) / Opt key (Mac) / two fingers (mobile) shows a grayscale preview.

The luminance **Detail** slider sets the noise threshold, so higher values preserve more detail but some noise may incorrectly be identified as detail.

The luminance **Contrast** slider at 0 is a much finer grain than 100. Higher values help to preserve texture, but can introduce a mottling effect, so lower values are usually a better choice.

The color **Detail** slider refines any fine color edges. At low values it reduces the number of color speckles in these edges but may slightly desaturate them, whereas at high values, it tries to retain the color detail but may introduce color speckles in the process.

The color **Smoothness** slider is similar to the main *Color Noise Reduction* slider, but it aims to remove larger areas of color mottling or splotchiness. You're most likely to see this on very underexposed images, where you've brightened an area considerably, or extreme contrast images that you're tone-mapping (using maximum - *Highlights* and + *Shadows* adjustments). The default is 50, which works very well on most images. Moving the slider to the right increases the smoothing, but can slow Lightroom down.

STEP-BY-STEP

Let's put this into practice on an "average" photo:

1. Zoom in to 1:1 view, as this provides the most accurate preview.

2. Check for color noise. For most raw files, the default *Color Noise Reduction* setting of 25 is spot on. It's set to 0 for JPEGs, but if there's still colored noise in your photo, particularly in the dark shadows, try increasing it slightly.

3. Adjust the *Noise Reduction* slider to reduce the noise without losing too much detail. If you're working on raw files, try a setting of around 15-20 on the main *Noise Reduction* slider as a starting point.

4. Leave the other sliders at their defaults unless you have an extremely noisy photo that will be printed as a billboard!

SELECTIVE NOISE REDUCTION

If your noise reduction is too strong in some areas, select the Brush tool (page 242), set the *Noise* sliders to between 0 and -100 and brush over those areas to reduce the noise reduction. Don't remove it entirely, as it'll look too grainy in comparison with the rest of the photo.

Likewise, if you only want to paint the noise reduction into certain areas, a brush set to + *Noise* applies additional noise reduction. (Contrary to the name of the slider, it doesn't really add noise!)

SELECTIVE EDITING

18

Most of Lightroom's sliders apply to the whole photo, but the selective adjustment tools allow you to apply settings to specific areas. This isn't a new concept. Photographers have been dodging and burning photos in the darkroom for years. The selective editing tools can be used for things like:

Dodging & Burning—The *Exposure* adjustment is similar to dodging and burning in a traditional darkroom, lightening and darkening areas of the photo.

Enhancing Faces—Settings such as *Sharpness, Texture* and *Noise Reduction* can be used for softening skin on portraits without softening the eyes.

Mixed Lighting—*Temp* and *Tint* are useful when adjusting for mixed lighting situations, or changing the color of specific regions.

Enhancing Sunset Skies—Settings can be combined, so a combination of - *Exposure*, + *Saturation* and + *Clarity* can enhance a sunset.

But how do you decide what to adjust, and where to draw the eye? It comes back to the decisions you made when you were analyzing the photo. Did you find any distractions that need to be minimized, for example, bright areas in a dark scene, or warm saturated colors in the wrong spot? And what did you decide to enhance, to

draw the viewer's eye around the photo?

Before you start applying settings, however, you need to create a selection, and there are three tools to do this:

• The **Brush** offers complete flexibility to correct uneven lighting, dodge and burn to draw the eye and enhance people's faces.

• The **Linear Gradient** is ideal for darkening skies and lightening foregrounds.

• The **Radial Gradient** creates off-center vignettes and can put a "spotlight" on certain areas of the photo.

IN THIS SECTION, WE'LL CONSIDER:

• How to create brushed selections.

• How to create linear selections.

• How to create radial selections.

• Examples of the adjustments you can make using selective adjustments.

MAKING SELECTIONS USING THE BRUSH

The Brush tool allows you to create a freeform selection by painting on the photo. Unlike the gradient tools, it's not constrained to a specific shape, so it's very flexible.

The brush is a powerful tool, with lots of useful tricks, so in this lesson we'll look at:

- The basics of creating a brush selection.

- How to choose the right brush for the job.

- How to manage multiple brush selections.

CREATING BRUSH SELECTIONS

To **open the Brush tool** on the desktop, click on the brush icon in the right panel bar or press the B key.

← Brush tool

On mobile, select the Selective Editing tool, then tap the **+** button and select the brush icon.

Select the Selective Editing tool then the Brush

When you select the brush, it's automatically ready to start a new selection. To **paint with the brush** on the desktop, hold down the mouse button and drag the cursor across the photo then release the mouse. On mobile, drag your finger or stylus/pen across the photo. Holding down the Shift key while you paint draws the stroke in a straight vertical or horizontal line (desktop only).

To **apply adjustments** to the selection, so

you can see where you're painting, adjust the sliders. You can tweak them again later, when you've perfected your selection.

If you make a mistake when brushing, it's not a problem. To **erase part of the selection,** select the *Eraser* from the Brush panel (desktop) / icons (mobile).

← Brush (add to selection)
← Eraser (remove from selection)

On the desktop, you can also hold down the Alt (Windows) / Opt (Mac) key to select the eraser temporarily, and brush away the selection. Of course, if you've only just painted a stroke, Ctrl-Z (Windows) / Cmd-Z (Mac) / undo icon (mobile) will also undo your last action.

By creating multiple selections, you can apply different edits to different areas of the photo, and they can be overlapped and layered to build up the effect. To **create an additional brush selection**, click the **+** button at the top of the Brush panel (desktop) / tap the **+** button and select the brush icon again (mobile).

THE BRUSH TOOL (WINDOWS/MAC)

Reset All Brush Selections

Open Brush tool

New Brush Selection

Brush tool (add to selection)

Eraser (remove from selection)

Brush Size

Feather (brush softness)

Flow (build up gradually)

Density (maximum stroke strength)

Auto mask (limit to similar pixels)

Sliders

Automatically reset sliders to 0 when starting a new selection

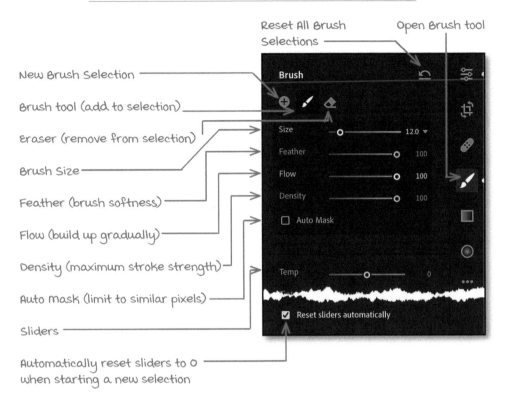

CHOOSING THE RIGHT BRUSH

If you're doing some painting at home, you'll pick the right brush for the job. Perhaps a large brush for the wall, and a small brush to paint along the edges. Lightroom offers similar controls. On the desktop, these are selected using sliders in the Brush panel (some are hidden under a disclosure triangle), and the size and feathering are previewed on the cursor, with two lines close together for minimal feathering, and further apart for greater feathering.

On mobile, hold your finger on the *Size*,

Feather or *Flow* icon and drag up or down to increase or decrease the slider value. The numeric value displays at the top of the screen, and a red preview displays in the center of the screen, so you can see how big or hard the brush will be.

Size runs from 0.1, which is a tiny brush, to a maximum size of 100. You can use multiple different brush sizes on the same selection, perhaps using a large brush to cover a large area, then a small brush for detailed edges. On the desktop, you can also use the [and] keyboard shortcuts or your mouse scroll wheel to adjust the size.

Feather runs from 1, which is a hard edged brush, to 100 which is soft. A harder edged brush is useful when you're brushing up against the edge of an object in the photo,

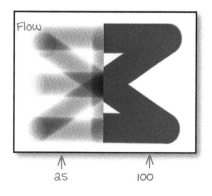

whereas a soft brush is better for blending your adjustments into the rest of the photo. On the desktop, the Shift-[and Shift-] keys also adjust the feathering.

Flow controls the rate at which the adjustment is applied. With *Flow* at 100, the brush behaves like a paintbrush, laying down the maximum effect with each stroke. With *Flow* at a lower value, such as 25, the

THE BRUSH TOOL (IOS/ANDROID)

New Brush Selection (Tap + button and select the brush)

Brush tool (add to selection)

Eraser (remove from selection)

Brush Size

Feather (brush softness)

Flow (build up gradually)

Hold finger on buttons and drag up/down to adjust

Delete Selection

Sliders

Undo/Redo

Tap on gray (unselected) pin to reselect it (turns blue)

Drag pin to move selection

Hold finger on pin to view menu

Duplicate Brush
Remove Brush
Reset Current Adjustments
Auto Show Red Overlay
Never Show Red Overlay

Tap to confirm the changes or cancel. (Buttons at the top on Android, or a Done button on tablets)

Light   Color   Effects   Detail   Optics   Previous   Reset

✕   Selective Edits   ✓

Density

0

25

100

brush behaves more like an airbrush, building up the effect gradually.

Density (desktop only) limits the maximum strength of the stroke. Regardless of how many times you paint, the mask can never be stronger than the maximum density setting. Unless you need the *Density* control for a specific purpose, I'd suggest leaving it set at 100.

If you're brushing over the photo and nothing seems to be happening, it's usually because either the *Flow* or *Density* sliders are set too low.

Some photographers like to use a graphics tablet/pen (desktop) / Apple Pencil (iOS) / stylus (Android) to paint on the photo. It can take some practice, but it's a more natural and accurate way of drawing. The flow/opacity of the stroke can be controlled by how hard you press, just like drawing with a pencil on paper.

The **Auto Mask** checkbox (desktop only) confines your brush strokes to areas of

similar color, based on the tones that the center of the brush passes over. This helps to prevent your mask spilling over into other areas of the photo, for example, you can paint over a child's shirt to selectively adjust the color, without having to carefully brush around the edges.

It can cause halos, for example, trying to darken a bright sky with a silhouette of a tree in the foreground may leave a halo around the edge of the tree.

MASK & PINS

Each brush selection is marked with a small icon called a pin. On the desktop, they're all circular and the colors are reversed depending on whether the pin is selected or not.

Unselected   Selected

On mobile, there's a different pin for each type of selective edit, and they have a blue center when selected, or a gray center when deselected.

← Brush pin

← Radial Gradient pin

← Linear Gradient pin

To **hide the pins**, float the cursor away from the photo (desktop) / click *Done* to exit the Selective Editing tools (mobile).

The **mask overlay** is a colored tint that shows the location and opacity of your selection.

On the desktop, you can temporarily **show**

Pin   mask Overlay

the mask overlay by floating the cursor over a pin. If you can't see the pins and overlays on the desktop, press the O key or go to *View menu > Edit Tools > Show Overlay*. The O key cycles through four states—*Hide Overlays* (pins), *Show Tool Overlay* (pins), *Show Mask Overlay* (red/green mask) and *Show Tool and Mask Overlays* (pins and mask). You can also use Shift-O to switch between a red overlay and a green one, which can be useful when you're painting over a red object.

On mobile, the mask shows automatically, but disappears when you apply edits to the selection using the sliders. To hide the red mask overlay, long press on the pin to show the menu and switch from *Auto Show Red Overlay* to *Never Show Red Overlay*.

EDITING SELECTIONS

To **reselect an existing brush selection**, click/tap on its pin.

If you've reached the limit of a slider, you can duplicate the selection without having to paint a new selection. To **duplicate a selection**, right-click (desktop) / long press (mobile) on the pin and select *Duplicate*. There isn't an easy way to access the bottom mask again, however. To do so, you must move the top pin, so get the first pin right

before duplicating it.

Duplicating a selection is also useful if you want to replicate an effect somewhere else on the photo, for example, if you've enhanced the iris of one eye, you can duplicate the selection and move it to the other eye.

To **move the brush selection**, click/tap and drag the pin.

You can't **invert the brush selection**, but you can use a large brush to paint over everything, and then use a small brush to erase from that mask. For example, you can paint the entire photo using a negative *Saturation* brush to partially desaturate the background and then erase to show a small amount of the original color photo below, to draw the eye to that area.

To **fade the edits (desktop only)**, hold the Alt (Windows) / Opt key while dragging left<>right on the pin to move multiple adjustment sliders at once.

To **delete a brush selection** on the desktop, select the pin then press the Delete key or right-click on the pin and select *Delete*. On mobile, select the pin then tap the Delete icon or long press on the pin and select *Remove Brush*.

To **delete all brush selections**, press the *Reset* button in the Brush panel (desktop) / toolbar (mobile). On the desktop, this only deletes the brush strokes, whereas on mobile, choosing *Selective Edits* (iOS) / *Selection* (Android) clears all selective edits.

There's a multitude of keyboard shortcuts and modifiers for the Selective Editing tools on the desktop, so we won't list them all here. They're all listed on the Keyboard Shortcuts sheets available in the Members Area (see page 378).

MAKING SELECTIONS USING A DEPTH MASK ON IOS

If you own an iPhone with dual cameras, you can create a depth mask which can be used for blurring and darkening backgrounds. It's a quicker way of making a selection.

To **capture a photo with a depth mask**, you must either use the Apple Camera app (or similar) set to Portrait mode with *iOS Settings > Camera > Formats* set to *High Efficiency* mode so it captures in HEIC format, or select *Depth Capture* from the pop-up in Lightroom's camera (page 38).

To **use the depth mask**, select the Selective Editing tool, then tap the **+** button and select the depth mask icon. It only appears for HEIC format photos that have a depth mask.

Select the Selective Editing
tool then the Depth Mask

The selected areas are shown using a red mask. To invert the selection, tap the *Invert* button.

At the bottom, the histogram shows the number of pixels at each depth, from distant pixels on the left to nearby pixels on the right.

The curved line allows you to choose how many of the pixels should be included in the selection.

THE DEPTH MASK TOOL (IOS)

Invert selection

Red mask shows selected area

Depth Histogram with distant pixels on the left, nearby pixels on the right

Range – spread or contract affected area using bottom handles or by dragging left/right on the photo

Smoothness of the transition from selected to unselected is controlled using top handle, or by dragging up/down on the photo

Tap to confirm the changes or cancel

The range is selected using the handles at the bottom, and the smoothness of the transition from selected to unselected is controlled by the top handle. For example, moving the handles to the right selects the pixels closest to you.

When you tap the checkmark, the mask is turned into a normal brush mask, which you can edit further using the brush tools discussed in the previous lesson (page 242).

Dragged apart widens the range

Dragged together narrows the range

Dragged to the right selects areas near the camera

Dragged to the left selects areas further away from the camera

When you're done, it becomes a normal brush selection

MAKING SELECTIONS USING A GRADIENT

There are two kinds of gradients—Linear (straight) and Radial (round/oval). Since the behavior is similar, we'll discuss both at once.

LINEAR GRADIENT

The Linear Gradient is particularly useful for darkening the sky in a sunset photo or blurring a distracting foreground. It can also be useful if the lighting on one side of the photo is different to the other side.

RADIAL GRADIENT

The Radial Gradient is particularly useful for off-center vignettes, to draw the eye to a specific area of the photo. It can also be used to lighten faces in photos or put a "spotlight" on one area of the photo, among other things.

CREATING A GRADIENT

To **open the Linear and Radial Gradient tools**, click the buttons in the right panel bar or press the L key (Linear) or R key (Radial).

Linear Gradient tool

Radial Gradient tool

On mobile, select the Selective Editing tool, then tap the + button and select the Radial Gradient or Linear Gradient icon.

Select the Selective Editing tool then the Linear or Radial Gradient

To **create a linear gradient** on the desktop, click at the gradient starting point, and drag to the gradient end point before releasing the mouse button. To drag out from the center of the gradient, instead of setting the start/end points, hold down the Alt (Windows) / Opt (Mac) key while dragging. The gradient then expands equally from both sides of your starting point. If the horizon is straight, hold down the Shift key while creating the gradient to constrain it to a 90° angle.

On mobile, drag your finger or stylus/pen across the photo, from the start of the gradient to the end.

To **create a radial gradient** on the desktop, click in the center of your new circle/oval, and drag out towards the edge of the photo before releasing the mouse button. On mobile, drag your finger or stylus/pen out from the center of your radial gradient.

To **apply adjustments** to the selection, so

you can see the effect, adjust the sliders. You can tweak them again later, when you've perfected your selection.

By creating multiple gradients, you can apply different edits to different areas of the photo, and they can be overlapped and layered to build up the effect.

To **create an additional gradient** on the desktop, just click and drag again. On mobile, tap the **+** button and select the Linear or Radial Gradient icon again, then drag across the photo.

OVERLAYS, PINS & MASKS

The gradients are controlled using an overlay—three lines for the Linear Gradient and a circle with four small handles for the Radial Gradient. They allow you to adjust the size, rotation and position of the gradient.

Each brush selection is marked with a small icon called a pin. On the desktop, they're all circular and the colors are reversed depending on whether the pin is selected or not.

unselected Selected

On mobile, there's a different pin for each type of selective edit, and they have a blue center when selected, or a gray center when deselected.

← Brush pin

← Radial Gradient pin

← Linear Gradient pin

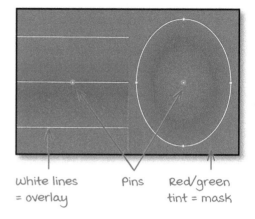

White lines   Pins   Red/green
= overlay   tint = mask

To **hide the pins**, float the cursor away from the photo (desktop) / click *Done* to exit the Selective Editing tools (mobile).

The **mask overlay** is a colored tint that shows the location and opacity of your selection.

On the desktop, you can temporarily **show the mask overlay** by floating the cursor over a pin. If you can't see the pins and overlays on the desktop, press the O key or go to *View menu > Edit Tools > Show Overlay*. The O key cycles through four states—*Hide Overlays* (pins), *Show Tool Overlay* (pins), *Show Mask Overlay* (red/green mask) and *Show Tool and Mask Overlays* (pins and mask). You can also use Shift-O to switch between a red overlay and a green one, which can be useful when you're painting over a red object.

On mobile, the mask shows automatically, but disappears when you apply edits to the selection using the sliders. To hide the red mask overlay, long press on the pin to show the menu and switch from *Auto Show Red Overlay* to *Never Show Red Overlay*.

EDITING GRADIENTS

Like the Brush tool, you can go back and edit

the selection or settings later. To **reselect an existing gradient**, click/tap on the pin.

To **feather/stretch a linear gradient**, drag the outer lines further apart. Moving them closer together reduces the feathering.

To **feather a radial gradient**, adjust the *Feather* slider (desktop) / hold your finger on the *Feather* icon and drag up or down to increase or decrease the slider value (mobile).

To **resize a radial gradient**, drag the handles on the oval line.

To **rotate the gradient** on the desktop, float over ends of the central line (linear) / oval line (radial). The cursor changes to a curved double-headed arrow, then click and drag

to adjust the rotation of the gradient. On mobile, simply drag the central line (linear) / oval line (radial).

If the gradient is the wrong way round, for example, the effect is applied to the inside of a radial gradient instead of the outside, **invert the gradient** by clicking the *Invert*

LINEAR & RADIAL GRADIENT (WINDOWS/MAC)

checkbox (desktop) / tapping the *Invert* icon (mobile).

To **move the gradient**, drag the central pin.

If you've reached the limit of a slider, you may want to **duplicate the gradient**. To do so, right-click (desktop) / long press (mobile) on the pin and select *Duplicate* from the menu.

To **fade the edits** (desktop only), hold the

Alt (Windows) / Opt key while dragging left<>right on the pin to move multiple adjustment sliders at once.

To **delete a gradient** on the desktop, select the pin then press the Delete key or right-click on the pin and select *Delete*. On mobile, select the pin then tap the Delete icon or long press on the pin and select *Remove Linear/Radial Gradient*.

To **delete all gradients**, press the **Reset**

LINEAR GRADIENT (IOS/ANDROID)

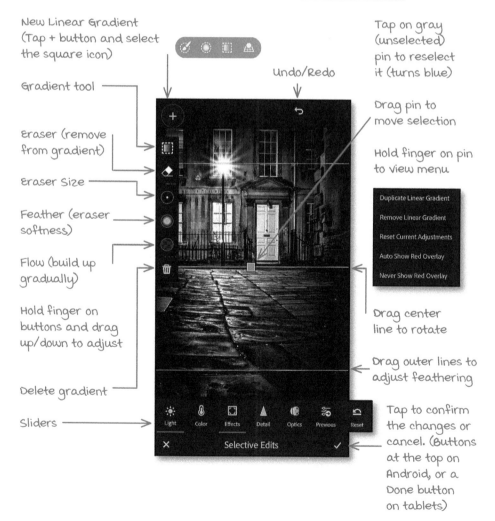

New Linear Gradient (Tap + button and select the square icon)

Gradient tool

Eraser (remove from gradient)

Eraser Size

Feather (eraser softness)

Flow (build up gradually)

Hold finger on buttons and drag up/down to adjust

Delete gradient

Sliders

Tap on gray (unselected) pin to reselect it (turns blue)

Undo/Redo

Drag pin to move selection

Hold finger on pin to view menu

Duplicate Linear Gradient
Remove Linear Gradient
Reset Current Adjustments
Auto Show Red Overlay
Never Show Red Overlay

Drag center line to rotate

Drag outer lines to adjust feathering

Tap to confirm the changes or cancel. (Buttons at the top on Android, or a Done button on tablets)

Light   Color   Effects   Detail   Optics   Previous   Reset

Selective Edits

button in the Linear/Radial Gradient panel (desktop) / toolbar (mobile).

ADDING TO OR ERASING PART OF THE GRADIENT

At times, you may want to prevent parts of the photo being affected by a gradient, or add an extra brush stroke to the gradient. For example, if you're darkening the sky, you may not want to darken the building on the horizon at the same time. In this case, you can brush away part of the gradient.

To **add to or erase part of the gradient**, select the **Brush** or **Eraser** icon in the Gradient panel (desktop) / sidebar (mobile), then click and drag across the photo. (On mobile, you can only erase from the gradient.) The brush/eraser options (size/ feather, etc.) in the gradients work like the main Brush tool (page 242).

RADIAL GRADIENT (IOS/ANDROID)

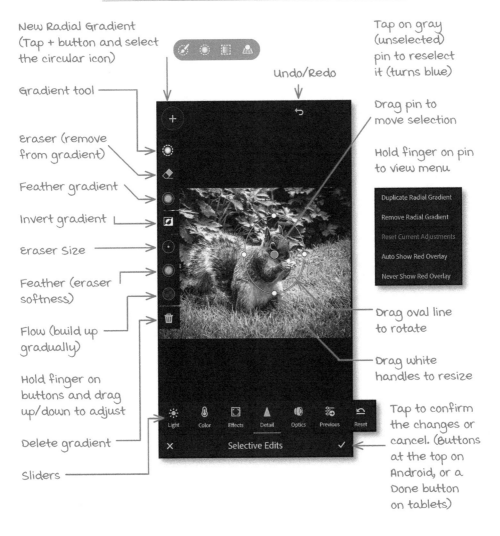

New Radial Gradient (Tap + button and select the circular icon)

Gradient tool

Eraser (remove from gradient)

Feather gradient

Invert gradient

Eraser Size

Feather (eraser softness)

Flow (build up gradually)

Hold finger on buttons and drag up/down to adjust

Delete gradient

Sliders

Tap on gray (unselected) pin to reselect it (turns blue)

Undo/Redo

Drag pin to move selection

Hold finger on pin to view menu

Duplicate Radial Gradient
Remove Radial Gradient
Reset Current Adjustments
Auto Show Red Overlay
Never Show Red Overlay

Drag oval line to rotate

Drag white handles to resize

Light   Color   Effects   Detail   Optics   Previous   Reset

Selective Edits

Tap to confirm the changes or cancel. (Buttons at the top on Android, or a Done button on tablets)

LIGHT ADJUSTMENTS (INCL. DODGING & BURNING)

One of the most logical uses for local adjustments is tonal changes—**Exposure, Contrast, Highlights, Shadows, Whites, Blacks, Clarity** and **Dehaze**. They can be used for darkening skies, brightening shadows, reducing bright highlights, darkening edges like an off-center vignette, and many other adjustments.

The word 'dodging' comes from the

darkroom printing process and refers to lightening areas of the image. Many photos benefit from a little dodging, for example, lightening faces.

The opposite of dodging is 'burning in' or selectively darkening areas of the photo that are too bright, attracting your attention more than the main subject.

−1 Exposure & −39 Highlights on a linear gradient brings back the detail in the sky without darkening the foreground, like an ND Grad filter. For some skies, we might also add Clarity, Dehaze, Saturation or a different color tint

+0.6 Exposure & +45 Saturation lightens and warms up the cub's face & body

−1.0 Exposure & −80 Highlights darkens the light patch on the cub's face

−40 Temp & +20 Saturation enhances the cub's blue eyes

−3.2 Exposure evens out lighting on wall

LOCAL COLOR ADJUSTMENTS

The *Temp, Tint, Hue* and *Saturation* sliders and the *Colorize* picker are useful for local color adjustments.

Temp makes the selected area warmer or cooler, while **Tint** moves between green and pink, like the main White Balance sliders. This helps to compensate for mixed lighting situations, where the white balance is different in specific areas of the photo.

The **Hue** gradient behaves like the *Hue* sliders in the Color Mixer panel, but has a much wider range of adjustment. Unlike the other sliders, the *Hue* slider is a pair of gradients. The bottom gradient shows the color that you started with, and the static top gradient shows the resulting color after the hue adjustment. They're just a guide, and it's often easier to see the result on the photo itself.

The slider offers an additional helping hand by automatically adjusting its starting point based on the masked pixels. For example, when you've selected something red, the color gradients move along to put red under the slider handle.

You may remember that we used the main *Hue* sliders to change the color of a car on page 212, but we could only shift it from red towards pink or orange. With the local *Hue* slider, and a very careful brush selection, you could change the car to any color. You might also check the *Use Fine Adjustment* checkbox to make smaller adjustments, such as tweaking the color of the sky without affecting the other blue tones in a photo, or reducing ruddy cheeks without changing lip color.

The **Saturation** slider acts like the intelligent *Vibrance* slider when dragged to the right (+), but dragged to the left (-), it behaves like negative *Saturation*, allowing you to desaturate the selected area to B&W. Adjusting the saturation in limited areas of the photo can help to draw the eye towards the subject or away from a distraction. Some like to use *Saturation* for a selective color effect, for example, a B&W or partially saturated photo with a small area of the

Whereas the Color mixer sliders (page 209) could only shift the red car toward pink or orange, the local Hue slider can change it to any color.

photo in its original color.

The **Colorize** option applies a specific color tint of your choice, without the brightness changes that would happen with *Temp/Tint*. It's a much more subtle shift than *Hue*, but can apply color to neutral areas of the photo, whereas *Hue* can only adjust existing color. You might use it to apply a hand-colored effect to old black & white photos.

To create an effect known as B&W with Spot Color or Selective Color, we've used a brush to paint negative Saturation. I've exaggerated the effect for print, but aim for a more subtle touch rather than complete desaturation for a more natural look. Also, avoid desaturating skin when applying this effect, as it always looks odd!

In this photo, we've used the Colorize slider to apply some "pink lipstick." Saturation has also been used to subtly enhance the color of her eyes

LOCAL DETAIL

The *Sharpening, Texture, Noise Reduction* and *Defringe* sliders are ideal for selectively sharpening, blurring, reducing noise and removing colored fringes.

Brushing on **Sharpness** or **Texture** can be useful for sharpening eyes and other facial features without over-sharpening the skin, or enhancing fine texture on specific areas of a photo, such as brickwork.

Moved in the opposite direction, setting the *Sharpness* slider between -50 and -100 applies a blur similar to a lens blur, allowing you to blur the background of a photo.

Negative *Texture* creates a slightly different softening effect, which works brilliantly for smoothing skin without losing its natural texture.

Contrary to the name, the **Noise** slider doesn't add noise, but decreases or increases any global noise reduction that you've applied, for example, the shadows may benefit from extra noise reduction.

The **Defringe** slider can be used to remove color fringes along high contrast edges, or reduce the effect of the Optics panel's *Defringe* sliders (page 262).

The wires of the enclosure walls in the tiger sanctuary are distracting

–Clarity, –Sharpness, –Saturation and –Exposure tone down the background, focusing attention on the tiger

In this grab shot, the camera focused on the grass at the front, so the eyes are soft

A high sharpness value just made it look "crunchy," but a combination of +35 Texture and +35 Clarity works

REDUCING A MOIRÉ PATTERN

The **Moiré** removal slider in the Brush tool allows you to paint a moiré rainbow away. It can only usually remove the color rainbow, not any luminosity changes, but it works very well. It works on both raw and rendered photos, although the additional data in a raw file means that it is far more effective on raw files.

STEP-BY-STEP

1. Temporarily increase the Saturation slider in the Color panel (page 208) to make the moiré easier to see.

2. Open the Brush tool (page 242).

3. Set the *Feather* slider to 0 to create a hard edged brush, adjust the *Size* to suit and turn off *Auto Mask*.

The rainbow-colored pattern sometimes found on fabrics is called moiré. It can't be removed completely, but it can be reduced

4. Set the *Moiré* slider to +100. (If you set the *Moiré* slider to a negative value, it won't do anything—that's only used to reduce the effect of another brush stroke which already has positive moiré removal applied.)

5. Paint carefully over the photo. If you cross a boundary of another color in the photo, it can blur or smudge.

6. Set the Color panel's *Saturation* slider back to your preferred setting for the photo.

7. Reduce the brush selection's *Moiré* slider if the full +100 setting is too strong.

ENHANCING FACES

Most facial retouching can be done faster using a pixel-based editor such as Photoshop, but if you don't have access to such a tool, the brush tool allows you to do some enhancement. Here's a few examples, using a mix of different sliders:

SHARPEN EYES

To sharpen the eyes (or other facial features) without over-sharpening the rest of the face, use a soft-edged brush set to +*Texture* or *Sharpness*.

FIX RED EYE

Red eye—or green eye in dogs—is caused by the flash being too close to the lens. To fix it, use a small, relatively hard edged brush set to roughly -4 *Exposure* and -*Saturation* and paint over the highlight on the pupil.

REDUCE BLOOD SHOT EYES

If the subject's eyes are blood shot, the redness can be reduced using a small brush set to + *Exposure*, + *Shadows* and - *Saturation*.

Exposure and -60 *Saturation*. You may need to increase or decrease the *Exposure* slider to suit the photo.

ENHANCE THE IRIS COLOR

To brighten the iris of the eyes (the colored bit!), paint a selection using a small brush and try settings like +0.35 *Exposure*, +10 *Clarity* and +40 *Saturation*. You might also want to adjust the *Hue* slider to change the color slightly.

WHITEN TEETH

To whiten yellowing teeth, try around +0.20

SOFTEN THE SKIN

To soften skin over the face, use a soft edged brush set to around -70 *Texture* (amount adjusted to taste), avoiding the eyes, eyebrows, nostrils, mouth, hair and clothing. (In the past, -*Clarity* and +*Sharpening* was often used, but -*Texture* looks more natural.)

On page 286, we'll also discuss how to remove blemishes and bags under eyes using the Healing Brush, and then we'll do a start-to-finish edit on page 314.

FIXING DISTORTION

19

Distortions caused by lens imperfections and the angle of the camera are really quick and easy to fix, and can make a big difference to the quality of your photos.

IN THIS SECTION, WE'LL CONSIDER:

• How to remove chromatic aberration and other fringing.

• How to use lens profiles to remove vignetting and barrel/pincushion distortion.

• How to automatically correct geometric distortions.

• How to draw lines on the photo to correct geometric distortions.

• How to manually warp the photo.

∨ Optics

☑ Remove Chromatic Aberration
☑ Enable Lens Corrections   ▾

Adobe (Canon EF 50mm f/2.5 Co... 📷

Distortion... ─────○───── 100

Lens Vigne... ─────○───── 100

⚡ Defringe   ◄

∨ Geometry

Upright Off ∨   ✛

Distortion   ────○──── 0

Vertical   ────○──── 0

Horizontal   ────○──── 0

Rotate   ────○──── 0

Aspect   ────○──── 0

Scale   ────○──── 100

X Offset   ────○──── 0

Y Offset   ────○──── 0

☐ Constrain Crop

REMOVING CHROMATIC ABERRATION & FRINGING

Chromatic aberration, or CA, refers to the little fringes of color that can appear along high contrast edges in your photo. They're caused by the red, green and blue light wavelengths being unable to focus at the same point.

There are two types of chromatic aberration, with slightly different causes and treatments.

Lateral chromatic aberration creates opposing colored fringes, whereas Axial chromatic aberration fringing is a single color

LATERAL CHROMATIC ABERRATION

Lateral or transverse chromatic aberration results from color wavelengths hitting the focal plane next to each other. It causes two different colored fringes (purple/green) to appear on opposite sides of your image details. It's most noticeable around the corners of photos taken with a lower quality wide angle lens, and doesn't appear in the center of the photo.

This type of chromatic aberration is fixed using the **Remove Chromatic Aberration** checkbox in the Optics panel. It's disabled by default as it can slow Lightroom down slightly, and in rare cases may introduce new fringing, but if you find any chromatic aberration in the corners of your photo, simply check the box.

AXIAL CHROMATIC ABERRATION & PURPLE FRINGING

Axial or longitudinal chromatic aberration results from the color wavelengths focusing at different lengths. It causes a halo of a single color—purple in front of the focal plane or green behind it—which can be

Cause of Lateral (Transverse) Chromatic Aberration

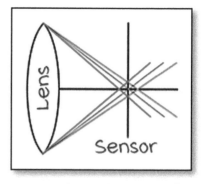

Cause of Axial (Longitudinal) Chromatic Aberration

present anywhere on the photo.

Flare and sensor issues can also cause fringing, usually along high contrast backlit edges, but the treatment of these fringes is the same regardless of the cause.

This type of chromatic aberration is fixed using the **Defringe** sliders and Fringe Selector Tool. These allow you to target specific hues to remove the fringing. (They're currently only available on the desktop apps.)

FRINGE SELECTOR TOOL

The easiest way to select the right hue is using the eyedropper, called the **Fringe Selector** tool.

Click on the eyedropper in the Optics panel and float the cursor over the purple and

green fringes. The edge of the magnified view becomes purple or green, depending on the color of the pixels below. If the edge is white, clicking won't do anything.

The outside of the Fringe Selector changes to purple or green based on the color of the underlying pixels

Click on the purple fringe to automatically remove it, then repeat on the green fringe. When you sample the fringes using the eyedropper, the *Defringe* sliders are automatically adjusted. When you're done, return the eyedropper to its panel (or hit the Escape key).

DEFRINGE (WINDOWS/MAC)

Remove Lateral Chromatic Aberration

Alt/Opt click to Reset

Switch sliders Purple <> Green

Amount of desaturation

Hue range affected

Fringe Selector tool

FINE TUNE USING THE DEFRINGE SLIDERS

If there's a small amount of purple or green fringing still showing, you can fine tune the selection further using the sliders. There are two pairs of sliders, and you can switch between them by clicking on the purple and green circles.

The **Amount** sliders affects the strength of the adjustment, and the **Hue** sliders affects the range of colors being corrected. As you move the *Hue* sliders further apart, the fringe removal affects a wider range of colors.

At first glance, you may be tempted to simply set the *Amount* to the maximum (20) with the widest *Hue* range possible, but doing so would also desaturate the edges of other objects in your image. To avoid this, use the lowest *Amount* and narrowest *Hue* range possible, while still removing the fringing.

Defringe correction can desaturate other edges in your photo, so it must be used with caution

If you're tweaking the sliders manually, the easiest way to check that you've captured all the fringe pixels is to hold down the Alt key (Windows) / Opt key (Mac) while dragging the *Defringe* sliders. The aim is to turn the purple/green fringes black on the masked image.

BRUSH AWAY FRINGING

Another way to avoid this accidental edge desaturation is to limit the correction to a selected area using the Selective Editing tools.

If the **fringing is limited to a small area** of the photo, use a +*Defringe* slider with the Brush tool (page 242) to brush away the fringing, instead of using the global *Defringe* sliders. Positive values on the selective *Defringe* slider remove fringing of any color, not just purple and green, and it's available in the mobile apps as well as the desktop.

If the **fringing affects more of the photo**, use the *Defringe* sliders in the Optics panel to remove the fringing, and then use a -*Defringe* brush to protect areas like the edge of the building from desaturation.

STEP-BY-STEP

Let's put these steps into practice on a real photo...

1. Correct any lens distortion by checking the *Enable Lens Corrections* checkbox in the Optics panel, as the distortion corrections can affect the chromatic aberration. We'll investigate this checkbox in more detail in the next lesson starting on page 266.

2. Enable the **Remove Chromatic Aberration** checkbox to remove the purple and green fringing that's still visible in the corners of the photo.

3. After removing the lateral chromatic aberration, this photo still exhibits purple fringing along the backlit edges. To clearly see the fringe pixels, click on the photo to zoom into 1:1 and then use the keyboard shortcut Ctrl = (Windows) / Cmd = (Mac) to access the hidden 2:1 view.

4. Look around the photo to see whether the fringing is localized (perhaps to a backlit area of the photo) or covers most of the photo.

If the leftover chromatic aberration is limited to a small area, the fringe is not purple/green, or you're using a mobile device, select the brush tool, set it to *+Defringe* and roughly paint the fringe away.

If the leftover fringing is purple or green, and appears across the photo, select the eyedropper from the Optics panel and click on the purple and green fringes. Fine tune the corrections further using the **Defringe** sliders if needed, then check for any edges that need painting back using the brush tool set to *-Defringe*.

FIXING OPTICAL DISTORTION & LENS VIGNETTING

The physical limitations of lenses can create distortion in your images. Lightroom corrects three types of optical distortions— vignetting (darkening around the edges of the photo), barrel and pincushion distortion (curved lines that should be straight) and chromatic aberration (colored halos, which we fixed in the previous lesson). JPEGs are usually fixed by the camera, so these corrections mainly apply to raw files.

This photo has vignetting in the corner and barrel distortion

These distortions can be removed using Lightroom's Optics panel

BUILT-IN LENS CORRECTIONS FOR MIRRORLESS CAMERAS

Most compact and mirrorless cameras have lens profile information embedded in the raw file by the manufacturer and applied by Lightroom. To check which corrections are being automatically corrected, click on

Built-in Lens Profile Applied at the bottom of the Optics panel on a desktop computer. (The information isn't visible on mobile, but the built-in lens profiles are still applied).

The built-in profile can apply corrections for distortion, chromatic aberration and/or vignetting. For example, the Sony RX100 applies corrections for distortion and chromatic aberration behind the scenes, but you might still want to apply a lens profile to remove vignetting.

LENS CORRECTIONS FOR DSLR'S

If you're shooting with a DSLR or another camera that doesn't embed lens data, you can apply a lens profile by checking the

Enable Lens Corrections checkbox.

Lightroom checks the EXIF metadata to try to identify the lens. If it finds a matching profile, it automatically selects the right profile, and fixes the distortions.

Lens metadata standards are quite new, so Lightroom may need some help to identify the right lens. If so, it says ***Change profile....*** (desktop) / ***Manually Select a Profile...*** (Android). (This option isn't currently available on iOS.)

Click on that text to show the Select Lens Profile dialog, then select the correct lens profile in the ***Make, Model*** and ***Profile*** pop-ups.

Some newer mirrorless cameras (added after August 2020) also use the *Enable Lens Corrections* checkbox, even though the lens profile is embedded in the files. This makes it possible to disable the built-in lens corrections. Applicable cameras show *Camera Settings* as the profile name when lens corrections are enabled.

NO PROFILE AVAILABLE

To create a profile, Adobe must have access to the lens, or the manufacturer can create the profile and send it to Adobe. This means that profiles are available for many current lenses, but older lenses may not have profiles.

If your lens doesn't appear in the Lens Profile pop-up menus and isn't built into the image file, you have a couple of different options:

• Wait for Adobe to create a profile for that lens. Lens profiles are being added gradually in each dot release.

• (Advanced users) Switch to the Geometry panel's *Manual Transforms* and adjust the sliders manually (page 271).

Many of the lens profiles are built for raw files only. If a profile is usually available for your lens, check the format of your selected photo in the Info panel (page 95), as it may be a JPEG or TIFF/PSD.

REDUCING THE EFFECT

In some cases, you might want to use some of the profiled correction, but not all of it. For example, if you're using a fisheye lens, you might want to remove the vignetting automatically, but keep the fisheye distortion. The ***Distortion Correction*** and ***Lens Vignetting*** sliders (not currently available on iOS) act as a volume control, increasing or decreasing the amount of profiled correction that's being applied. 0 doesn't apply the correction at all, 100 applies the profile as it was designed, and higher values increase the effect of the correction.

FIXING PERSPECTIVE USING UPRIGHT

If you've ever shot a photo of a building, you've probably noticed it seems to be leaning backwards. This is called keystoning.

To avoid it, you'd have to keep the camera sensor perfectly aligned with the subject, but unless you like to go around climbing trees or you carry an expensive tilt-shift lens, that's probably not realistic. Instead, Lightroom helps you fix the distortion, using a tool called *Upright* in the Geometry panel.

UPRIGHT OPTIONS

In the **Upright** pop-up, there's a series of automatic adjustments:

Off is simple—*Upright* is disabled, so no adjustments are made.

Guided allows you to draw lines directly on the image to show Lightroom which lines

should be horizontal or vertical. We'll come back to this option shortly.

Auto is the most artificially intelligent option. It not only tries to level the photo and correct converging horizontal and vertical lines, but it also takes into account the amount of distortion that's created by the correction. It aims to get the best visual result, even if that's not perfectly straight.

Level only tries to level the photo, fixing tilted horizons or vertical lines. It's similar to straightening the photo when cropping. It doesn't try to adjust for converging lines.

Auto Upright Correction

Full Upright Correction

Vertical not only levels the horizon, but also fixes converging verticals.

Full is the most extreme option. It levels the photos and fixes converging horizontal and vertical lines, even if that means using very strong 3D corrections which distort image features.

More often than not, the *Auto* button gives the best fully automated result.

USING THE GUIDED UPRIGHT TOOL

Upright's Guided mode allows you to draw lines on the image, so you can decide which lines should be vertical or horizontal. The resulting correction is usually better than automatic Upright corrections.

Windows/Mac

1. First, enable the lens profile in the Optics panel (page 266). This results in a more accurate correction.

2. In the Geometry panel, click the **Guided Upright Tool** button, which looks like a hand-drawn + symbol.

Guided Upright tool

3. To **draw a line**, click at the beginning of your vertical or horizontal line (for example, the wall of a building) and drag to the end of the line.

As you float over the photo, the floating Loupe tool displays a zoomed section to help you make an accurate selection.

Click and drag   Zoomed section helps
to draw a line   you draw accurately

Hold down Alt (Windows) / Opt (Mac) to slow down the Upright cursor for greater accuracy.

4. Repeat to add additional lines—a maximum of two horizontal and two vertical. As you add the second and any subsequent lines, Lightroom updates the perspective of the image so you can preview the effect.

5. When you're finished, click on the *Guided Upright Tool* button again to hide the tool.

To **adjust an existing line**, click on the square at the end of the line and move it to a new position.

To **delete a line**, click on it to select it and press the Delete key on the keyboard. To remove all of the lines, right-click on the photo and select *Reset Upright Guides*.

iOS/Android

The principles are the same on mobile, but the interface is slightly different.

1. First, enable the lens profile in the Optics panel (page 266). This results in a more accurate correction.

2. In the Geometry panel, click the **Guided Upright Tool** button, which looks like a hand-drawn + symbol.

Guided Upright tool

3. Drag your finger across the photo to **draw the line**. It's easiest if you zoom in so you can see the line. The two-finger pinch/spread gestures work while the Guided Upright tool is active, or you can turn the *Add Line* button off to move around the photo without drawing accidental lines.

4. Repeat to add additional lines—a maximum of two horizontal and two vertical. As you add the second and any subsequent lines, Lightroom updates the perspective of the image so you can preview the effect.

5. When you're finished, tap the *Done* button.

To **adjust an existing line**, tap on the line to reselect it, then drag the circles at the end of the line and move them to a new position.

To **delete a line**, tap on it to select it and press the Delete (trashcan) icon.

REDUCE THE EFFECT

We're used to seeing converging verticals in everyday life, so full correction can look unnatural. Using the *Manual Transform* sliders, you can adjust individual axes of rotation, reducing their effect. For example, setting the *Vertical* slider to +10 reintroduces some converging verticals, giving a more natural appearance. We'll discuss these sliders in the next lesson (page 271).

CONSTRAIN CROP

When you pull the pixels around to fix the geometry of a photo, white areas appear. You can crop these white areas away manually using the Crop tool (page 153), but the **Constrain Crop** checkbox does it for you automatically. Unchecking the *Constrain Crop* checkbox doesn't remove the crop, but if you don't like the result of the automatic crop, you can adjust it using the Crop tool.

Tap and drag to draw a line

White space caused by distortion correction

Add new line (highlighted) or view only (+ sign only)

Delete selected line

Close Guided Upright tool

FIXING LENS DISTORTION MANUALLY

The *Manual Transform* sliders are not often needed, however they can be useful for slimming people and recovering pixels pushed out of the frame by other lens and perspective corrections.

The **Distortion** slider corrects for barrel or pincushion distortion, which can be useful if you don't have a lens profile. It can also be used to create a fisheye type effect.

The **Vertical** and **Horizontal** sliders adjust for perspective. They're most useful for reducing the effect of Upright corrections, to make it look more natural.

The **Rotate** slider adjusts for camera tilt. It's applied at a much earlier stage in the processing than the crop, with a different result. *Rotate* pivots on the center of the uncropped photo instead of the center of the crop.

If you're using these *Manual* sliders to correct perspective and your camera wasn't level, it's better to use *Upright* or the *Rotate* slider to level the camera rather than *Straighten* in the Crop tool. If you're not using the other *Manual* sliders, don't worry about this slider!

The **Aspect** slider squashes or stretches the photo to improve the appearance. Strong keystone corrections (such as the *Upright* tool) can make a photo look unnatural,

especially when they include people. The slider direction depends on the image rotation, but in most cases, dragging the slider to the left makes things look wider, and dragging the slider to the right makes them look taller and thinner.

Even if you haven't used the other perspective corrections, moving the *Aspect* slider slightly (usually to the right) slims down the subject, reversing "the camera adds 10lbs!"

The **X Offset** and **Y Offset** sliders shift the photo left/right/up/down. This is useful when a geometric adjustment has pushed the important section of the photo out of the frame. The *Offset* sliders move the important section of the photo back into the frame without interpolation, retaining the best image quality possible.

The **Scale** slider shrinks the image within the frame to recover pixels which have been pushed out of the frame by geometric corrections.

Lightroom has to interpolate the data (create new pixels based on surrounding pixels) to resize the image within the frame, which can reduce image quality, so it's best avoided where possible.

Scale can also "zoom in" to remove blank areas of the photo caused by the lens and perspective corrections, however using the Crop tool (page 153) to remove these blank areas maintains the quality, and is therefore a better choice.

STITCHING PANORAMIC PHOTOS

When you see the most incredible view, you may be frustrated to find that you can't fit it all into a single photo.

One option is to use a super wide angle lens. However, this can introduce distortion, and often leaves far too much foreground and sky to crop out, reducing the size of the final photo.

Lightroom's Panorama Merge tool allows you to shoot a series of photos and then merge them into a single large photo. It's currently only available on the Windows/ Mac apps.

If the source photos were captured in the raw file format, other stitching software has to convert the raw data before merging, reducing the dynamic range and applying

the white balance color adjustments to the image data. Lightroom's merge tool, on the other hand, retains the editing flexibility of the original raw files, for the best image quality.

SHOOTING FOR PANORAMIC PHOTOS

Before you can start merging, you need to **shoot some photos**. They must all be the same file type, and ideally captured at the same time using the same camera.

It's best to use a **standard length lens** to minimize distortion, for example, around 20mm-50mm. If you're using a zoom lens, don't zoom in or out between photos.

Remove any filters from your lens,

Shoot multiple photos and merge them using Lightroom

especially polarizers, because they can leave gradients across the finished photo.

You can use the camera's auto/assisted modes to work out the best exposure for the lightest part of the scene, but then, if you can, switch the camera to **manual mode** so the exposure doesn't change for each photo. If you forget, Lightroom does try to normalize the exposures when you merge.

If you can set your camera to **manual focus**, this also helps to maintain the sharpness throughout the photo.

For the best quality, shoot in your camera's **raw file format**. This gives you some flexibility when merging, especially if you've forgotten to switch to Manual mode.

Most photographers shoot from left to right, or right to left, depending on whether they're right or left handed. Some even capture a photo of their hand pointing in the direction of travel, to make it easy to identify the photos they intend to merge later.

As you shoot the pictures, **overlap them** by around 30% so they blend smoothly. For the best results, use a tripod to ensure the photos are correctly aligned. If you're shooting hand-held, leave extra space at the top and bottom to crop out later.

Panoramas don't have to be horizontal. You may shoot a vertical panorama of a tall building, or even shoot multiple rows to create a super-size image for very large prints.

If you're shooting in a very high contrast situation, you can use your camera's **auto exposure bracketing** to capture multiple exposures for each image (discussed on page 200), and then merge these into a panoramic HDR file to retain detail in both

This huge panorama was created using 24 very roughly captured photos, and is now ready to be edited. As a linear DNG, it retains the editing flexibility of the original raw files.

the highlights and the shadows.

PREPARING TO MERGE

There's no need to edit the photos before you merge them, with two exceptions: lens corrections and sensor dust.

Lightroom applies the default **lens profile** and chromatic aberration correction to the raw data before merging the panorama to get the best result, whether you've enabled it for the selected files or not.

Dust or sensor spots appear in the same place on every image, and retouching them individually can take a long time on a huge panorama. You can fix your dust spots on one photo (page 280), paste the corrections to the other photos (page 151), and they'll be applied during the merge process.

One thing to note is that these spot corrections are 'baked in' to the resulting merged image data, so you can't go back and edit them in the finished panorama. Other spots that only need to be removed on a single image are best left until the finished merged image is available.

If you do choose to edit the photos before merging, Lightroom automatically copies the edits from one of the photos onto the merged photo. It skips things like the crop, perspective corrections and local adjustments as these would have a different effect on the merged photo.

Finally, select the photos, right-click and choose *Photo Merge > Panorama Merge* or *HDR Panorama Merge* to open the Panorama Merge dialog. You'll also find these commands under the Photo menu.

Lightroom automatically downloads the originals from the cloud. If the originals are unavailable, perhaps because you're offline, then Smart Previews will be used instead, and the resulting panorama will be smaller.

SELECTING THE PROJECTION

In the Panorama Merge dialog, there are three projection options to choose from:

Spherical aligns and transforms the photos as if they were mapping the inside of a sphere. This is often the best choice for 360° panoramas.

Cylindrical displays the images as if they're on an unfolded cylinder, using the middle image as the reference point

and transforming the photos where they overlap. It reduces the bow-tie type distortion you can get with *Perspective* mode. It's a good choice for most photos, especially wide panoramas.

Perspective uses the middle image as the reference point and transforms the other images where they overlap, but it can result in a bow-tie type distortion. It's better at keeping vertical lines straight, so it's often used for architectural photography.

There's no right or wrong choice here, so just select the one that looks best on your photo. If one projection mode fails to merge, sometimes another one will work.

FILLING THE EDGES

Unless every source photo was perfectly aligned at the time of capture, there will be **blank white areas** around the edges.

One option is to crop the photo to remove these white areas, and the **Auto Crop** checkbox will do this automatically for you. All of the pixel detail is retained and you can reset or edit the crop later using the normal Crop tool.

Alternatively, you can adjust the **Boundary Warp** slider. This analyzes the photo and warps/stretches it to fill the empty space,

When filling the white gaps, a mixture of tools generally works best. Only using Fill Edges on this Perspective merge made a complete mess of the foreground.

but straight lines in the image can become a little wavy.

The **Fill Edges** checkbox uses content aware fill technology to create new pixels to fill the gaps, but its artificial intelligence is limited, so it may create artifacts and blending problems, especially when there are larger areas to fill.

In many cases, the best solution is a mix of tools: bend it a little using *Boundary Warp*, fill in what's left with *Fill Edges*, and manually crop away any leftover distorted areas.

THE RESULTING IMAGE

The resulting panorama is saved as 16-bit

DNG file. Lightroom automatically adds -pano to the end of the filename to help identify them, and displays a thumbnail badge. If you were viewing an album, the source photos are automatically stacked, with the merged panorama at the top of the stack.

There is a limit to the file size that Lightroom can handle. Photos have to be no more than 65,000 pixels along the longest edge or no more than 512 megapixels, whichever is smaller. Large panoramas can sometimes hit these limits, but Lightroom automatically shrinks them to fit, so you don't have to think about it.

The photo can be edited using the normal editing tools, however Lightroom may feel a little slower to respond, due to the size of the image.

STEP-BY-STEP

There's a set of photos in the demo images download in the Members Area, so let's give it a try:

1. Select a series of photos. The order of the photos in the Filmstrip doesn't matter,

Panorama badge   Stack

as Lightroom matches the photos visually.

2. Right-click on the photos and select *Photo Merge > Panorama Merge* or *HDR Panorama Merge*.

3. Select a projection mode that looks good.

4. Check the *Auto Crop* checkbox to remove the blank white space, drag the *Boundary Warp* slider to warp the photo to fill the white space, check the *Fill Edges* checkbox, or combine settings for the best result.

5. Click *Merge* to created the stitched file.

RETOUCHING DISTRACTIONS

20

Retouching has long been the domain of pixel-based photo editors such as Photoshop, but Lightroom has advanced healing tools that can remove many distractions without a round trip to Photoshop.

The Healing Brush can remove sensor dust spots in the sky, litter on the ground, rain drops on the lens, acne on faces, or even more complex distractions. If there's something more complicated to retouch, Lightroom can send the photo to Photoshop.

PROS AND CONS

There are pros and cons to retouching in Lightroom. Being able to edit the raw file in Lightroom means you don't need another large TIFF file taking up space in the cloud or on your hard drive, and it's non-destructive,

so you can go back and change your edits again later.

On the down side, Lightroom is a parametric editor, which means it has to constantly re-run text instructions, so it gets slower with the more local adjustments (spots, brushes) that you apply.

The point where a pixel editor becomes more efficient than Lightroom depends on your computer hardware, as well as the retouching you're trying to do. As a rule of thumb, when it gets frustrating, stop and switch to Photoshop!

IN THIS SECTION, WE'LL CONSIDER:

• How to retouch spots as well as larger distractions using Lightroom.

• How to send a photo to Photoshop for more extensive editing.

RETOUCHING SPOTS

The Healing Brush is ideal for removing distractions against plain backgrounds, such as sensor dust in the sky. We'll look at more complex retouching in the next lesson, but first, let's get an overview of how the Healing Brush works.

HEALING SPOTS

To **open the Healing Brush tool** and show the Healing Brush panel on the desktop, click the icon in the right panel bar or press the H key.

← Healing Brush

On mobile, select the Healing tool from the Edit view toolbar.

↳ Select the Healing tool

Lightroom can do two different kinds of repair, selected using the **Mode** pop-up on the desktop, or using the buttons on mobile.

← Heal
← Clone

Clone simply picks up the pixels and drops them in another location.

Heal attempts to intelligently match the texture, lighting and shading to blend the repaired pixels seamlessly into the surrounding area.

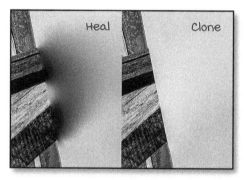
Heal   Clone

Against hard edges, Heal mode can smudge, so Clone is a better choice

HEALING BRUSH (WINDOWS/MAC)

Healing mode (Clone vs. Heal)

Brush Size

Brush Feathering

Opacity of Heal

Visualize Spots

Visualize Spots Threshold

Reset Healing Brush

Open Healing Brush

For most spots, the *Heal* option works best, particularly in clean areas such as sky. If you're trying to retouch a spot along an edge in the photo, for example, a roof line against the sky, the *Heal* tool can smudge, in which case the *Clone* option may work better.

CHOOSING THE RIGHT BRUSH

Before you start retouching, you need to decide on the size and feathering of the brush you'll use.

On the desktop, these are controlled using sliders in the Healing Brush panel, and the size and feathering are previewed on the cursor, with two lines close together for minimal feathering, and further apart for greater feathering.

On mobile, hold your finger on the *Size*, *Feather* or *Opacity* icon and drag up or down to increase or decrease the slider value. The numeric value displays at the top of the screen, and a red preview displays in the center of the screen, so you can see how big or hard the brush will be.

Size runs from 0, which is a tiny brush, to a maximum size of 100. On the desktop, you can also use the [and] keyboard shortcuts or your mouse scroll wheel to adjust the size.

Feather runs from 1, which is a hard edged brush, to 100 which is soft. On the desktop, the Shift-[and Shift-] keys also adjust the feathering.

A *Clone* spot stands out if it has hard edges, so select a higher feathering value, such as 90-100. The *Heal* mode works best with *Feather* set to 0 as it automatically attempts to blend the edges into the surroundings. If you feather a *Heal* spot, you may end up with unhealed patches in the center of the healed area.

To prevent gaps in the middle of repaired areas, set feathering to 0 when using Heal mode

The **Opacity** slider allows you to fade the retouching, for example, you may not want to completely remove the lines on a person's face, but just fade them slightly. If you want to remove a blemish completely, leave it set to 100.

DRAWING SPOTS

There are two kinds of spot repair that you can apply to your photo, depending on whether the distraction is circular or not.

To **create a circle spot**, for example, to remove sensor dust, simply click/tap on the distraction. Circle spots display as single

HEALING BRUSH (IOS/ANDROID)

Undo/Redo

Full screen view

Heal mode

Clone mode

Brush Size

Feather (brush softness)

Opacity

Brush spot pin

Circle spot pin

Arrow shows source > target

Tap on pin to reselect it

Drag pin to move spot

Hold finger on pin to view menu

Heal ✓
Clone
Delete
Reset Healing Brush

Hold finger on buttons and drag up/down to adjust

Delete spot

Tap to confirm the changes or cancel. (Buttons at the top on Android, or a Done button on tablets)

Healing Brush

round spots and they can be moved and resized later.

To **create a brush spot** (non-circular healing), click/tap and drag over the distraction. A brush stroke appears, and it's then replaced by two white outlines showing the source and target. Brush spots can have an arbitrary shape, and you can change the feathering after creation, but the brush stroke can't be resized later.

To create straight lines on the desktop, click at the beginning of the line to create a circle spot, and then hold down the Shift key and click at the end of the line. Lightroom joins

the spots using a straight brush spot. It's a handy trick for power or telephone lines.

When you create a circle or brush spot, Lightroom intelligently searches for the most suitable **source of replacement pixels**, even if that's outside of the current crop boundary. If the suggested replacement pixels are not a great match, press the / key to make Lightroom try again (desktop only), or click and drag the source spot to a better source.

It's easiest to zoom in before creating the brush spot, so you can see the photo in detail. On the desktop, hold down the

Source of new pixels   Retouched area

Spacebar while clicking and dragging, to move around the photo without accidentally creating extra spots. On mobile, pinch, spread and drag the photo around using two fingers.

STEP-BY-STEP

We'll look at more complex retouching in the next lesson, but for now, let's focus on sensor dust and other distractions against plain backgrounds, such as this one:

1. Select the Healing Brush tool.

2. Using the options in the Healing Brush panel, set the brush options to:

Mode: Heal

Size: to suit the size of the distraction

Feather: 0 (because we're using Heal)

Opacity: 100 (because we want the distraction completely gone)

3. Click/tap on the spot in the photo.

4. The spot overlay appears on the screen, showing the outline of the retouched area and the source of the new pixels. Lightroom automatically tries to find a good source, but you can drag the overlays to fine tune the correction.

5. For non-circular distractions, click/tap and drag over the distraction to display the overlay, then drag the overlays to find a good source.

EDITING EXISTING SPOTS

Because Lightroom is a non-destructive editor, you can come back and change your retouching later.

To **find existing retouched spots**, you'll need to see the overlay. If it isn't showing on the desktop, press the O key and float the cursor over the photo.

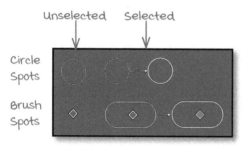

The pins and overlays look slightly different on mobile.

To **resize a circle spot** on the desktop, hover over the edge of the outline, so the cursor changes to a double-headed arrow, and then drag the edge to adjust the size.

On mobile, select the circle spot and then drag up/down on the brush size icon. (Remember you can't resize non-circular brush strokes.)

To **move a spot**, drag the center of a spot or its source to a new location.

To **delete a spot** on the desktop, click on the spot to make it active, and then press the Delete key on your keyboard, or right-click on the spot to delete using the menu. On mobile, select the pin and then tap the trashcan icon.

To **delete multiple spots** on the desktop, hold down the Alt key (Windows) / Opt key (Mac) so the cursor changes to a pair of scissors, then drag a rectangular shape around the spots to delete them.

To **delete all spots**, press the *Reset* button in the Healing Brush panel on the desktop, or hold your finger on a pin and select *Reset Healing Brush* from the menu.

DON'T MISS A SPOT

On the desktop, there's a handy trick to view the entire photo at 1:1 zoom without missing any spots. Zoom into 1:1 and view the top left corner and then press the Page Down key (Windows) / Fn down arrow key (Mac). Lightroom divides the photo up into an imaginary grid, so when you reach the bottom of the first column, it automatically returns to the top of the photo and starts on the next column. By the time you reach the bottom right corner, you'll have checked the entire photo without missing any spots.

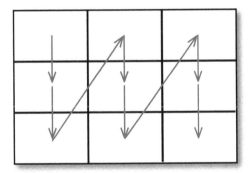

VISUALIZE SPOTS

By checking the **Visualize Spots** checkbox in the Healing Brush panel (desktop only), Lightroom displays a black and white edge mask of your photo, which makes it easier to spot any dust spots. You can adjust the **Threshold** slider to increase or decrease the amount of white borders displayed.

ADVANCED RETOUCHING USING LIGHTROOM

In the previous lesson, we learned how to remove simple distractions using the Healing Brush tool, but it gets more complicated when the distraction isn't on a plain background or borders against something else.

REMOVING LARGE DISTRACTIONS AND EDGES

Complicated distractions are quicker and easier to retouch using a pixel-based editing tool such as Photoshop, but with a bit of patience, it is possible to do it in Lightroom. The trick is to chop the distraction up into bite-size pieces, and handle each section individually.

The duck photo-bombed this photo of a pelican, so let's remove him...

If we just brush up to the edge of the beak and sign in *Heal* mode, it leaves a dark smudge, but using *Clone* mode doesn't match the texture and leaves harsh edges.

Retouching against an edge using Heal mode leaves a dark smudge

What we need is the best of both worlds. To remove the duck, we'll use both the *Clone* and *Heal* modes.

1. Use two thin *Clone* lines along the edge of the beak and sign. When you then paint a large *Heal* stroke over the duck's head and body, and slightly overlap the these *Clone* strokes, you'll get a much cleaner result, as there won't be any adjacent dark pixels to smudge.

Retouch the edge using Clone lines to create a clean boundary

2. In this case, there's only one suitable small clone source to the right of the duck's head, which isn't big enough to clone over his whole head and body. To solve this, we'll divide him up using additional *Clone* strokes.

Add additional Clone lines to divide the area into smaller chunks if it's too big

3. Brush over the individual duck sections one at a time using a *Heal* brush, slightly overlapping the clone dividers. This step is tricky, because Lightroom tries to select the existing brush strokes when you get close to them. Start the brush stroke from the center of the section and brush toward the *Clone* strokes, and zoom in closer if necessary.

Use Heal brush strokes to fill each individual section, overlapping the clone strokes

4. Additional strokes can be used to heal any leftover artifacts. Repeat the same process for the duck's body and legs to remove him completely.

RETOUCHING FACES

Faces also need slightly more advanced retouching. For softening skin, brightening eyes, whitening teeth and similar retouching, you'll need to use the Selective Editing tools (page 259). Spot removal, however, can be useful for reducing wrinkles and bags under eyes and removing pimples and scars.

If you remove bags and wrinkles completely, it looks unnatural, so try a brush set to *Clone* mode, and reduce the *Opacity* to around 20-25. Select a source that's similar in tone and texture, such as the skin immediately underneath.

For blemishes, use a *Heal* brush slightly larger than the pimple, set to full *Opacity*. (Severe acne may still need the power of Photoshop.)

SENDING PHOTOS TO PHOTOSHOP ON THE DESKTOP

Lightroom offers a wide range of tools to cater for most of your editing needs, but sometimes you'll need a pixel-based photo editor such as Photoshop. For example:

• Swapping heads, changing backgrounds and merging photos are jobs for Photoshop.

• Some distractions, such as flare on glasses, can be reduced in Lightroom, but can be removed more effectively in Photoshop.

• Removing some distractions, particularly when they're on a complex or detailed background, is much faster and easier in Photoshop.

• Doing lots of retouching on a single photo is faster in Photoshop, as Lightroom slows

down with lots of edits.

Lightroom and Photoshop handle the color and file management, so you only need to worry about editing skills. Since this is not a Photoshop book, we won't go into detail, but we'll learn how to hand the files off to Photoshop...

The signs, van and people couldn't have been easily removed using Lightroom alone

LIGHTROOM EDITS FIRST

Lightroom's editing tools work best on raw files, because they have the largest amount of data available. For this reason, it's usually best to do most (if not all) of your Lightroom adjustments before moving to Photoshop or other editing software.

There are a couple of exceptions:

• You may prefer to leave cropping until after your external edits, leaving you the flexibility to non-destructively crop to different ratios without having to repeat your retouching and other edits.

• If the photo is going to be in both B&W and color, you may want to retouch the color version and then convert the retouched TIFF to B&W so that you only have to do the retouching once.

• If your photo was shot in JPEG, or it's a scan, the workflow order isn't as important. For example, you may decide to retouch dust on negative scans in Photoshop before adding them to Lightroom.

SENDING PHOTOS TO PHOTOSHOP

To open a photo in Photoshop (CS6 or later), right-click and select **Edit in Photoshop** or use the shortcut Ctrl-Shift-E (Windows) / Cmd-Shift-E (Mac). You'll also find it in the *File* menu. The photo opens in Photoshop with your Lightroom edits applied. Leave Lightroom open in the background so it can keep track of the file and automatically add it to your library.

REDUCING FILE SIZE

By default, Lightroom opens the photo in Photoshop as a 16-bit ProPhoto RGB file, which it then saves a TIFF.

16-bit ProPhoto RGB TIFFs are the best choice for quality, retaining the largest amount of data and smooth color gradations (e.g. in the sky). However, they're large files, especially when you add layers, so they'll take up a lot of space in the cloud.

If it's your favorite photo, and you've spent hours working on it in Photoshop, keep the full 16-bit TIFFs, because it leaves your options open for the future. However, if you only flipped into Photoshop to quickly remove a distraction, and you're just going to post it on social media, you may decide to reduce the file size before saving the photo. To do so, follow these steps in Photoshop:

1. Go to *Image menu > Convert to Profile > Adobe RGB* (because ProPhotoRGB is too wide a color space for an 8-bit file).

2. Go to *Image menu > Mode > 8-Bits/Channel* to reduce the bit depth.

3. If you no longer need the layers, go to *Layers menu > Flatten Image* to flatten the layers.

RETURNING TO LIGHTROOM

To return to Lightroom after editing in Photoshop, go to *File menu > Save.* This saves the file back to Lightroom with *-Edit* on the end of the file name. You can use *Save As* to change the file name if you prefer, but don't change the file type or Lightroom will lose track of it.

Close the file in Photoshop and switch back to Lightroom. The edited photo is automatically stacked on top of the original in the selected album and *All Photos,* but not in other albums.

RETAINING LAYERS

If you open a layered TIFF/PSD into Photoshop again later, the behavior depends on whether you've done further editing in Lightroom:

If you haven't edited the TIFF/PSD in Lightroom, it opens in Photoshop with its layers intact.

If you've applied edits to the TIFF/PSD in Lightroom, the layers are flattened when you open it in Photoshop.

SENDING PHOTOS TO OTHER EDITING APPS ON MOBILE

Like the desktop version, there are occasions when you might want to switch to a pixel-based editing app.

Photoshop aims to bring many of the desktop Photoshop features to the iPad. It's early days, but it shows great promise.

Photoshop Express creates collages, adds text and borders, and applies graphical watermarks.

EDIT IN PHOTOSHOP ON IPAD

There's a direct link from Lightroom to Photoshop on iPad.

1. In Detail view, tap on the cloud icon and ensure that *Local* says you're viewing the *Original* format. If it says *Smart Preview*, tap on **Get This Original** to download the full size file.

If *Get This Original* is missing, the full resolution image isn't available to download, because you've uploaded it using Lightroom Classic. You can still send the photo to Photoshop, but the image will be a maximum of 2560px long edge.

2. Tap on the Share menu and select **Edit In Photoshop**.

 ← Share menu

3. The image opens into Photoshop, where you can edit to your heart's content.

4. When you've finished editing, you have three choices:

Cancel asks for confirmation and then closes the document without saving your edits.

Send to Lightroom saves the file as a PSD file with *-Edit* at the end of the filename, and returns the image to Lightroom. If you were viewing the photo in an album, the edited copy is automatically added to the album too.

... > Create Photoshop cloud document saves your edited photo to Photoshop's Cloud Documents storage space (found at https:// assets.adobe.com/cloud-documents). This is useful if you want to continue editing the same layered file in Photoshop later, before manually sending it back to your Lightroom library.

SEND AN IMAGE FROM PHOTOSHOP TO LIGHTROOM ON IPAD

If you've been working on a photo that's stored in Photoshop's Cloud Documents space, and then want to send it to your Lightroom Catalog, you can use Photoshop's share sheet.

1. Tap on the Share menu and select *Publish and Export*.

2. If you've used layers in Photoshop, select the TIFF or PSD format. If the finished photo is flattened, you may save it back as a JPEG (quality 12) file, which will be much smaller than a TIFF.

3. Select the Lightroom app from the Share sheet. If the icon isn't available, scroll along to *More* to find it.

4. Tap *Launch Lightroom Now* to complete the file transfer.

The edited file appears in the *Recently Added* album as well as *All Photographs*.

OPEN IN OTHER PHOTO EDITING APPS

On Android, and for other photo editing apps on iOS, you'll need to copy the photo to the app via the Share sheet. To do so...

1. From Detail view, tap on the Share menu.

2. Tap the Presets icon next to *Open In* (iOS) / *Share To...* (Android). On iOS, the file type settings you choose will depend on the editing app. Android always sends a full resolution JPEG. Turn off the watermark, include all of the metadata and in most cases, disable output sharpening.

3. Select *Open In* (iOS) / *Share To...* (Android) to show available apps.

4. Select the app of your choice, for example, Photoshop Express. The options will depend on which photo editing apps are installed on your device, and you may need to swipe through the apps or press the *More* button to find the app you require.

5. When you've finished editing save the result back to the camera roll (iOS) / gallery (Android) and add it to Lightroom.

START-TO-FINISH EDITS

21

So far, we've learned how to use the sliders individually and how they interact within their panels.

Now it's time to start putting it all together and edit a series of photos from start to finish, using a whole range of different tools.

We'll start each lesson with an image analysis, and then briefly cover the thought process behind each slider adjustment.

You can download most of these images from the Members Area, so you can follow along on your own computer.

You might prefer a different end result, and that's fine, because editing is subjective and we're all continually learning and changing.

IN THIS SECTION, WE'LL CONSIDER:

• How to edit a whole range of photos using different Lightroom tools.

EARLY MORNING COUNTRYSIDE

No true black, but
otherwise good range

TECHNICAL

Exposure

Underexposed, very
flat, no true black.

Color

Needs warming, and more vibrant.

Detail

Shot at low ISO, so no notable noise,
and using fast shutter speed.

Optical & Geometric Distortion

Micro four thirds, so lens
corrections automatically applied.

Sensor Dust

None noted.

Output

Lounge wall, 20"x 16".

ARTISTIC INTENT

Purpose

I liked the empty winding road
leading off into the rolling
hills in the background.

Story

Early morning solitude.

Mood/Emotion

Peaceful, soft.

Simplify the Scene & Draw the Eye

Couple of road signs are
distracting and need removing.

Draw the eye along the road and
the fence towards the rolling hills.

1. Change the profile to **Adobe Landscape** to enhance colors and detail in the greenery.

    Steps 1–5 brightness/ contrast adjustments

2. **Highlights -80** to pull back the cloud detail.

3. **Shadows +45** to bring out verge detail.

4. **Whites +23** & **Blacks -50** to bring back global contrast.

5. **Clarity +70** to add more local contrast to highlight the textures.

    Steps 6–7 color adjustments

6. **Temp 6100** to warm it up.

7. **Vibrance +50** to make the colors more punchy.

8. **Linear Gradient** from top to half way down, with central line on horizon, set to *Temp -10, Exposure -0.20, Clarity 100* to enhance the cloud detail and reduce the yellow in the sky.

    Step 8 Linear Gradient (red mask shown)

9. **Sharpen 50, Radius 0.8, Masking 77** to sharpen the foreground without over-sharpening the sky.

10. **Healing Brush** to remove distracting road signs and debris on the road.

11. **Crop** to 4x5 ratio for 16"x20" print.

    Steps 9–11 Sharpen, retouch & crop

KANIKA THE LEOPARD CUB

Highlights are clipped

TECHNICAL

Exposure

Cub is too dark as in the shadows, but foreground is too bright. Some detail in the leaves is clipped.

Color

Needs increase of saturation and warmth to enhance cub's coat.

Detail

Sharpen to highlight whiskers. High ISO and heavy crop will make noise more noticeable.

Optical & Geometric Distortion

Not needed.

Sensor Dust

None found.

Output

Square crop to match set.

ARTISTIC INTENT

Purpose

Create ongoing series of photos of Kanika growing up.

Story

This was Kanika's first trip out of her den, so she was shy but also inquisitive and playful.

Mood/Emotion

Excitement of first outing, so use plenty of contrast and punchy colors.

Simplify the Scene & Draw the Eye

Needs a heavy crop to remove excess background and zoom in on leopard cub.

Reduce brightness of foreground to reduce distraction.

Lighten cub's face to draw the eye toward her.

1. **Crop** first to zoom in on subject.

2. **Exposure +0.80** to brighten overall.

Steps 1–5
incl. Crop
& tonal
adjustments

3. **Highlights -100** to reduce glare of light falling through the tress.

4. **Shadows +80** to bring up the shadow detail.

5. **Blacks -60** to bring back the contrast lost by *Highlights/Shadows* adjustments.

6. **Clarity +54** to add punch and bring out the detail in the cub's coat.

Steps 6–9
incl. Clarity
& color
adjustments

7. **Contrast +8** to add midtone contrast.

8. **Temp 4577** and **Tint +31** to warm it up, as auto white balance left the photo too cool.

9. **Vibrance +48** and **Saturation +9** to bring out the color in her coat.

Steps 10–12
Selective
edits

10. **Radial Gradient** set to -1.84 *Exposure*, -73 *Contrast*, -100 *Highlights*, -52 *Clarity* to create an off-center vignette, drawing the eye to the cub.

11. **Brush** set to *Temp +10, Contrast +20* and *Saturation +32*, brushed over the cub's face and legs to warm her up further.

12. **Healing Brush** used to patch the light patch on her den to reduce the distraction.

Step 13
Noise
Reduction

13. **Noise Reduction +25** to minimize noise.

14. **Send to Photoshop**. The leaves at the front were completely clipped, and trying to recover them has just turned them gray, but these could be retouched using Photoshop.

SUNSET AT STEEPHILL COVE

Full range of tones, but not a lot in the midtones

TECHNICAL

Exposure

Shadows need brightening, while retaining highlight detail.

Color

The sun had already set, so light was cool, but clouds in the sky would look great warmer.

Detail

Slight noise on the rocks, but it just adds texture.

Optical & Geometric Distortion

Some barrel distortion. Chromatic aberration visible along tree line.

Sensor Dust

Spots in the sky on the right.

Output

Framed print on the lounge wall.

ARTISTIC INTENT

Purpose

Capture this pretty hidden cove at sunset.

Story

This perfect little cove can't be reached by road, so at the end of the day, when everyone's gone home, it's a beautiful little spot.

Mood/Emotion

Relaxed and peaceful, but wonder at the power of the waves and beauty of the sunset.

Simplify the Scene & Draw the Eye

Start with the eye on the setting sun (warmth, brightness), then go to the warm reflection, then the buildings (bright) then run round the curve of the rocks (lines, contrast, reflected warmth).

1. Change the profile to **Adobe Vivid**, as we want to enhance the sunset.

2. **Straighten 0.80**, using *Straighten* tool to draw line down central building.

3. **Healing Brush** (*Heal, size 46, feather 0, opacity 100*) to remove spots in sky.

4. **Enable Profile Corrections** (Canon 18-200) to remove barrel distortion and check **Remove Chromatic Aberration**.

⌐ Steps 1–6 incl. Highlights & Shadows

5. **Highlights -100** to recover and enhance the detail in the sky and **Shadows -80** to bring out detail in rocks and houses.

6. **Whites +14** so the sun is just short of clipping and **Blacks -26** blocks the darkest shadows in the rocks, where I'm willing to sacrifice the detail to increase the overall contrast.

⌐ Steps 7–8 Clarity & Saturation

7. **Clarity +100** is an extreme adjustment, but it's just flat and boring, and using too much *Contrast* would lose sky/rocks detail. The local contrast created strong halos along the tree line, so I reduce it with a soft **-Highlights -Whites brush**.

8. **Saturation +70** to make it much more colorful. *Vibrance* would have enhanced the blues on the building and protected the yellows, whereas I want to pump up the yellow tones. Doing this before white balance will help me set *Temp & Tint* to taste.

⌐ Steps 9–10 White Balance & Vignette

9. **Temp 5450** and **Tint +18** to warm it up.

10. **Vignette -30** with **Feather 70** to bring down the brightness of the corners, especially on the left.

11. It's still a little flat and dark, so **Contrast +20** and **Exposure +0.20** to finish.

⌐ Step 11 Contrast & Exposure

UNDERGROUND HOSPITAL

↑ Slight spike of white strip light, and some blocked blacks ↑

TECHNICAL

Exposure

Exposure's not bad, but enhance the shadow detail in the walls. Light is clipped, but that's expected.

Color

Adjust white balance to cool blues.

Detail

It was shot at ISO 800 on a small sensor, so it is noisy, but that adds to the gritty dramatic feel.

Optical & Geometric Distortion

Micro four thirds, so no profile needed.

Sensor Dust

None found.

Output

Portfolio?

ARTISTIC INTENT

Purpose

Capture the eerie feeling and interesting lines.

Story

This was an underground hospital in Guernsey used to care for German soldiers during World War 2.

Mood/Emotion

It was cold, damp and eerie. I'd have hated to be a patient there! Enhance that feeling using cool blues.

Simplify the Scene & Draw the Eye

The lines of the tunnel lead the eye towards the person at the end, but could do with enhancing.

There's a fire exit sign which wouldn't have been there in the 1940's.

1. **Exposure -0.25** because it's a little bright.

Step 1 Exposure →

2. **Temp 2400** and **Tint +22** to make it a really cool blue.

3. **Clarity +40** to bring out the detail in the brickwork and increase the "wet" look.

4. **Healing Brush** used to remove the fire exit sign.

5. **Send to Photoshop**. The man at the end of the tunnel was pulling up his sock, so I'd also take the photo to Photoshop to move his leg too.

Step 2 White Balance →

Step 3 Clarity →

Step 4 Healing Brush →

NIGHTTIME COBBLES

Blue channel clipping in the shadows

TECHNICAL

Exposure

Overall exposure is ok but enhance shadow detail.

Color

Yellow street lighting doesn't add anything. B&W would enhance lines of cobbles and texture of brickwork.

Detail

No notable noise, but sharpen to enhance local contrast.

Optical & Geometric Distortion

Micro four thirds, so already applied.

Sensor Dust

None found.

Output

Wall with other B&W photos.

ARTISTIC INTENT

Purpose

To illustrate the timeless beauty of the historic English town of Bath, with its detailed architecture and cobbled streets.

Story

Welcome home!

Mood/Emotion

A quiet street in the middle of town, but still felt quite safe.

Simplify the Scene & Draw the Eye

Enhance the diagonal lines of the wet cobbles, leading toward the light and doorway.

Crop to remove some of the blank wall on the right to draw the eye to light at the end of the alleyway and the doorway.

Darken the light slab on the left.

1. **Highlights -34** to reduce the glare of the light.

2. **Shadows +100** to bring out the detail in the cobbles & brickwork.

    Steps 1-5 Brightness/ contrast adjustments →

3. **Whites +56** and **Blacks -3** to bring back the contrast lost by *Highlights* and *Shadows*.

4. **Clarity +100** to enhance the local contrast further.

5. **Contrast +22** to add a little more global contrast.

    Step 6 Fix white balance →

6. **Temp 2500** and **Tint +34** to remove the worst of the strong yellow color cast.

7. **Upright Auto** to straighten it.

8. **Crop** to remove the brickwork on the right.

9. Switch to **B&W** mode. I like the default **Adobe Monochrome** conversion, and playing with the B&W mix doesn't improve it due to the lack of different colors in the original capture.

    Steps 7-9 Geometric corrections, crop and B&W conversion →

10. **Dehaze +13** to add a little more local contrast.

    Steps 10-13 Selective Edits →

11. **Vignette -21** to darken the corners and draw the eye into the photo.

12. **Healing Brush** to remove alarm on wall.

13. **Brush** (*Highlights -100 Whites -100*) to darken slab on left that now stands out.

THE HUNGRY CATERPILLAR

Great tonal range, no true black

TECHNICAL

Exposure

Whites are a little bright, but otherwise pretty good.

Color

White balance is good, but increase vibrancy of yellows.

Detail

Sharpen carefully to enhance fine hairs.

Optical & Geometric Distortion

Micro four thirds, so automatically applied.

Sensor Dust

None found.

Output

Nothing specific.

ARTISTIC INTENT

Purpose

Capture the incredible detail of this scary little beast.

Story

I had a new camera and wanted to try the automatic focus stacking, and this little guy was busy eating all the leaves on my birch tree.

Mood/Emotion

Awe at the amount of detail on this tiny little creature.

Simplify the Scene & Draw the Eye

Reduce the brightness of the white background. Focus attention on the tiny hairs.

1. **Exposure -0.20** to reduce brightness slightly.

2. **Highlights -25** and **Shadows +15** to bring back a little more detail.

Steps 1-4 Brightness & Contrast

3. Since this is a JPEG, there's no detail to recover in the clipped highlights, so **Whites -15** just brings down their brightness slightly.

4. **Blacks -20** to make some pixels truly black.

5. **Temp +3** to warm it up very slightly and **Vibrance +15** to strengthen the yellow.

Step 5 Color Adjustments

6. **Clarity +30** to add more definition, especially to the fine hairs.

7. **Radial Filter** on the caterpillar, set to *Exposure +0.50, Clarity +48, Sharpness +20* and *Saturation +25.*

Steps 6-8 Clarity & Selective Edits

8. Second **Radial Filter inverted** to affect the background, set to *Exposure -0.80, Clarity -84, Saturation -57.*

9. **Vignette -28, Midpoint +60, Roundness -46** to reduce the edge distractions.

10. **Healing Brush** to remove the tiny brown spots on the leaf.

Steps 9-10 Vignette & Healing brush

SUNNY COAST

Low dynamic range

TECHNICAL

Exposure

A little too bright, very hazy
and lacking contrast.

Color

White balance is about right, but I'd
like a little more depth to the color.

Detail

Sharpen to bring out the
detail in the stones.

Optical & Geometric Distortion

Some vignetting visible,
apply lens profile.

Sensor Dust

None found.

Output

Framed print on the wall.

ARTISTIC INTENT

Purpose

Capture the lovely cove
where we stopped for lunch.
Loved the turquoise blue sea
against the green grass.

Story

A peaceful walk along the
coast on a summer's day.

Mood/Emotion

Warm, happy, majestic.

Simplify the Scene & Draw the Eye

Too much sky, crop some out.

Focus on the island outcrop
between the two coves.

Highlight the movement in the sea.

1. Apply **Camera Landscape** profile, because the stones are too red in *Adobe Landscape*.

2. **Enable Lens Corrections** to remove vignetting and distortion.

3. **Dehaze +40** to reduce the atmospheric haze.

4. **Highlights -100** to bring detail back into the waves on the shoreline.

5. **Shadows +40** to increase detail in the rock face.

6. **Auto Whites +17** and **Blacks -56** to expand the tonal range, compressing the deepest shadows.

7. **Brush** over breaking waves and rocks with +100 *Clarity* for impact.

8. **Crop** to 16x9 ratio for panoramic effect.

Steps 1-2 Profile & Lens Profile

Step 3 Dehaze

Steps 4-6 Tonal Adjustments

Step 7-8 Selective Edits & Crop

KIDS LOVE BOXES!

Data to left of histogram
= photo is dark

ARTISTIC INTENT

Purpose

Capture the little girl having fun.

Story

Every child loves a cardboard box!

Mood/Emotion

Cute, mischievous.

Simplify the Scene & Draw the Eye

Remove distraction of tear and slot so eye goes to her face instead of the bright spots.

TECHNICAL

Exposure

It's underexposed and lacking contrast.

Color

White balance isn't great, and the color doesn't really add to the photo, so try in B&W.

Detail

Very high ISO (6400 on a micro four thirds sensor) so lots of noise reduction needed.

Optical & Geometric Distortion

Profile applied automatically but needs straightening.

Sensor Dust

None found.

Output

Framed shelf portrait.

1. **Exposure +0.50** as underexposed.

2. **Auto Whites +15** and **Auto Blacks -22** to expand to fill tonal range. *Steps 1-4 → Brightness & color*

3. **Clarity +20** to add contrast. No wrinkles to worry about here, and it'll enhance the lines in the box.

4. **Temp 3050** and **Tint -1** to improve white balance to give a cleaner starting point for the B&W conversion.

5. Convert to **B&W** by selecting the **B&W Orange Filter** profile, because red/orange filters traditionally lightened skin tones. *Step 5 B&W →*

6. **Linear Gradient** diagonally from bottom left corner, set to *Exposure -1.27* and *Clarity +88* to even up the lighting. **Brush** to lighten and define eyes slightly, set to *Exposure +0.3* and *Clarity +10*.

7. **Healing Brush** set to *Clone* mode to retouch the top and bottom of bright line, as *Heal* mode would smudge where it meets other image detail. Then use *Heal* mode for the rest of the bright line and tear in the box. (Due to the noise levels, Photoshop would work better.) *Step 6-7 → Selective edits & retouching*

8. **Noise Reduction 35** to reduce high ISO noise. (*Color Noise Reduction* is fine at the default of 25.)

9. **Crop** to straighten lines and remove bright knees. *Steps 8-9 → Noise Reduction & Crop*

ORANGE WINDOWS

Lacking pure white. After crop,
may not have pure black either

TECHNICAL

Exposure

Needs a little more contrast.

Color

White balance is good, but
shift orange tones toward red
to fit in with office decor.

Detail

Light noise reduction
as small sensor.

Optical & Geometric Distortion

Major geometric distortions.

Sensor Dust

None found.

Output

Abstract square print for office wall.

ARTISTIC INTENT

Purpose

I was waiting for a bus and noticed
these odd orange windows. No
time to compose properly, but I
thought they could be interesting.

Story

Unusual abstract pattern to these
windows. Architect with imagination!

Mood/Emotion

Hard, clean, repetitive pattern.

Simplify the Scene & Draw the Eye

Needs a heavy crop to
emphasize the repetition.

1. Draw four **Guided Upright** lines using the windows for guides to correct the geometric distortion.

2. **Crop** to 1:1 ratio.

3. **Whites +34** and **Blacks -41** to extend the tonal range.

4. **Clarity +35** and **Contrast +15** to highlight the clean lines.

5. **Color Mix** to change orange to a deeper red to find in with office decor.
   Hue: Red -20, Orange -60
   Saturation: Red +20, Orange +14
   Luminance: Red +22, Orange -50

6. **Sharpening 45, Radius 2, Detail 11, Masking 50** to emphasize the strong edges without sharpening the panels.

7. **Noise Reduction 10**.

8. **Healing Brush** to remove tiny spot in bottom window.

Step 1
Guided
Upright

Step 2
Crop

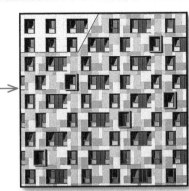

Steps 3-4
Brightness
& contrast
adjustments

Steps 5-8
HSL and
Detail
adjustments

THE GUY ON THE STEPS

Good dynamic range, no
notable clipping

TECHNICAL

Exposure

Needs a little more detail
in his clothes. No pure white
expected in the photo.

Color

Color doesn't add to the photo.
The strong lines and stone
texture would work well in B&W.

Detail

Shot at low ISO in good light, so no
notable noise. Texture of stone can
take some crunchy sharpening.

Optical & Geometric Distortion

Horizon needs straightening
(use bricks in background).

Sensor Dust

None found.

Output

Nothing specific planned.

ARTISTIC INTENT

Purpose

The guy looked small and
insignificant against the huge
pillars of the government building.

Story

Is he homeless? Or just
waiting for a friend?

Mood/Emotion

Very cold day (hat). Feeling lonely?
High contrast B&W with lots of local
contrast for a gritty urban look?

Simplify the Scene & Draw the Eye

Notes scribbled on photo.

Crop to remove the door
and sign on the left.

Even up lighting on the pillars, front
step and bricks in the background
to reduce background contrast.

Increase contrast on face/
clothing of man to draw the eye
in that direction even more.

1. **Crop** to remove dark door at side and excessive foreground.

2. **Exposure 0.71** to lighten photo overall.

3. **Highlights -80** to reduce brightness of pillars.

4. **Shadows +60** to show more detail in his clothes.

5. **Whites +7** and **Blacks -23** to compensate for loss of contrast.

6. Convert to B&W using the **Adobe Monochrome** profile. There are no contrasting colors in the photo, so manually mixing the channels won't help much.

7. **Clarity +100** and **Contrast +70** to give a gritty feel.

8. **Vignette -23, Feather 63** to darken the bright edges and draw the eye into the photo.

9. **Exposure** increased to **1.04** as it looked too dark in B&W.

10. **Grain 57** to add to gritty urban look.

11. **Linear Gradient** from right side of photo to darken, set to *Exposure -0.80* and *Highlights -36*.

12. **Brush** used with multiple different strokes, mainly set to varying Exposure values to lighten and darken different areas of the photo.

13. **Noise Reduction 20** as many areas have been significantly lightened and therefore show more noise.

Steps 1-5 Crop & tonal adjustments

Steps 6-10 Gritty B&W effect

Step 11 multiple brush selections

Steps 11-13 Selective edits applied

FAMILY DAY OUT

Good dynamic range, slight
highlight clipping

ARTISTIC INTENT

Purpose

Capture the family together
while the children are still
small (and clean!)

Story

This is a family day out
with the grandchildren.

Mood/Emotion

Happy, relaxed.

Simplify the Scene & Draw the Eye

There are some light areas in the
background that are distracting.

Some facial wrinkles to
reduce but not remove.

Draw the viewer's eye to
the people's eyes.

Don't make it look retouched!

TECHNICAL

Exposure

The exposure is fine and
this is a JPEG so we're not
going to mess with it.

Color

The color's fine as it is.

Detail

Child bottom right is slightly out
of focus, but otherwise good.

Optical & Geometric Distortion

None as it's a JPEG, so
corrected in-camera.

Sensor Dust

None noted.

Output

Small print on the fireplace.

1. Using **Brush** set to *Exposure -1.95* and *Highlights -87*, brush over the light areas in the background to stop them competing for the viewer's attention.

2. Using **Healing Brush** set to *Clone* mode, *Feather 100, Opacity 25*, retouch the bags/lines under the eyes, selecting nearby skin as the source to avoid changing the texture. We don't want to remove the lines, but just lighten them slightly.

3. Using the **Brush** tool set to *Exposure +0.33* and *Texture 25*, brush over the eyes to brighten and sharpen them slightly to draw the eye.

4. Using another **Brush**, paint over the skin with *Texture -47*. This softens the skin a little bit, reducing some of the contrast, but still looks natural. The red mask overlay helps you see where you're painting, as you don't want to soften the eyes or other facial features.

⌐Step 1 Brush distractions at back

⌐Steps 2-3 Brush & Healing Brush around eyes

⌐Step 4 Brush over skin to soften

PULTENEY BRIDGE

High dynamic range

TECHNICAL

Exposure

There is highlight and shadow detail but the contrast is far too high.

Color

The cool white balance doesn't show off the warm Bath stone.

Detail

No noticeable noise, but the textures would benefit from sharpening.

Optical & Geometric Distortion

The lamp on the left leans out of the frame due to perspective.

Sensor Dust

None found.

Output

Hang in the dining room.

ARTISTIC INTENT

Purpose

Capture the beautiful Georgian architecture in soft evening light, when most of the tourists have gone home.

Story

This is an early evening stroll after a relaxing dinner, enjoying the sunset.

Mood/Emotion

Calm, relaxed, peaceful.

Simplify the Scene & Draw the Eye

There's a little yellow flower bottom left that is slightly distracting.

1. Select **Adobe Landscape** profile, as we want the extended dynamic range.

2. **Highlights -100** to bring back the detail in the clouds.

Steps 1-5 Brightness → *and Clarity*

3. **Shadows +100** to bring back detail in the buildings.

4. **Exposure -0.45** to darken the photo overall.

5. **Clarity +80** for extreme local contrast, to give it that crunchy HDR feel.

Steps 6-7 Color → *adjustments*

6. **Temp 9650** and **Tint +30** to warm it up to show off the reflected sunset in the clouds and the warm Bath stone.

7. **Vibrance +68** to enhance the colors.

Step 8 Tone curve →

8. **Tone Curve** (Parametric) set to **Highlights +43, Darks -45, Shadows -7**. This increases the contrast in the buildings and brightest clouds, while sacrificing contrast in the deepest shadows.

9. Use **Upright** to correct the perspective, drawing a line up the center of the light stand and another up the central building.

10. **Crop** to remove the flower in the bottom left corner.

Steps 9&10 → *Upright & Crop*

BACK TO THE OLD DAYS

Clipped whites

TECHNICAL

Exposure

There's a large expanse of white sky, but the train is lacking shadow detail.

Color

The white balance is fine, but I want a sepia tone to suit the old-fashioned feel.

Detail

Low ISO, so there's no notable noise to worry about.

Optical & Geometric Distortion

Shot on a DSLR, so will need a lens profile.

Sensor Dust

No visible dust.

Output

Vacation album, only a small print.

ARTISTIC INTENT

Purpose

Visiting a steam railway, seeing how things were done in the past.

Story

The guy had just hopped out to change the points to go along a different track. No modern technology here!

Mood/Emotion

Historical scene, so go for a sepia toned monochrome with plenty with grain, to imitate photographs of that time period.

Simplify the Scene & Draw the Eye

Remove all the plain white sky at the top.

Might be worth removing the wires in the background.

Draw the eye to the train driver, and retain detail in the train itself.

Highlight the steam.

Leading lines of train tracks.

1. **Enable Lens Profile** to correct the distortion. It's automatically selected the right profile.

   Steps 1-3 Lens profile,
   Crop and Toned B&W

2. **Crop** the photo to remove the sky, cable and left hand side.

3. Convert to B&W using **Adobe Monochrome** profile, then use Color Grading to add a sepia tone to the shadows (**Shadow Hue 40**, **Saturation 30, Blending 100**).

4. Use **Dehaze +20** to remove some of the atmospheric haze.

   Steps 4-5
   Tonal
   Adjustments

5. Bring back highlight and shadow detail using **Highlights -90** and **Shadows +80**.

6. In the B&W Mix, set to **Orange +11** and **Yellow +25** to lighten the grass, creating a greater contrast with the train driver.

   Steps 6-7 B&W mix
   and Tone Curve

7. Adjust the parametric Tone Curve to **Highlights -43**, **Lights -17**, **Darks +4** and **Shadows -20** to increase the contrast in the steam, at the expense of the midtones (which is mainly the background trees).

8. Add a **Vignette -30** to darken the edges, with **Highlights 80** so the sky doesn't get too dark.

9. Add **Grain 38**, **Size 48** and **Roughness 78**, for a really rough grain.

   Steps 8-9
   Vignette
   and Grain

IN-APP TUTORIALS

Throughout the previous chapters, we've learned that there's no right or wrong in editing. While there are some technical issues that are generally worth fixing, the artistic choices are up to you.

Using Lightroom's Learn/Discover view, you can watch how a range of skilled photographers edit their photos. The exact settings won't work on your photos, but you can relate what they do to what you learned in the *Analyzing Your Image* chapters (pages 123 to 135) to see how to apply the principles to your own photos.

You'll find Learn and Discover in the left panel on the desktop, or at the bottom of the screen on mobile.

TYPES OF TUTORIAL

There are two different kinds of tutorials:

Learn or Guided Tutorials are interactive tutorials, which tell you to move specific sliders to specific values, so you can edit the photo yourself. The idea is similar to the start-to-finish tutorials in this chapter, allowing you to follow along with a specific edit, and understand the principles of editing.

Discovery Files, or Interactive Edits, allow you to simply watch the photographer work. These are more useful when the photographer has a very distinct style that you want to understand how to reproduce. Lightroom automatically displays a brief slideshow of the different stages of development, and you can play/pause it by clicking on the photo. Click on each edit step (desktop) / scroll to each edit step (mobile) to view the effect of the adjustment. If you Ctrl-click (desktop only) to exclude the step

Learn Tutorials tell you what to do, whereas Discovery Files let you watch the photographer.

from the preview, you can see what would have happened if that step wasn't included. The *Info* view also shows the camera settings used to capture the photo.

FOLLOW A PHOTOGRAPHER

If you like a particular photographer's style, click/tap on their avatar to view their other tutorials and social media pages. There's also a *Follow* button, so you can bookmark photographers you like. To find them again, click on your own avatar or the *Following* tab in the Discover view.

You can view my tutorials by visiting https://www.Lrq.me/lrtutorials

SUBMIT YOUR OWN PHOTOS

If you're particularly pleased with how a photo has turned out, and you want to **share your edits** to help others learn, go to the Share menu and select *Share Edit (Beta)*. Fill out the form, giving the photo a name, description and categories to help other people find your Discovery images.

There are some rules governing the kinds of photos that can be uploaded, as they may be seen by a wide age range. You can read the guidelines at https://lightroom.adobe.com/lightroom-community-guidelines

To **update your profile** with your bio and social media links, tap your own avatar at the top of the Discover view and then click/tap the edit button at the top.

Recent tutorials from photographers you're following ↓

Access & edit your own profile ↓

SAVING & SHARING PHOTOS 22

Having selected all of your best photos and edited them until you're proud of the result, don't keep them to yourself. Share them with the world!

Lightroom offers a number of different ways of sharing your photos. At the time of writing, you can't print directly from Lightroom on the desktop, but you can save the photo as a JPEG to send to an online lab or open into another program to print. You can also save a smaller file to email to a friend or share on Facebook, Instagram or other social media apps.

If you have a whole selection of photos to share, you can share the entire album as a web gallery, and even add additional text to describe the photos and tell the story.

IN THIS SECTION, WE'LL CONSIDER:

• How to save edited photos to your hard drive.

• How to share photos to social media.

• How to share entire albums of photos using Lightroom Web.

EXPORTING PHOTOS

You might want to save edited copies of your photos for different purposes, including:

- Send to other people.

- Upload to photo sharing websites.

- Upload to online labs or take to local photo labs to be printed as photographic prints.

- Upload to online printers to create books, calendars and other products.

- Print using other software.

- Open in other software for further editing, such as Nik, On1, Topaz, etc.

There's no need to keep these copies once they've served their purpose, as you can save a new copy at any time.

SAVING A PHOTO ON THE DESKTOP

To **save one or more photos to the hard drive**:

1. Go to *File menu > Export* or click the Share icon and select *Custom...*

2. In the Export dialog, you have a number of choices, so we'll take a look at the individual options in more detail in the next lesson starting on page 328.

You can preview the effect your settings will have on your photo using the Export dialog's preview area. Below the image is the filename and file size for the selected photo. You can also zoom in to 1:1 to see a more accurate preview.

However, note that the options you select apply to all of the photos you're exporting, not just the one you're viewing.

There's also a few presets for quick exports, which are available in the Share menu and Export dialog. You can't create your own presets at this point in time. The *Previous Settings* preset provides quick access to your last-used export settings, complete with a keyboard shortcut Ctrl-E (Windows) / Cmd-E (Mac).

3. Once you've set your Export options, click *Export Photo* to choose where to store the exported photos. By default, it saves to *Pictures/Lightroom Saved Photos*.

SAVING A PHOTO ON IOS

To **save one or more photos to the Camera Roll or other file storage space**:

1. Go to Grid view, hold your finger on a photo to enter selection mode, then tap or drag across the photos you want to save. Alternatively open a single photo in Detail view.

2. Tap on the Share menu.

 ← Share menu (iOS)

3. Select *Export As...* to access the export

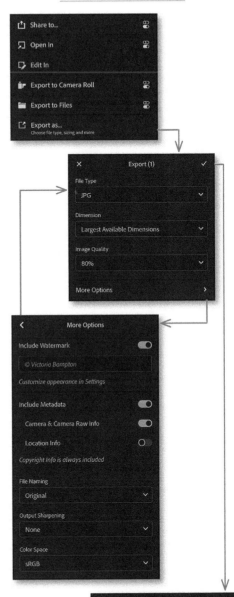

EXPORT (iOS)

options. We'll take a look at the individual options in more detail in the next lesson starting on page 328.

4. Tap the checkmark to choose where to store the exported photos. You can send the photos to other apps such as Mail, Messages, Facebook, Instagram, or WhatsApp. If your chosen app isn't showing, scroll along the app icons to tap the *More* button.

You can also *Save Images* to the Camera Roll, so you can access the photos directly from other apps.

Save to Files allows you to select any storage locations you've mounted in the Files app, such iCloud, Dropbox or external storage drives.

If you're wondering about the other export menu commands, they all do very similar things, with slight variations:

Share to... is the same as *Export As*, but it allows you to save export options using the Preset button to the right, for example, you may set *Share* to always output a 2048px JPEG with a watermark and no metadata.

Open In uses the export options set using the Preset button to its right and then asks which app should open the exported photo. We used this on page 290 to open photos into other editing apps.

Export to Camera Roll and **Export to Files** are like presets. They use the export options set using the Preset buttons to the right. *Camera Roll* automatically saves the exported photo to the Lightroom album in the Photos app, whereas *Files* asks where to store the exported photo (for example, iCloud, Dropbox, etc.). If you're only saving a single photo to Files, you can set a new filename by tapping on the name at the top.

The old **Export Original** option is gone, but you can get the same result by selecting the *Original* format using any of the export options.

SAVING A PHOTO ON ANDROID

To **save one or more photos to the Pictures folder**:

1. Go to Grid view, hold your finger on a photo to enter selection mode, then tap or drag across the photos you want to save. Alternatively open a single photo in Detail view.

2. Tap on the Share menu.

 ← Share menu (Android)

3. Select **Export As...** to access the export options. We'll take a look at the individual options in more detail in the next lesson starting on page 328.

4. Tap the checkmark to save the photos to your Internal Storage/Pictures/ AdobeLightroom folder. They'll appear in the Gallery app.

The other export menu commands act like presets for specific purposes:

Share to... sends the photos to other apps such as Email, Messages, Facebook, Instagram, or WhatsApp. It allows you to save the photos to cloud storage such as Google Drive or Dropbox. It doesn't offer a choice of file formats, always saving a full resolution JPEG, but it does allow you to set the metadata and watermark options using the Preset button to the right.

Share & Invite shares the photos as a web gallery, which we'll come back to on page 339.

Save to Device skips the settings and just saves a full resolution JPEG to the photo gallery. You can choose which metadata to include and whether to apply a watermark using the Preset button to the right.

Saving/sharing videos is not currently possible using the Android app, but there is a partial workaround. To save a video on Android, share the web gallery (page 339), then visit the gallery link using your device's web browser. View the video, then tap the ... button in the corner of the video to download it from the cloud.

EXPORT (ANDROID)

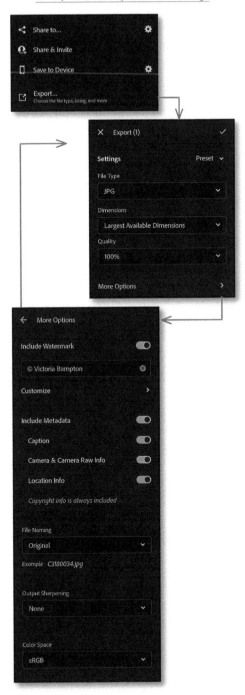

SETTING OPTIMAL EXPORT OPTIONS

The array of export options can be slightly overwhelming, so let's find out what they actually mean, and how you can decide which settings are best for your intended purpose.

FILE TYPE

There are a few different file formats to choose from:

Original (mobile only) creates a copy of the photos without any of your updated metadata. This is useful for editing in other apps that can handle raw files.

Original + Settings (desktop only) creates a copy of the photos with updated metadata (stars, keywords, Info panel contents) but doesn't apply any edits to the photo image data. This is useful for editing in other software that can handle raw files.

JPEG and TIFF both create a copy of the photo with the updated metadata and with your edits applied to the image.

JPEG (or JPG) is an excellent choice for emailing photos or posting them on the web. It applies a lossy compression, so the files are much smaller than TIFF format, but compression artifacts may become visible at lower quality settings.

You can control the amount of compression applied using the **Quality** pop-up, and check

the result by clicking on the Export preview to zoom into 1:1. 100% is maximum quality, but has the largest file size, whereas 10% is a small file but square compression artifacts may be visible.

JPEG compression can create square compression artifacts at very low values (enhanced here so you can see them clearly)

TIFF (or TIF) is a lossless format, so it's the best choice for opening in other photo editing apps for pixel-based retouching and special effects.

The choice of **Bit Depth** is a trade-off between smoother gradients (16-bit) or a smaller file size (8-bit). You're most likely to notice a difference on smooth gradients, such as a sky at sunset, like this extreme example:

Posterization/banding can show up in smooth gradients (enhanced here for visibility)

You can apply Lossless **Compression** when saving a TIFF file. This reduces the file size considerably, without any loss of quality.

ZIP is almost always the best choice, but occasionally you may come across old software that can't open a ZIP compressed TIFF. In that case, you might need to select LZW compression (an older algorithm which may be supported) or None.

TIFF format can also **Save Transparency**, for example, the blank areas around a panoramic photo, rather than filling them with white.

DNG stands for Digital Negative. It's an openly-documented file format designed primarily for raw image data. It contains the original image data and metadata (excluding flags/album membership). Since this can include the edit settings, it's a good way of non-destructively sending your images and their edits to Lightroom on another device or backup drive, when you can't use Lightroom's cloud sync.

DIMENSIONS

The **Dimensions** pop-up controls the file resolution. We'll learn more about resolution on page 332.

Full Size uses the pixels created by the camera, without creating new ones or throwing any away (other than those you've cropped). This is also known as "full resolution" or "native resolution."

Small is 2048px along the long edge. It's a relatively small file, ideal for emailing or posting on the web.

Custom asks for the length of the long edge in pixels. We'll learn how to calculate custom file dimensions in the next lesson on page 332, but the desktop app also allows you to specify the long edge in inches/cm with the resolution (PPI) to save you doing the calculations manually.

WATERMARKING

Include Watermark allows you to add a text watermark to the photos as they're exported. We'll design your watermark on page 333.

METADATA

Under *More Options*, the Metadata options control how much information is included with the photos.

All Metadata includes everything: the EXIF data captured by the camera, the metadata you added in the Info and Keyword panels, names added in People view, the GPS location (if available) and the edit settings applied.

Copyright Only just includes the copyright entered in the Info panel, and strips the rest of the information. This is useful if you're going to post the photos online and are concerned about privacy.

The mobile apps break the Metadata options down a little further.

FILE NAMING

The File Naming options allow you to rename the photos as you export them.

Original retains the existing filename.

Custom Name renames the photos using the custom text you enter in the Export dialog. If you're exporting more than 1 photo, it adds a sequence number, starting with the number you specify. Lightroom automatically adds padding zeros if you have more than 9 photos, so the photos sort correctly in other software. This is particularly useful if you've sorted the photos into a custom sort order.

Date-Filename renames the photo using the capture date and then the existing filename.

An example filename is shown, so you can see exactly how the photo will be named. It also displays in the toolbar beneath the photo preview.

OUTPUT SHARPENING

Output sharpening applies additional

sharpening that's optimized for how the photo will be used, on top of the capture sharpening you've applied using the Detail panel sliders (page 234). It's far smarter than the two simple pop-ups suggest. It calculates the optimal sharpening settings based on the size of the original file, the size of the exported photo, the type of screen/paper, and the strength of sharpening you prefer.

Screen is optimized for computer monitors, which are very good at showing fine details.

Glossy is ideal for typical glossy, metallic and lustre prints, and **Matte** is designed to compensate for the softer appearance of matte and fine art papers.

The **Amount** setting (*Low*, *Standard* or *High*) is purely down to personal taste.

If you have no idea how the photos will be used, perhaps because you're giving them to a friend or client, *Glossy Standard* is a good average.

COLOR SPACE

The Color Space pop-up allows you to choose between *sRGB*, *Adobe RGB*, *Display P3* and *ProPhoto RGB* color spaces.

We'll explain the differences in a little more detail on page 337, but if in doubt, use the default *sRGB*. It's the most common color space (although not necessarily the best).

TYPICAL SETTINGS

If you're still not sure which combination of settings to use for different purposes, try these settings:

Email or social media
Dimensions: custom 2048px.
File type: JPEG, quality 60 for email or 90 for social media (as they're compressed again during upload).
Color Space: sRGB.

4" x 6" digital print
File type: JPEG, quality 70.
Dimensions: custom 1800px.
Color Space: sRGB (some labs may accept Adobe RGB too).

8" x 10" digital print
File type: JPEG, quality 80.
Dimensions 3000px or Full Size.
Color Space: sRGB (some labs may accept Adobe RGB too).

Full resolution file
File Type: JPEG, quality 90-100.
Dimensions: Full Size.
Color Space: sRGB.

Edit in another color managed program
File type: TIFF, ZIP compressed.
Dimensions: Full Size.
Bit Depth: 16 bits (if your software is able to handle 16 bit)
Color Space: ProPhoto RGB.

UNDERSTANDING FILE RESOLUTION

When it comes to saving files, you need to work out the size you need, and this depends on how the file will be used. For example, you'll need a big file to print a poster, but there's no point sending a file that big if it's only going to be displayed on a computer monitor or mobile device.

WHAT IS RESOLUTION?

When digital photographers speak of image size, they're usually referring to the pixel dimensions—the number of pixels along a photo's width and height.

Pixels don't have a fixed physical size. They expand or contract to fill the space available. If you expand them too far, the photo appears blurry and pixelated (you can see the squares), so the aim is to keep the pixels smaller than or equal to the monitor pixels or printer dots.

For example, this smiley face looks sharp when it's printed small, but the individual pixels are visible when it's enlarged too far.

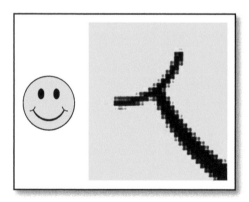

When you set a size in the Save dialog, Lightroom creates new pixels or selectively throws away spare pixels to fit your chosen size. This process is called resampling (but the original file isn't touched!)

CALCULATING THE SIZE YOU NEED FOR PRINT

To work out how many pixels you need for a specific print size, it's a simple calculation. Let's use a 8" x 10" print:

$$10" \times 300ppi = 3000px$$
$$8" \times 300ppi = 2400px$$

Inches—The length/width of the print size in inches.

PPI (pixels per inch)—300ppi is traditionally the resolution used for printing. (If you prefer to use cm in your calculations, use 118ppcm instead of 300ppi.) For very large prints, you can get away with a lower value as you view them from a distance, but even then, aim for no less than 200ppi.

Result—The minimum number of pixels you need along that edge, to get a high quality print.

You can reverse the calculation, dividing the number of pixels by 300ppi / 118ppcm to get an idea of how large a print you can make.

SIZES FOR SCREEN IMAGES

For displaying on computer screens, the files can be much smaller. Relatively few screens display more than 2048px along the longest edge, so there's no point sending someone a larger photo unless they're likely to print it.

Likewise, Facebook recommends uploading photos that are 720px, 960px or 2048px along the long edge. Instagram suggests up to 1080px wide and up to 1350px high. Other photo sharing websites make similar recommendations.

ADDING A WATERMARK

Some photographers use a subtle watermark to 'sign' their artwork. Others use it as part of their branding, promoting their website. Many believe a watermark helps to discourage people from stealing photographs, however remember that if the watermark is large enough to be difficult to remove, it can also be a significant distraction for the people viewing your photo. Other people feel that a watermark is tacky and should never be used.

Whether you should watermark is the subject of many flame wars online, so I'll leave you to make your own decision!

Lightroom allows you to add a text or graphical watermark to photos as you export them. Your watermark syncs across all of your devices, but you can only save a single watermark at this time.

To **design your watermark** on the desktop, enable *Include Watermark* in the Export dialog and click on the cog icon to access the watermark settings.

On mobile, enable the *Include Watermark* switch in the Export Options (page 324), then tap *Customize* to design your watermark.

You can select between a text or graphic watermark, and we'll cover the individual options shortly. On the desktop, you can test the watermark on multiple photos in the filmstrip, to ensure it works well on a range of photos.

Watermark

When you're happy with your watermark, **save the settings** by pressing *Done*, or click *Cancel* to return to the Export dialog without saving your changes.

To **apply your watermark** to photos as you save or share them, ensure that the *Include Watermark* switch is enabled when exporting. Note that watermarks don't display on shared web galleries (page 339).

DESIGNING YOUR TEXT WATERMARK

The text watermark options include:

Text—Depending on your reason for watermarking, you may decide to use your name and copyright symbol, your business name, your website, your social media handle, or any combination. You may find that the text is less distracting in all capital letters, rather than a mix of upper and lower case.

Font & Style—On the desktop, Lightroom can access many of the fonts installed on your system. The mobile apps are more limited, so for consistency, you may want to choose one that's available on all of your devices. You can also choose a bold or italic

WATERMARK (WINDOWS/MAC)

Preview watermark
on selected photo

Ignore changes &
go back to Export

Save watermark &
go back to Export

Try your settings on a variety of photos

Watermark settings

variant.

Color & Drop Shadow—Neutral tones are less distracting than color, so Lightroom only offers black or white. These can be toned down to shades of gray using the *Opacity* slider. Adding a drop shadow to a white watermark can help it remain legible on a light area of the photo.

DESIGNING YOUR GRAPHIC WATERMARK

The graphic watermark offers additional flexibility, because you can design the watermark in other software (such as

Photoshop). This means you're not only limited to text, but you may include your logo, or perhaps a stylized signature such as those created by https://www.photologo.co.

File—You can select a PNG or JPG image as your watermark file. A PNG is usually the most useful, as it contains transparency.

WATERMARK (IOS/ANDROID)

Include Watermark ← Enable/disable watermark

Customize › ← Edit Watermark

Back to Export Options →

Customize Watermark

Text Graphic ← Switch Text vs. Graphic Watermark

© Victoria Bampton ← Watermark text

Lock watermark to corner, center of edge or dead center →

Watermark position preview →

© Victoria Bampton

Font →

Bold / Italic →

Drop Shadow →

T B I C ▢ ▢

Rotate text →

White/Black font color →

Use Drop Shadow

Font size → Size 14

Opacity → Opacity 77

Offset from edge → Horizontal Offset 3

Vertical Offset

Double-tap slider handle to reset

Text Graphic

Victoria-Bampton_white-bevel.png

Select watermark image file →

SETTING THE WATERMARK PLACEMENT

Once you've decided on the content of your text or graphic watermark, you can set the size and placement on the photo.

Size—The *Size* slider is relative to the size of the photo, so it automatically adjusts for horizontal and vertical photos. Some watermarks are so small they're illegible, which defeats the purpose. On the other hand, you don't want the watermark to distract the viewer, so set your size carefully for its intended purpose. For example, if you're putting the photo on Instagram, it will probably be viewed on a smaller screen than on your website.

Opacity—Depending on the purpose of the watermark, you may want to reduce the opacity to fade it into the photo, making it less obvious.

Anchor & Offset—Even if your watermark is small, you're adding a focal point to your photo, so think about the placement carefully. Traditionally, artists have signed their work in the lower left or right corner, inset slightly from the edges of the frame.

Rotation—On page 133, we learned that text has significant visual mass. By rotating the watermark by 90°, you may find it's less distracting, as your viewers will be less inclined to stop and read it.

UNDERSTANDING COLOR SPACE

Color management is a huge topic in its own right, but Lightroom handles most of it for you. It's only when you come to export photos that you need to pick the right color space for your purpose, so we'll just cover a quick introduction to the subject.

We already know that photos are made up of pixels, and each pixel has a number value for each of the color channels (red, green and blue). For example, 0-0-0 on an 8-bit scale is pure black and 255-255-255 is pure white. The numbers in between are open to interpretation. Who decides exactly which shade of green 10-190-10 equates to? That's where color profiles come into play: they define how these numbers should translate to colors.

Some color spaces contain a larger number of colors than others, so we refer to the 'size' of the color space. If a color in your photo falls outside of the gamut of your chosen color space, it's automatically remapped to fit into the smaller gamut.

sRGB is a small color space, but it's the most widely used. It's a great choice for screen output, emailing or uploading to the web. It's also the safest choice if you don't know where the photos will end up.

Adobe RGB is a slightly larger color space, but it's a good choice if you're sending photos for printing at a color managed lab, if your editing software can only handle 8-bit files, or if you're saving as JPEG.

Display P3 is a wide gamut color space used on the latest Apple devices. It's a similar size to Adobe RGB, but it's shifted slightly towards reds/oranges and loses some of the greens/blues. It's primarily useful when exporting photos for display on the latest Apple devices.

ProPhoto RGB is the largest color space, so it's the best choice when transferring photos to Photoshop or other photo editing software, as long as they're color managed. ProPhoto RGB photos look dull and flat in programs that aren't color managed, such as web browsers.

A ProPhoto RGB photo is dull and flat when opened in a program that doesn't understand color management

SHARING SLIDESHOWS ON MOBILE

If you hand your phone or tablet over to someone to show them your photos, you may be worried that they'll change your flags or star ratings with an accidental swipe. The best way to avoid this is to put Lightroom into Slideshow mode.

To **access the Slideshow view**, go to ... *menu > Slideshow*.

On iOS, a Grid view shows initially, then when you tap the triangular play button, it starts playing the slideshow. On Android, it immediately starts playing the slideshow.

If you tap the ... icon at the top, you can **change the slide transition** effect and the slide duration.

If you **pause the slideshow** using the Play/Pause button, the viewer can swipe through the photos without worrying that they'll accidentally change your ratings.

It's not a completely failsafe way of protecting your photos, as tapping the X in the top left corner returns to the normal Lightroom interface, but it's a handy protection against accidents.

SLIDESHOW VIEW (IOS/ANDROID)

Close Slideshow view

Play / Pause

Back to Slideshow Grid (iOS only)

... menu

No Transition

Cross Fade

Wipe

Flip

2.0 Sec

Slideshow Grid (iOS only)

Swipe left <> to move manually

SHARING WEB GALLERIES

Entire albums or smaller groups of photos can be shared with friends, family or clients by sending them a link to a web gallery. They can then:

- View the photos in Grid or Detail view.

- View the photos as a slideshow.

- Like or comment on the photos (optional).

- Download full resolution JPEGs (optional).

- Upload their photos to your Lightroom album (optional).

Desktop

mobile

SHARING ALBUMS OR PHOTOS

To **share an album or specific photos**:

1. On the desktop, select an album in the Albums panel, or one or more photos in the Grid view, right-click and choose **Share & Invite**.

On mobile, select an album in the Library or Grid view. Or to share individual photos as a web gallery, hold your finger on a photo to enter selection mode then tap on the photos you want to save, or drag your finger across multiple photos. Tap the ... menu and select **Share & Invite**.

2. Click/tap **Enable Sharing** to show and set the sharing preferences. All of these preferences are detailed on the following pages.

3. If the **Link Access** is set to *Anyone Can View*, copy the link to the clipboard and send it by email, text message, Facebook, etc.

If you prefer to restrict access to specific people, set the *Link Access* pop-up to *Invite only* and enter their email address to send an invitation by email. They'll need to sign in to view the gallery.

4. Click *Done*.

In addition to setting these options when creating the gallery, you can **access the settings again later** on the desktop by returning the to Share & Invite dialog.

To **stop sharing an album** on the desktop, right-click on it again and choose *Stop*

SHARE & INVITE

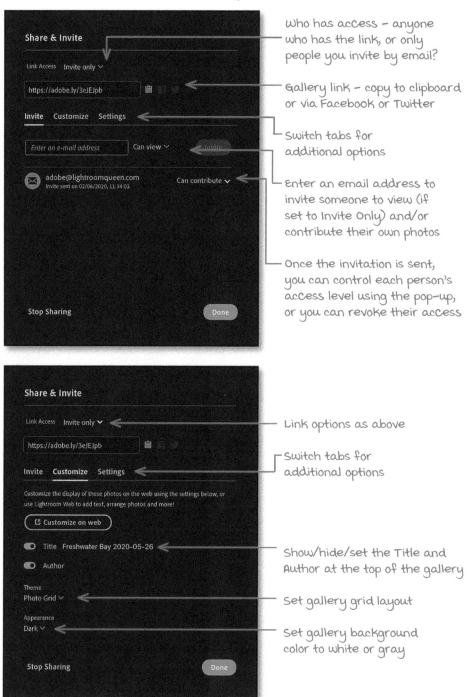

Who has access – anyone who has the link, or only people you invite by email?

Gallery link – copy to clipboard or via Facebook or Twitter

Switch tabs for additional options

Enter an email address to invite someone to view (if set to Invite Only) and/or contribute their own photos

Once the invitation is sent, you can control each person's access level using the pop-up, or you can revoke their access

Link options as above

Switch tabs for additional options

Show/hide/set the Title and Author at the top of the gallery

Set gallery grid layout

Set gallery background color to white or gray

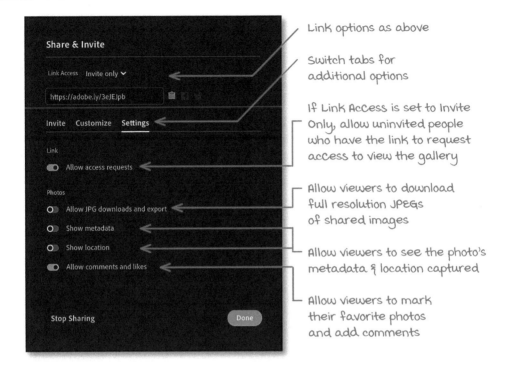

Link options as above

Switch tabs for additional options

If Link Access is set to Invite Only, allow uninvited people who have the link to request access to view the gallery

Allow viewers to download full resolution JPEGs of shared images

Allow viewers to see the photo's metadata & location captured

Allow viewers to mark their favorite photos and add comments

Sharing. On mobile, tap the *... menu > Share & Invite* and choose *Stop Sharing.*

SHARING FROM THE WEB

To **share an album** from the web interface:

1. Select an album in the Albums panel, click the *Share & Invite* icon in the top right corner and then *Enable Sharing.*

 Share & Invite

2. Click/tap **Enable Sharing** to show and set the sharing preferences and link access options, as we did in the previous section.

3. Copy the link to the clipboard and send it by email, text message, Facebook, etc.

To **share specific photos** from the web interface:

1. Click/tap the checkmarks in the corners of the thumbnails to select multiple photos.

2. From the blue options bar, choose *Share.*

3. Give the new ad-hoc album a name.

4. Set the sharing preferences and link access options, as we did in the previous section.

5. Copy the link to the clipboard and send it by email, text message, Facebook, etc.

LINK ACCESS & INVITATIONS

If the **Link Access** is set to **Anyone Can View**, it doesn't mean your photos are being broadcast across the web, but simply that anyone with the link can view the gallery.

Set to **Invite only**, the gallery is kept private,

except for the people you invite by email. To view the photos, they must click the link in their email and sign in using their Adobe ID or Facebook/Google login.

If the gallery is set to *Invite only*, but an uninvited viewer visits the link (perhaps because it was previously shared as *Anyone Can View*), they'll be asked to log in, and then be given the option to **Request Access**.

This sends you a request by email, giving you the choice to approve or deny their request. They won't be able to view the gallery until you grant access from the Share & Invite dialog.

Once you've invited someone to a shared album, you can set their access level to *Can View* or *Can Contribute*. The **Can Contribute** option adds an *Add Photos* button to the top of the web gallery, so they can upload their own photos to your album. For example, if you're the designated photographer at a family event, you may invite family members to upload their photos to the shared album, so the whole family can enjoy them. These contributed photos show a small profile photo in the corner, so you know who uploaded them. The contributed photos take up space in your cloud storage, just as if you'd uploaded the photos yourself.

DISPLAY & SETTINGS

There's a growing list of settings available for the shared web galleries, found under the **Display/Customize** and **Settings** tabs, although the exact names vary slightly by operating system.

Allow JPG Downloads and Export displays a download button in the viewer's web gallery, allowing them to download full resolution JPEGs of the photos.

Show Metadata and **Show Location** limit the amount of metadata your viewers can see in the Info panel of the web gallery.

Allow Comments and Likes allows your viewers to share their thoughts on your photos.

The **Theme**—*Photo Grid, Column* or *One-Up*—controls the layout of the gallery, and the **Appearance** options allow you to switch between a light and dark design. Further customization is available in the Web interface, but we'll come back to these settings on page 347.

CHANGES TO FILTERING

In some earlier Lightroom versions, you could filter the photos to share only those with a certain number of stars, or only the flagged photos. This filtering was later removed. Now, you just select the photos you want to share and create a new shared album.

You'll notice a yellow exclamation point on filtered shared albums, warning of this change, but you don't need to do anything. Lightroom will maintain the privacy of your existing filtered albums by automatically creating new shared albums containing only the filtered photos, but reusing the existing link and settings.

 Shoot - Lepe 2019-02-15   133

VIEWING A SHARED GALLERY

When your friends, family or clients visit a web gallery link, they can view the photos in a Grid or Detail view, or watch a slideshow of your photos.

Depending on the gallery settings, they may be able to download some or all of the photos.

If they sign in using an Adobe ID, or a Facebook/Google account, they can like and comment on your photos too.

If their access level is set to *Can Contribute*, they can upload their own photos to your album using the *Add Photos* button.

If they've installed the Lightroom app and you've invited them to view the gallery using their email address, the shared gallery also appears in the *Shared with You* section of the Shared Photos panel in their Lightroom app.

PUBLIC VIEW (WEB)

Other Shared Albums

Upload photos (if set to Can Contribute)

Holiday 2015-09 Guernsey
by Victoria Bampton

Sign in/out

menu incl. Download

Play Slideshow

Open in Detail view

Back to Grid view

Download JPEG

Info panel

Comments panel

Sign in to Like/Comment

Number of comments/likes

Previous/Next Photo

MANAGING SHARED ALBUMS

The Shared Photos panel allows you to see all of your shared albums in one location, without having to search through your folders of albums. You can add and remove photos, just as you would with any other album.

Select the Shared Photos panel using the button on the left of the Windows/Mac apps and the web interface, or at the bottom of the mobile apps.

←Shared (desktop)

← Shared (mobile)

VIEWING VISITOR'S ACTIVITY

To **view notifications of recent activity**, such as likes and comments, click/tap on the bell icon at the top of the screen. A blue dot on the icon means that there are new notifications that you haven't seen. You'll receive notifications for any albums you own, plus any photos you've contributed to other people's albums.

← Notifications

Lightroom lists all of the recent activity, and clicking/tapping on a notification opens the photo.

In the Grid view on desktop, **thumbnail badges** are automatically displayed on photos with likes or comments. In the iOS Grid view, go to the ... *menu > View Options > Activity* to display the icons on the thumbnails. These icons aren't currently available on Android.

When you're viewing a shared album on mobile, you can go to ... *menu > Activity* to show a list of activity in the selected album.

In the Detail view, select the Activity panel (desktop) / Activity view (mobile) to see and reply to the likes and comments for the selected photo.

CONTRIBUTING TO OTHER PEOPLE'S ALBUMS

If someone has invited you to view or contribute to one or more of their albums (page 341), you'll find the albums listed in the Shared Photos panel, under the **Shared with You** heading. You can like and comment on their photos from within the Lightroom app.

If your link access is set to *Can Contribute*, you can drag your photos to their album, just as if you're adding photos to one of your own albums. When you add photos to someone else's album, Lightroom asks which of your metadata you wish to include.

The owner of the album is the only person who can edit the contributed photo, and it's duplicated into their cloud space, disconnected from your original.

You can only export a JPEG copy of the photo if the album is set to allow downloads.

SHARED PHOTOS PANEL (WINDOWS/MAC)

Open Shared Photos

Other people's albums that have been shared with you

Shared albums

Groups of shared photos not in shared albums

SHARED PHOTOS VIEW (IOS/ANDROID)

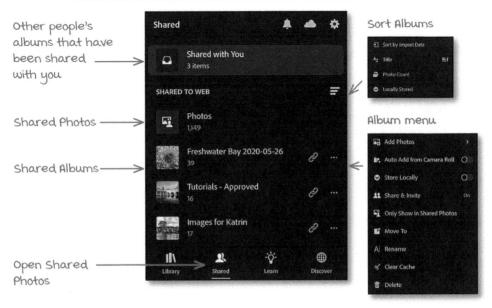

Other people's albums that have been shared with you

Sort Albums

Shared Photos

Album menu

Shared Albums

Open Shared Photos

NOTIFICATIONS & ACTIVITY VIEW (WINDOWS/MAC)

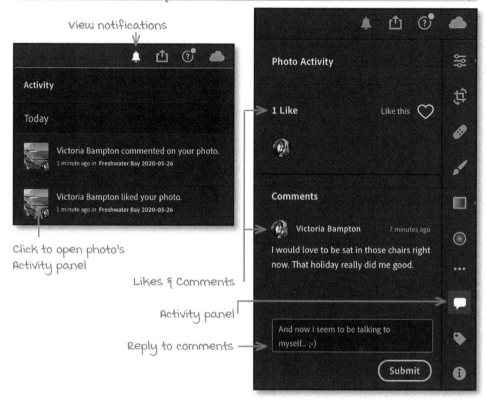

View notifications

Click to open photo's
Activity panel

Likes & Comments

Activity panel

Reply to comments

NOTIFICATIONS & ACTIVITY VIEW (IOS/ANDROID)

View notifications

Select Activity view

Tap to open photo's
Activity view

Likes &
Comments

Tap to reply to comments

ENHANCING WEB GALLERIES

To access additional share preferences, visit Lightroom Web at https://lightroom.adobe.com and sign in to your account.

ADDING CUSTOM TEXT & LAYOUT

You can create a more interesting web gallery by splitting the grid of photos and inserting descriptive text to tell a story.

Select the *Display* view at the bottom of the album's Grid view and choose your prefered layout, then click between images to **split the photos and add text**. Further options are available in the floating panel at the bottom of the page, including a **cover photo** that can be placed at the top of the page or in the background.

CUSTOM SHARE (WEB)

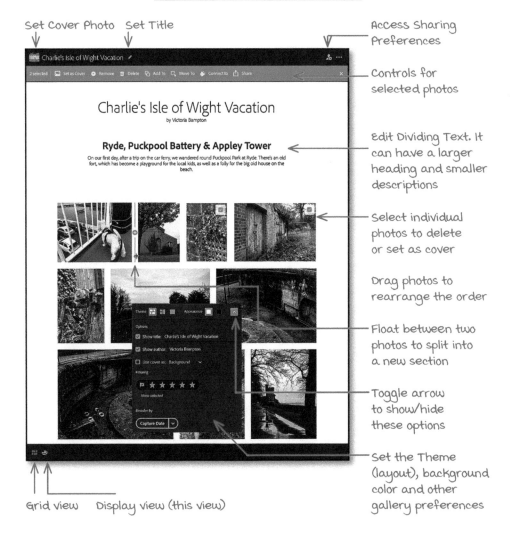

Set Cover Photo   Set Title

Access Sharing Preferences

Controls for selected photos

Edit Dividing Text. It can have a larger heading and smaller descriptions

Select individual photos to delete or set as cover

Drag photos to rearrange the order

Float between two photos to split into a new section

Toggle arrow to show/hide these options

Set the Theme (layout), background color and other gallery preferences

Grid view   Display view (this view)

CREATING A GALLERY INDEX PAGE

You can also create an index page of chosen shared galleries, perhaps to use as your portfolio.

To do so, open the Shared Photos panel using the icon on the left. Click *Gallery* at the top (above the shared albums), enable the index and add the albums of your choice.

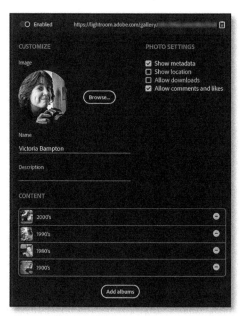

EMBEDDING A SLIDESHOW

If you have your own website or blog, you can embed a slideshow of a web gallery into an existing web page.

Copy the *Embed Code* from the Sharing Preferences to the clipboard, then paste into your webpage's HTML code.

If you're familiar with basic coding, you can tweak the default embed code, for example, you might change *background_color=%23191919* to *background_color=white* to change the slideshow background to match the background color of your page.

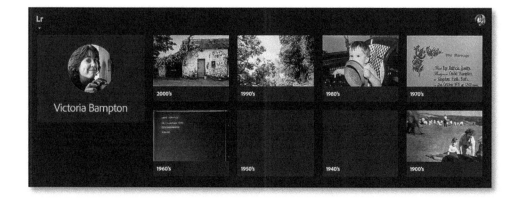

CONNECTING TO OTHER SERVICES

Under *All Photos* on the desktop is a section marked **Connections**. These are connections to external web services.

Initially, there was only an Adobe Portfolio connection available, and Blurb and WHCC have been added since. There's potential to link to many different companies, for example, to:

- order photo prints

- design & order photo books

- design & order calendars and other photo gifts

- create advanced slideshows

- publish photos on other social media/ photo sharing websites

- publish photos on stock websites

- integrate with your own website

In time, it may even be possible to access advanced metadata manipulation plug-ins for more specialized tasks such as duplicate detection.

These additional options are simply waiting on companies building these connections using Adobe's API. If you want to see your favorite photo lab or website supported, you may want to send them an email to encourage their developers to start work on the integration.

CREATING CONNECTIONS

The principles are the same for all connections, so we'll look at the basic setup and then the variations for specific connections.

To **create or view connections**, click on *All Photos* to show *Connections* on the left of the Windows/Mac apps (and in the Web interface too, for Portfolio connections).

To **add a new connection**, click the + button, add the connection(s) of your choice and then close the dialog.

To **share a whole album**, right-click and choose *Share To > [your connection name, e.g. Adobe Portfolio]*.

To **share specific photos**, select one or more photos in the Grid view, right-click and choose *Share To > [your connection name, e.g. Adobe Portfolio]*. Decide whether to create a new project (similar to an album, but specific to that connection) or add them to an existing project.

What happens next depends on the specific connection...

ADOBE PORTFOLIO

Adobe Portfolio is an advanced portfolio website, that can hold up to 200 images, and is free with your Creative Cloud subscription. You can learn about Adobe Portfolio at https://www.myportfolio.com

When you've shared an album or photos to Portfolio, Lightroom automatically opens the project in a web browser so you can **customize the layout** and appearance.

To **remove an album** from an Adobe Portfolio connection, visit the Adobe Portfolio website.

BOOKS FROM BLURB

Blurb is a well-known photobook company who print and ship high quality books to photographers worldwide.

With your permission, Blurb's Photo Manager website can browse the photos stored in your Lightroom cloud and automatically import them into its own BookWright book design software.

There's **no need to create a connection** in the Lightroom desktop app before switching to BookWright, but it's a handy way of keeping track of which photos you've used in a book.

At this point in time, Blurb just sees the connected project as another album. Photos sent to BookWright aren't updated when you make changes in Lightroom, but there's potential for this to develop further in future.

To **create your book**, download the BookWright software from Blurb's website https://www.blurb.co.uk/bookwright. Create a book project, choosing your size, paper and cover style.

To **add your photos to the book**, click on *Photos* at the top of the BookWright software and then click the cloud icon below. This opens Blurb's website, allowing you to connect your Lightroom cloud account.

Browse your albums and select photos, and then click *Import Selected* to send them to the BookWright software, where you can **design your book** and send it to be printed.

You'll find an introductory video and help guide under BookWright's Help menu, in case you get stuck with the design process.

MOUNTED PRINTS FROM WHCC

WHCC, or White House Custom Color, is a US-based online lab that produces photographic prints and other photo products.

Like Blurb, if you give permission, WHCC can access the photos stored in your Lightroom cloud, making it easy to order mounted or framed prints.

You can create a new connection for each order, to help you keep track of which photos you've ordered, or you can simply visit https://lightroom.whcc.com to browse your albums and photos and decide how you'd like them to be presented.

MANAGING CONNECTED PROJECTS

You can view the connected projects from within Lightroom by returning to the Connections section and clicking on the connection. Lightroom displays a list of your projects.

The connections don't update automatically when you add new photos, remove photos or edit photos, just in case you're experimenting with your photos. To **update a connected project** with your changes, click the *Resend* button. For Portfolio, this updates Portfolio your changes. For Blurb and WHCC, this just adds/removes photos, but doesn't update any edits.

CONNECTIONS VIEW (WINDOWS/MAC)

VIEWING PHOTOS ON APPLE TV

Lightroom for Apple TV allows you to view your photos and videos on your big TV screen, so you can view them with your friends, family or clients.

INSTALLING LIGHTROOM

To run the Apple TV app, you'll need an Apple TV 4th generation or newer, running on tvOS 11.0 or later.

To get started, search the App Store for *Lightroom* and click *Install*, then click *Open*.

To sign in, the app asks you to use a web browser on another device to visit https://lightroom.adobe.com/tv, sign in, and type in the number shown on your TV screen. No fiddling with entering passwords on your remote!

LIBRARY VIEW

The first screen displays folders and below that, any root-level albums (that's albums that aren't inside folders).

Navigate around the screen using the touch surface on your remote, then click the touch surface to open the selected folder or album. To go back up a level, press the Menu button.

GRID VIEW

In Grid view, you can scroll up and down the thumbnails of the photos to view them in context. When viewing a large album, swipe along the right edge of the remote's touch surface to quickly scroll.

Click the Sort icon on the left to sort by capture date (*Newest First* or *Oldest First*) or by a *Custom* order set using the iOS app, or click the Refine icon to filter by flags or star rating, and click again to clear the filters.

To return to the Library view, press the Menu button, or click on a photo to open it in Detail view.

DETAIL VIEW

Detail view displays the photo in full screen. Clicking the remote again zooms in so you can see all of the detail, and you can pan around using the touch surface.

If you swipe down from the top of the touch surface of the remote, Lightroom displays a Filmstrip view at the top the screen. Swipe left or right on the touch surface to quickly navigate through the photos and videos, and swipe up to hide it again.

APPLE TV

In Library view, click on a folder to show the albums inside.

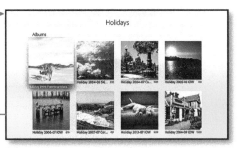

Click on an album to show its photos in Grid view.

Click on a thumbnail to enlarge it in Detail view.

Click again to zoom in and out again, or long-press to start a slideshow.

Swipe down from the top to view the filmstrip.

When you're done, press the Menu button to return to Grid view.

SLIDESHOW

In Grid or Detail view, click the Play/Pause button on the remote or long-press the touch surface to start a slideshow of photos or play the selected video, and again to pause it. Swiping left <> right manually switches photos.

You can change the Slideshow Speed in Lightroom's Settings, accessed through the menu at the top of the Library or Grid view.

You can't add music to your slideshow in Lightroom, however, you can keep playing the background music from another app. To do so, start the music playing, switch back to Lightroom and start or pause the slideshow by long pressing on the remote's touch surface, rather than using the Play/Pause button.

ALL PHOTOS VIEW

The **All Photos** view is divided by month, and like the album grid view, you can change the sort order or filtering, and swipe along the right edge of the remote to quickly scroll.

SEARCHING PHOTOS

To search for photos, select **Search** from the

menu at the top of the Albums/All Photos view and then use the on-screen keyboard to search for words such as *dog, cat* or combinations like *sunset boat*. To dictate the search words, highlight the on-screen keyboard and hold down the Siri button while speaking.

RANKING & EDITING PHOTOS

The Apple TV app is designed for viewing photos, rather than editing them, but if you're working on a photo on another device, it should also update on the tv screen. If they don't update correctly, go to *Settings > Reload Albums*.

If you need the full Lightroom iOS interface on your Apple TV, perhaps to flag the photos while you're viewing them, you could enable Screen Mirroring instead of using the Apple TV app. To do so, swipe up from the bottom of the phone/tablet to reveal Control Center, then should tap *Screen Mirroring* and select *Apple TV*.

REFERENCE INFORMATION

23

We'll finish the book with some reference information you may need in the future.

There aren't too many preferences, but it's handy to know what they do.

Computers don't always behave the way they're designed to work, so we'll also discuss how to handle the most frequent problems.

IN THIS SECTION, WE'LL CONSIDER:

• What the different preference settings do.

• How to solve the most likely problems.

• How to move to a new computer.

SETTING PREFERENCES

There aren't too many preferences to worry about, and the default settings are good, but here's what all of the sliders, buttons and checkboxes do:

ACCOUNT PREFERENCES (WINDOWS/MAC)

Subscription Status

Opens the Adobe website to manage your account

Check how much cloud storage space is available. If you run out of space, you can buy more

Diagnostic Log buttons only show when you hold down Alt (Windows) / Opt (Mac). They help Adobe staff figure out sync issues

LOCAL STORAGE PREFERENCES (WINDOWS/MAC)

Click to show your local cache folder (page 57)

Limit the amount of space Lightroom uses to store photos on your hard drive (page 57)

Keep a copy of the smart previews and/or originals on your hard drive, in case your internet connection goes offline (page 57)

View additional information about storing your originals

Decide where to store the local cache of original image files (page 58)

Reset moves the original photos back to the default library location (page 58)

GENERAL PREFERENCES (WINDOWS/MAC)

Prevent system sleep during sync
keeps the computer awake so the
photos can be safely uploaded

Enable/disable
People view if
you're worried
about privacy
(page 102)

IMPORT PREFERENCES (WINDOWS/MAC)

Add your copyright metadata to new
photos, as long as they don't have existing
copyright metadata (page 94)

Set default edit
settings for
new raw photos
(page 175)

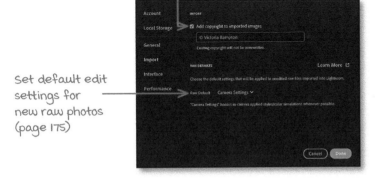

PERFORMANCE PREFERENCES (WINDOWS/MAC)

Use Graphics Processor allows you
to override the default Auto setting
to optimize
performance or
solve problems
caused by
buggy graphics
card drivers.

Selecting Custom
displays additional
options (page 364)

INTERFACE PREFERENCES (WINDOWS/MAC)

By default, Lightroom uses the operating system
language. The language setting also determines
the text search language (page 108)

Change the size of
slider labels etc.

On a small screen,
change the Edit
Panel Layout to
Compact to fit
more sliders in a
smaller amount
of vertical space

Use simple
gestures to
flick through
the photos

Reset all warning
dialogs and tips
brings back any
dialogs that
you've hidden
using "Don't
Show Again"

By default, when you open a panel on one
side, the other side closes. Changing to
manual keeps the side panels open until
you choose to close them (page 18)

PREFERENCES/SETTINGS (IOS)

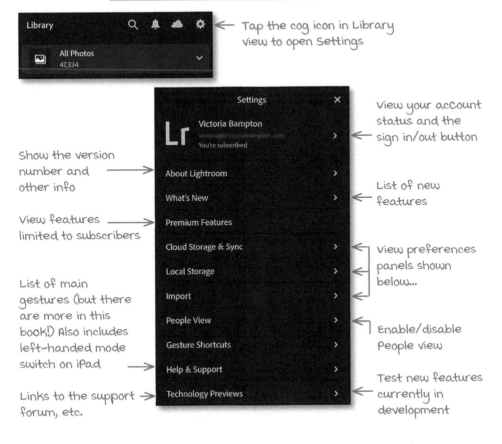

← Tap the cog icon in Library view to open Settings

View your account status and the sign in/out button

Show the version number and other info →

View features limited to subscribers →

List of main gestures (but there are more in this book!) Also includes left-handed mode switch on iPad →

Links to the support → forum, etc.

List of new features

View preferences panels shown below...

Enable/disable People view

Test new features currently in development

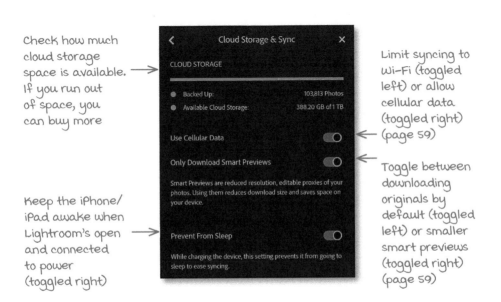

Check how much cloud storage space is available. If you run out of space, you can buy more

Keep the iPhone/ iPad awake when Lightroom's open and connected to power (toggled right)

Limit syncing to Wi-Fi (toggled left) or allow cellular data (toggled right) (page 59)

Toggle between downloading originals by default (toggled left) or smaller smart previews (toggled right) (page 59)

Local Storage shows how much space is available on your device →

Clear Cache clears space on your device, as long as the photos are safely stored in the cloud. It doesn't clear any albums you've marked for offline use (page 59)

Automatically add new photos and videos shot with other camera apps (page 31) →

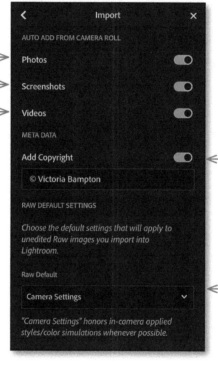

Automatically add your copyright to new photos as they're added (page 94)

Automatically apply your choice of default settings to new raw photos as they're added (page 175)

PREFERENCES/SETTINGS (ANDROID)

Tap the menu icon in Library view to open Settings

View your account status, amount of cloud storage space available, and the sign in/ out button

View features limited to subscribers

View Preferences screen shown below...

List of new features

Show the version number and other info

View Device Info & Storage preferences screen shown overleaf...

Links to the support forum, etc.

Test new features currently in development

Enable/Disable People view

View preferences screens shown on following page...

Limit syncing to Wi-Fi (toggled left) or allow cellular data (toggled right) (page 59)

Toggle between downloading originals by default (toggled left) or smaller smart previews (toggled right) (page 59)

Automatically add new photos of specified file formats shot with another camera app (page 31)

Automatically add photos from all locations

Specify which device folders are checked to auto add photos

Automatically apply your choice of default settings to new raw photos as they're added (page 175)

Automatically add your copyright to new photos as they're added (page 94)

Device Storage shows how much space is available on your device

Clear Cache clears space on your device, as long as the photos are safely stored in the cloud. It doesn't clear any albums you've marked for offline use (page 59)

move Lightroom data to expansion storage (SD card) where available (page 59)

view manage Storage screen to clear cached albums

System specifications, and information including whether your device can capture raw or HDR files

OPTIMIZING PERFORMANCE ON THE DESKTOP

Earlier in this book, on page 12, we discussed which computer hardware components are most beneficial when you're upgrading your computer.

There are also a few tweaks you can make to your preferences and workflow to optimize performance on your desktop. We've already covered many of these options earlier in the book, so we'll just summarize here.

IMPORT SPEED

When importing from a memory card, use a fast card reader (ideally USB3) rather than a camera cable, to speed up the import process.

HARD DRIVE SPEED

Lightroom's local database is stored on the boot drive, so ensuring you have a fast boot drive (ideally SSD) and plenty of space available on that drive can help with performance.

The originals can be stored on another drive (page 58). A standard internal or external hard drive is usually better for performance than a NAS (network accessible storage).

IMAGE LOADING SPEED

If your internet speed is slow or you want photos to load quicker, it's worth caching the photos locally (page 57), so they don't have to download from the cloud as you try to edit them. Depending on the hard drive space you have available, you may decide to only store specific albums locally, or all of your photos.

GPU ACCELERATION

Lightroom can use the GPU (page 13) to speed up certain tasks, such as how quickly the image preview updates on the screen when you switch photos or move an Edit slider. This is called GPU acceleration.

There are many possible combinations of graphics cards, drivers and driver settings, especially on Windows. A bad combination can cause slower performance, strange artifacts on the screen, or even crash the entire system.

There are a couple of preference settings in *Preferences > Performance tab*, to give you control over how Lightroom accesses your GPU, so you can select the best settings for your system.

Auto is the default setting. It only enables GPU performance enhancements that are expected to work well, and leaves potentially buggy options disabled.

Custom gives you control. If the pop-up is set to *Custom*, there are two options:

Use GPU for display uses the GPU to accelerate the drawing of pixels on the screen. It's the simplest option, and works well on most supported graphics cards, as long as the driver is updated regularly.

Use GPU for image processing uses the GPU to do the edits themselves, making slider movements smoother. It's much more advanced, and is therefore more likely to hit bugs in drivers, causing strange artifacts on the screen, slow performance or even system crashes.

Off disables these optimizations. You might select *Off* if your graphics card is underpowered, or continues to have issues (performance degradation, crashes or artifacts) after you've updated the driver.

FIXING IMPORT PROBLEMS ON THE DESKTOP

Import issues are fairly rare, but there are a couple of things you may run into on the desktop version of Lightroom.

CAN'T FIND DEVICE

If the camera or card reader doesn't show up in the Add Photos dialog, check that it's visible in Explorer (Windows) / Finder (Mac). Lightroom relies on the operating system to show the mobile device or memory card. Card readers are usually more reliable than camera cables.

FADED THUMBNAILS

If you can see thumbnails in the Add Photos dialog, but they're faded, then Lightroom knows that they're duplicates of existing photos. When you float the cursor over the photo, it reminds you that the photo is already in Lightroom.

Lightroom errs on the side of caution, calculating a checksum (hash) of the file to be sure that it's an exact duplicate. It won't identify duplicates that are edited versions of an existing photo, or if another program has changed the metadata in the file. If you believe a photo has been falsely identified as a duplicate, rename it in Explorer (Windows) / Finder (Mac) to force Lightroom to import it.

PREVIEW UNAVAILABLE

If you can't see thumbnails of your photos, but you can just see gray rectangles, go ahead and try to add them. Lightroom then provides additional information in an error message, or builds the previews from the full resolution file.

ERROR MESSAGES

If Lightroom is unable to add all of the selected images, it displays an error message at the end of the import. These are the most frequent error messages, their causes and solutions:

The file appears to be unsupported or damaged has a few possible causes:

• The raw file format isn't supported by your Lightroom version. To fix it, check for updates (page 17). If the camera is very new, you may need to wait for an update that supports your camera. You can check whether your camera is currently supported at https://www.Lrq.me/camerasupport

• The file is corrupted. There's usually nothing you can do to fix a corrupted file, other than adding the same file from an uncorrupted backup.

• The file format isn't on the list of supported file types (https://www.Lrq.me/file-formats), for example, it uses an unsupported color mode (e.g. duotone), it's too big, or it's a

PSD file that was saved without *Maximize Compatibility* enabled.

Error duplicate image within session means some of the thumbnails you checked in the Add Photos dialog are exact duplicates of other checked photos in the same import. This error message is for information only.

LOW DISK SPACE

When you add photos, Lightroom copies the selected photos to its own folder on your computer's hard drive and then uploads them to the cloud. Once they're uploaded, it can free up space on your hard drive again, but if you're doing a big import (such as all of your existing photos), you may run out of space.

If so, you can add the photos in smaller chunks and wait for these to finish uploading before adding more, or better still, change the location of the originals to another drive that has more space available (page 58).

SOLVING SYNC PROBLEMS

Syncing between multiple devices is complex, and although it usually "just works," there are a few hiccups that can arise. The most frequent issues have simple solutions, which we'll cover in this lesson, and I've included Adobe's contact details for more complex issues.

FREQUENT SYNC PROBLEMS

If Lightroom says it's syncing but nothing seems to be downloading, or edits made on other devices aren't showing up, check the other devices have finished uploading.

If edits made in the current version of Lightroom aren't uploading to other devices, check that sync isn't paused.

If you're not sure which device has the sync issue, check the web interface at https://lightroom.adobe.com to see whether the photos have safely uploaded to the cloud.

UNABLE TO DOWNLOAD ORIGINAL

If Lightroom says it's unable to download the original photo, there are three likely causes:

• You're offline (no internet connection) or sync is paused.

• The photo was added on another device and hasn't uploaded to the cloud yet.

• The photo was added on another device but you've run out of cloud storage space.

OUT OF SPACE

If Lightroom says you've run out of cloud space, click the cloud sync icon and then select the *Upgrade* button on the desktop to pay for additional cloud storage space, or log into your account on Adobe's website. Alternatively, you could delete photos you no longer want (e.g., the rejects or 1 star photos you kept "just in case") to clear space.

If it says you've run out of local hard drive space, you can move the originals to another drive (page 58). If you still don't have enough space, you'll need to clean up your boot drive using Windows/macOS tools or upgrade the size of your boot drive.

TROUBLESHOOTING WITH ADOBE

More unusual sync issues may require a little help from Adobe. This also allows them to investigate and figure out the cause of the problem, so they can avoid it in future releases.

To **request support from Adobe**, it's best to post at https://feedback.photoshop.com/ as the engineers themselves watch this forum. There are separate sections for the desktop apps (marked as Lightroom Desktop) and the mobile apps (marked as Lightroom Mobile).

When posting, don't forget to include your Lightroom version and operating system. The easiest way to find the information on the desktop is to go to *Help menu > System Info* and just copy the first block of text. On a mobile device, you'll find this information in Lightroom's *Preferences > About Lightroom*. And of course, don't forget to include a detailed description of what's wrong!

Adobe support staff may ask you to create a **Diagnostic Log**, **Mini Report** or **Full Report**.

To do so on the desktop, go to *Edit menu* (Windows) / *Lightroom menu* (Mac) > *Preferences* > *Account section* and hold down the Alt key (Windows) / Opt key (Mac) to display the buttons. Lightroom generates the log and offers to open it in your web browser or show it in Explorer (Windows) / Finder (Mac) ready to email to the support staff.

On mobile, go to *Settings > Help & Support* and hold your finger on the *Access our Support Forum* button. The diagnostic log is automatically attached to a draft email, ready to send.

RESETTING THE LOCAL CACHE

If you're having significant sync problems that Adobe can't solve, sometimes the "nuclear" option is the simplest solution. Obviously you'll need to ensure that all photos have finished syncing to the cloud or back them up before deleting the local cache.

Local Files (Desktop)—To reset the local cache, delete the following files from the problem computer:

Windows—C: \ Users \ [your username] \ AppData \ Local \ Adobe \ Lightroom CC \ Data \

Mac—Macintosh HD / Users / [username] / Pictures / Lightroom Library.lrlibrary

When you next open Lightroom, it will create a new local cache from the cloud.

Local Files (Mobile)—To clear the local cache on your iOS or Android device, simply delete the app and re-download from the App Store (iOS) / Play Store (Android), then sign in and allow it to sync the photos again.

DELETING EVERYTHING

If you want to wipe absolutely everything from the cloud and all devices, go to https://lightroom.adobe.com, sign in, click the LR icon in the top left corner, select *Account Info* and then press the *Delete Lightroom Catalog* button. But **make sure you have a copy of all of your photos and settings** on another disconnected hard drive because it really will delete them from everywhere that Lightroom controls.

STANDARD TROUBLESHOOTING STEPS

If your issue isn't covered by the previous sections, or in the specific topic area of the book, there are some general troubleshooting steps you can try, whether you're using a desktop computer or a mobile device.

DESKTOP

1. Restart Lightroom

Many issues fix themselves by simply quitting and reopening Lightroom.

2. Reboot the Computer

If you're having odd problems with any computer program, the age-old wisdom "turn it off and turn it on again" still works wonders.

3. Check for Lightroom Updates

Make sure you're running the latest updates, both for Lightroom (by going to *Help menu > Check for Updates*) and also for your operating system, as the issue you're running into could be a bug that's been fixed in a later release.

4. Check for Driver Updates

Buggy graphics card drivers can cause no end of trouble.

On Windows, check the graphics card manufacturer's website for an updated driver as Windows Update often has outdated drivers. It's best to uninstall the previous driver before installing the new one.

On macOS, check *System Preferences > Software Update* for an operating system update.

5. Turn off the GPU

If you continue to have problems, particularly with artifacts on the screen, slow performance or crashes, go to *Preferences > Performance* and set the *Use Graphics Processor* pop-up to *Off*. If this solves the problem, it's definitely a graphics card conflict.

6. Reset Preferences

If you're still having problems, resetting Lightroom's Preferences file can solve all sorts of 'weirdness,' so it's a good early step in troubleshooting. If you reset your Preferences file, the main settings that you lose are those in the Preferences dialog. Your photos, metadata, edits, presets and other important settings are unaffected by deleting the Preferences file.

There's a simple automated way of resetting preferences. Just hold down Alt and Shift (Windows) / Opt and Shift (Mac) while opening Lightroom and it will ask whether to reset the preferences. The timing is crucial—hold them down while clicking/double-clicking on the app/shortcut.

If you need to delete preferences manually, the preferences files are stored in hidden folders at:

Windows—C:\ Users \ [your username] \ AppData \ Roaming \ Adobe \ Lightroom CC \ Preferences \ Lightroom CC Preferences.

agprefs

Mac—Macintosh HD / Users / [your username] / Library / com.adobe. lightroomCC.plist and com.adobe. lightroomCC.mcat-daemon.plist. (Reboot the computer before reopening Lightroom, as the old preferences will be still cached if deleted manually.)

7. Uninstall/Reinstall Lightroom

Some problems can be caused by a corrupted installation. To rule this out, uninstall Lightroom by opening the CC app (page 16) in the system tray (Windows) / menu bar (Mac) and clicking the ... button to the right of Lightroom and selecting *Uninstall*. Restart your computer to clear out any gremlins, and then return to the CC app to reinstall Lightroom.

8. Ask for Help

If you're still stuck, post a description of your problem at https://feedback.photoshop.com/ tagged as Lightroom Desktop. Don't forget to include a full description of the problem, as well as your exact Lightroom version and operating system. You'll find this information under *Help menu > System Info* on the desktop.

MOBILE

1. Force Quit the App

If an app is misbehaving, one of the first things to try is quitting and reopening the app.

On most iOS devices, double-click the Home button to show your most recently used apps, swipe right or left to find the app that you want to close, then swipe up on the app's preview to close the app.

On Android, go to *Settings app > Apps > Lightroom* and tap *Force Stop*.

2. Reboot the Mobile Device

Like a desktop computer, rebooting a mobile device can often solve odd issues.

On iOS, a hard reset or force restart clears out RAM, which a standard restart doesn't. On older devices, hold down the Home button on the front and the power button, and keep them held down until the Apple logo appears, then let go of the buttons and wait for it to finish restarting. For newer devices without a Home button, hold the power button and volume down key until you see the Apple logo, then let go and wait for it to finish restarting.

On Android, hold down the power button and then press the *Restart* button on the screen.

3. Check for Updates

Check the App Store (iOS) / Play Store (Android) for an updated version of Lightroom, as you may be running into a bug that's already been fixed.

4. Ask for Help

If you're still stuck, post a description of your problem at https://feedback.photoshop.com/ tagged as Lightroom Mobile. Don't forget to include a full description of the problem, as well as your exact Lightroom version and operating system. You'll find this information under *Settings > About Lightroom.*

MOVING TO A NEW COMPUTER OR DEVICE

Since the cloud is the main repository for your photos, moving to a new computer/ device is simple, but if you've been managing files in folders on your local hard drive for years, it's a new thought process.

DECOMMISSIONING THE OLD COMPUTER

You can have Lightroom activated on two computers at a time (or five, if you have the Lightroom 1TB plan). To deactivate on an old computer, go to *Help menu > Sign Out* or uninstall the software.

Mobile devices don't have the same limitations, but if you're passing your old device onto someone else, you'll want to wipe your data by resetting your device back to factory defaults.

To avoid losing any photos or edits, ensure that your old computer or device has finished syncing with the cloud before you decommission it.

INSTALLING ON THE NEW COMPUTER

On the new computer or mobile device, install Lightroom and sign in (page 16), and allow Lightroom to download the photos and metadata from the cloud.

If you've cloned your whole boot drive (desktop) or restored from a backup (desktop or mobile), follow the instructions on page 369 to reset Lightroom's local cache, so that it syncs as a new device. This prevents sync problems that can result from working off a clone.

MINIMIZING BANDWIDTH

If you have many GB's of photos stored in the cloud and you had *Store a copy of all originals at the specified location* checked in *Preferences > Local Storage* on the old desktop computer, you can minimize the bandwidth by moving the originals to the new computer and telling Lightroom where to find them.

To do so, sign in on the new computer and then go to *Preferences > Local Storage*, check the same checkbox and navigate to the location of the originals. Lightroom will still need to sync the latest metadata from the cloud, but it won't need to download another copy of the originals.

MIGRATING TO LIGHTROOM CLASSIC

If you find that Lightroom is missing some features that you can't live without, or your internet connection is too slow to upload all of your photos, it is possible to migrate to Lightroom Classic. (That's the traditional desktop-based version of Lightroom.)

It's not as simple as migrating from Lightroom Classic (discussed on page 44), as it's not a direction Adobe intended people to take. There are two main options:

SAVING SETTINGS TO FILES

Saving settings to the files works well if you've added keywords to your photos and want to retain them when moving to Lightroom Classic (or any other photo cataloging software, for that matter).

1. Filter the photos to show the flagged photos and assign a star rating or a keyword (e.g., flagged) to help identify them later, as flags aren't written to the files metadata. Repeat for rejected photos.

2. Select all of the photos in an album and add a keyword to identify the album (e.g., album-vacation 2018), as album membership isn't written to the file metadata. Repeat for each album.

3. Select all of the photos and go to *File menu > Save To* (page 324). Select *Original & Settings* format and save the photos to a folder.

4. Open Lightroom Classic to a new catalog and go to *File menu > Import Photos*, then select *Move* at the top of the Import dialog. This will move the photos out of the large single folder into a more orderly folder structure that you select in the Destination panel.

SYNCING TO LIGHTROOM CLASSIC

Syncing photos from the cloud works well if you migrated from Lightroom Classic, or you haven't added keywords in Lightroom.

1. If you originally migrated from Lightroom Classic, open that migrated catalog. Otherwise, open Lightroom Classic to an empty catalog.

2. In *Edit menu* (Windows) / *Lightroom menu* (Mac) > *Preferences > Lightroom Sync*, set a custom location for mobile downloads.

3. Click on the Identity Plate and click the *Start* button next to *Lightroom Sync* to begin syncing. This downloads the original photos and metadata from the Lightroom cloud, storing them on your local hard drive. It doesn't sync keywords, or album folders, but it does sync the albums themselves.

Lightroom Classic is discussed in great detail in my book, *Adobe Photoshop Lightroom Classic - The Missing FAQ*. If you're going to continue syncing Lightroom Classic with the Lightroom cloud, I'd strongly recommend reading the Cloud Sync chapter of that book. Lightroom Classic is only a distant cousin of the Lightroom ecosystem, and therefore there are some things that don't sync, and some other unexpected behaviors to look out for.

GLOSSARY

Album—a set of photos grouped for a specific purpose.

AI (Artificial Intelligence)—a computer imitating intelligent human behavior.

All Photos—all of the photos and videos stored by Lightroom, found at the top of the Photos panel.

Aspect Ratio—the proportional relationship between the width and height of the photo, otherwise known as the shape.

Black Point—small area of the photo that is pure black.

Bounding Box—the edge of the crop.

Brightness—radiated or reflected perception of luminance of a subject.

Cache—a temporary storage location on your computer.

Chromatic Aberration—when a lens is unable to bring all wavelengths of color to the same focal plane point, causing fringes of color along high contrast edges.

Clipping—the loss of either highlight or shadow details when tonal information is driven to pure white or black.

Cloud—the server on the internet where your images are processed and stored.

Cloud-Native—photos are stored in the cloud and available on all connected devices.

Color Cast—an unwanted color shift in the photo.

Color Temperature—the color of the light source.

Contrast—the difference in brightness between light and dark areas of a photo.

Crop—to trim a portion of the photo.

Curve—a line graph that illustrates or controls the brightness and contrast of different image tones.

Deconvolution—type of sharpening which attempts to calculate and reverse the cause of blurring.

Demosaic—where raw image data is translated into a viewable color image.

Distortion—a warping or transformation of an object and its surrounding area.

DNG Format—open-source raw file format.

Dynamic Range—the difference between the brightest and darkest tones in a photo.

ETTR—stands for "expose to the right" and means setting the exposure to be as bright as possible without clipping the highlights to pure white.

Exposure—a measure of the amount of light in which a photo was taken, or the adjustment made in photo editing software.

Facets—used to limit search terms to specific criteria.

GPS data—the location co-ordinates captured using the Global Positioning System navigational satellites.

HDR (High Dynamic Range)—process that combines multiple exposure variations of an image to achieve a dynamic range exceeding that of a single exposure.

HEIC—a file format Apple has chosen for the HEIF (High Efficiency Image Format) standard. It enables smaller files by using advanced, modern compression methods while retaining higher image quality than a JPEG alternative.

Highlights—the light tones in the photo.

Histogram—a bar graph showing the relative population of pixels at each level.

Hue—the shade of a color.

JPEG—stands for Joint Photographic Experts Group, is a lossy compression technique for color photos (so photo data is compressed, resulting in smaller files with variable loss of data).

Keepers—photos you decide are worth keeping.

Kelvin Scale—unit of measure for temperature relating to color temperature of light sources.

Keystoning—where a building seems to lean backwards in a photo.

Lightroom—the new cloud-native version of Lightroom.

Lightroom Classic—the traditional folder-based version of Lightroom.

LUT (Look Up Tables)—used by profile developers for advanced color adjustments.

Members Area—password-protected area on the Lightroom Queen website at https://www.lightroomqueen.com/members

Metadata—data describing the photo, such as how the photo was taken (camera, shutter speed, aperture, lens, etc.), who took the photo (copyright), descriptive data about the content of the photo (keywords, caption), and edits made using Lightroom.

Midtones—range of tones that lie between highlights and shadow.

Moiré—a rainbow-like pattern which is often seen when photographing fabrics.

Noise—common term to describe visual distortion, equivalent of grain in film cameras.

Panorama—wide format (usually a landscape) made by overlapping individual shots and merging them into a long thin image.

Parametric tone curve—instead of a tone curve with points to adjust, this allows adjustment of Highlights, Lights, Dark and Shadows.

Pixel—a photo is made up of a number of pixels, each of them representing an individual dot of information.

Posterization— A visual defect (also called banding) in an image created by insufficient amounts of data to maintain the appearance of continuous tone.

Preset—a set of edit settings that can be applied to other photos.

Preview—a small copy of the edited photo for display within Lightroom.

Profile—a starting point for editing your raw photo, like choosing a film stock. Also used for special effects.

Raw File—the unprocessed sensor data from the camera.

Rendered File—the processed image data in a standard image file format.

Resample—changing the pixel dimensions of a photo.

Resolution—the number of pixels in an image.

Saturation—the intensity or purity of a color.

Shadows—darker tones in a photo.

Smart Preview—a small copy of the raw data for use within Lightroom.

Specular Highlights—areas of a photo that are meant to be pure white without detail, such as reflections on shiny objects.

Stack—a group of photos that appears as a single photo in the Grid view.

Sync—to synchronize data between the cloud server and other devices.

TAT—stands for Targeted Adjustment Tool. It allows you to drag on a photo to change color or tone curve while visually seeing the results.

TIFF—stands for Tagged Image File Format, a computer file format with lossless compression (so no detail lost).

Tone-mapping—redistributing tonal information to correspond more closely to the way our eyes see light.

USM (unsharp mask)—a type of sharpening that creates halos either side of an edge.

Vignette—a reduction or increase of brightness or saturation in the corners of a photo, which may be a lens defect or added for effect.

White Balance—removing unrealistic color casts so that objects the eye expects to be white appear so, for example, a white wedding dress.

White Point—pixels that are pure white.

Workflow—a series of steps undertaken in the same order each time.

Zoom—magnify or reduce the view of a photo.

THE LIGHTROOM CLOUD PREMIUM MEMBERS AREA

With your book purchase, you also get a year's access* to our Lightroom Cloud Premium Members Area.

YOUR LIGHTROOM CLOUD PREMIUM MEMBERS AREA ACCESS INCLUDES:

• **Multiple eBook formats** of this book.

• **New Lessons** in the Members Area, as Adobe adds new features to the Lightroom Cloud Ecosystem.

• **Email Support** from Victoria and Paul, in case you get stuck.

• **Blank Image Analysis Worksheet** to help you analyze your own photos.

• **Sample Images** so you can follow along with key editing examples.

• **Keyboard Shortcuts** to speed up your workflow.

• **Discounts** on future purchases on the Lightroom Queen website.

* Members Area access is valid for 365 days (from date of book purchase if new, or from date of publication if purchased used). When your Members Area access expires, you're welcome to extend it at a low cost, so you always have the most up to date information about the Lightroom cloud-based ecosystem.

ACCESS TO THE MEMBERS AREA & BONUS DOWNLOADS

If you purchased this book direct from https://www.lightroomqueen.com, your book is already registered, and you should have received your Members Area login details by email shortly after ordering. If you haven't received your login details, just send me an email.

If you purchased from a third-party retailer, such as Amazon or Book Depository, you'll need to register your book.

To register your book, I need both:

☐ Proof of Purchase, for example, your confirmation email, shipping confirmation, a scan/photograph of the packing slip, a screenshot of the order confirmation on Amazon's website, etc.

☐ The book reference code: **CC420201LS**

Send me the details using either:

• The book registration form: https://www.lightroomqueen.com/register

• Email: registration@lightroomqueen.com

What happens next?

We'll create your Members Area account and send you the login details. This can take up to 48 hours, as it requires a real human to press the buttons.

You can then log into the Members Area at https://www.lightroomqueen.com/members to access the bonus downloads and support contact form.

INDEX

CPSIA information can be obtained
at www.ICGtesting.com
Printed in the USA
BVHW050628140821
614244BV00001B/2